ECONOMICS
FOR PROFESSIONAL
INVESTORS

ECONOMICS FOR PROFESSIONAL INVESTORS

Second edition

TIM LEE

PRENTICE HALL EUROPE

London New York Toronto Sydney Tokyo Singapore
Madrid Mexico City Munich Paris

First published 1992 by Woodhead-Faulkner
Second edition published 1998
by Prentice Hall Europe
Campus 400, Maylands Avenue
Hemel Hempstead
Hertfordshire, HP2 7EZ

A division of
Simon & Schuster International Group

© Prentice Hall Europe 1998

All rights reserved. No part of this publication may be reproduced, stored in a retrieval system, or transmitted, in any form, or by any means, electronic, mechanical, photocopying, recording or otherwise, without prior permission, in writing, from the publisher.

Typeset in 10pt Caslon 224 by
T&A Typesetting Services, Rochdale

Printed and bound in Great Britain by MPG Books Limited, Bodmin

Library of Congress Cataloging-in-Publication Data

Available from the publisher

British Library Cataloguing-in-Publication Data

A catalogue record for this book is available from
the British Library

ISBN 0-13-792912-9

1 2 3 4 5   02 01 00 99 98

CONTENTS

List of figures   viii
Notation used in this book   x
Preface   xiii

1 MONEY, CREDIT AND INTEREST RATES
Introduction   1
What is money?   1
The monetary base   7
Difference between the demand for credit and the demand for money   13
Income velocity of circulation and the demand for money   16
Interest rates and the yield curve   21
    Long-term interest rates   21
    Short-term interest rates   23
    The yield curve   24

2 MONETARY EXPLANATION OF THE BUSINESS CYCLE
The business cycle   29
Asset price movements over the business cycle   39

3 REAL INTEREST RATE AND REAL EXCHANGE RATE
Real interest rates   45
Purchasing power parity and real exchange rate   52
Two-country model of real interest rate and real exchange rate determination   58

4 SAVINGS, INVESTMENT AND FLOWS OF FUNDS
Equivalence of savings and investment   65

Savings as a flow, assets as a stock   70
Assets and liabilities for the economy   72
Flows of funds   77
Difference between savings and money   80

5 THE BALANCE OF PAYMENTS AND EXCHANGE RATE
Introduction to the balance of payments   83
Current account balance, currency exposure and the forward exchange market   91
Relationship between the exchange rate and current account balance   96
Official intervention in currency markets   98

6 MONETARY POLICY UNDER FIXED EXCHANGE RATES
Limitations of monetary policy   103
Fixed rates in the foreign exchange markets   104
Fixed exchange rates in practice   110
Commodity and currency exchange standards or currency boards   117
International monetary systems   122
    Fixed exchange rates in a monetary system   122
    European economic and monetary union   129

7 IMPLEMENTATION OF AN INDEPENDENT MONETARY POLICY
Monetary policy under a floating exchange rate   137
    An independent monetary policy   137
    Reserve targeting in a fractional reserve monetary system   139
    Interest rate targeting in a fractional reserve monetary system   147
Monetary policy under a managed exchange rate   153
Monetary policy in a closed economy   161

8 PUBLIC SECTOR DEFICIT, ITS EFFECTS AND FINANCING
Public sector deficit   167
Macroeconomic impact of an increase in government spending   170
Financing the public sector deficit   174
    Borrowing to finance a deficit   174
    'Printing money' to finance a deficit   176
    Running down foreign reserves to finance a deficit   181

9 NATIONAL INCOME ACCOUNTING
Real and nominal GDP, GNP and national income   183
Expenditure components of GNP   186
    Consumer spending   186
    Treatment of debt and interest payments   187
    Treatment of housing   188
    Private investment spending   188
    Government spending   189
    External component of GNE   190
    Domestic and external contributions to GNE   192
Output components of GNP   193
Income components of GNP   196
Gross national savings   197

10 ECONOMIC INFLUENCES ON FINANCIAL MARKETS
Long-run stock market valuation and returns   201
    Real stock market returns   201
    Inflation and stock markets   204
Macroeconomic causes of excess returns   210
    Liquidity conditions and cyclical divergence   210
    Pegging of the exchange rate in an open economy   212
    Closed economies becoming open   215
    Commodity prices and the real exchange rate   219
    'Irrationality' and real exchange rate movements   220

Appendix   225
Bibliography   227
Index   229

LIST OF FIGURES

FIGURE 1	Spain: real M2 and domestic demand 5
FIGURE 2	Spain: real M3 and domestic demand 6
FIGURE 3	Germany: slope of the yield curve and GDP 26
FIGURE 4	France: tax burden and trend growth rate 30
FIGURE 5	UK: GDP and trend 31
FIGURE 6	UK: output gap and inflation 32
FIGURE 7	Stylized business cycle 34
FIGURE 8	United States: real M2 and GDP 35
FIGURE 9	Sweden: real M3 and inflation 36
FIGURE 10	Germany: composite liquidity indicator and consumption 37
FIGURE 11	Germany: composite liquidity indicator and inflation 38
FIGURE 12	Stylized monetary cycle 40
FIGURE 13	United States: money and credit cycle 41
FIGURE 14	Savings curve 47
FIGURE 15	Savings/investment equilibrium 49
FIGURE 16	OECD industrial production and global real rate 51
FIGURE 17	Sweden: krona/Deutschmark rate versus purchasing power parity 59
FIGURE 18	United States/Japan equilibrium 60
FIGURE 19	US public sector deficit increases 61
FIGURE 20	United States and Japan: debtor and creditor nations 63
FIGURE 21	France and Germany: inflation rates 112
FIGURE 22	France and Germany: yield curve slopes 113
FIGURE 23	France: franc/Deutschmark rate versus PPP 114
FIGURE 24	Europe: hard core money and GDP 134
FIGURE 25	United States: nonborrowed reserves and money growth 146

FIGURE 26	The demand for reserves 148
FIGURE 27	Reserve targeting 149
FIGURE 28	Interest rate targeting 150
FIGURE 29	United States: Federal funds rate 151
FIGURE 30	Interest rate targeting in a slowing economy 153
FIGURE 31	Effect of a public sector deficit in a closed economy 172
FIGURE 32	UK: profits from stock market and national accounts data 199
FIGURE 33	US: stock market price/earnings ratio and inflation 205
FIGURE 34	UK: equity risk premium and inflation 208
FIGURE 35	Thailand: balance of payments and money growth 214
FIGURE 36	Closed economy becoming open (1) 216
FIGURE 37	Closed economy becoming open (2) 218
FIGURE 38	Zimbabwe: real exchange rate and commodity prices 219
FIGURE 39	UK: savings rate and interest rate 222

NOTATION USED IN THIS BOOK

Δ	increase in
B	government bonds held by private sector
BD	bank deposits
BR	bank reserves
c	cash-to-deposit ratio
C	private consumption
CG	government consumption
Cp	cash currency in circulation
D	bank borrowings from the monetary authority
DV	dividends per share
E	earnings per share
ED	central government foreign debt
ER	exchange rate
$\dot{\text{ER}}$	(expected) change in exchange rate
ERP	equity risk premium
g	real growth rate of dividends per share/the economy
G	nominal growth rate of dividends per share/the economy
G	government expenditure
i	nominal interest rate
I	private investment
IG	government investment
I(Total)	gross capital formation
K	increase in private net foreign assets (capital outflow)
K	risk premium
M	imports of goods, services and payments of factor incomes
M	money supply
M0	monetary base
NFR	total government net foreign assets

x

NOTATION USED IN THIS BOOK • xi

P	level of stock market
P	general price level
Ṗ	(expected) inflation rate
PPP	purchasing power parity
PSD	public sector deficit
r	real interest rate
r	reserve ratio
R	central bank foreign reserves
REER	real effective exchange rate
RER	real exchange rate
S	private savings
SG	government savings
S(Total)	gross national savings
T	taxes net of transfers received
T	real transactions in goods and assets
V	velocity of circulation of money
W	weight
X	exports of goods, services and receipts of factor incomes
X − M	current account surplus
Y	real GNP
Z	sterilization instruments

PREFACE

Economics for Professional Investors was first published in 1992. This second edition is substantially revised and updated but its aim remains the same as before: to provide investors and those interested in financial affairs with a coherent economic framework for analyzing and understanding the behavior of the financial markets. The consistent analytical framework expounded is within the monetarist/classical tradition of economics. This approach encompasses the mainstream of financial market analysis and for more than two decades has been applied very successfully in economic forecasting by the economists at LGT Asset Management.

An additional and related aim is to explain the accounting relationships between the various macroeconomic concepts – GNP and its components, income, savings, public sector deficit, balance of payments and money supply. This is specifically the subject of Chapters 4, 5 and 9. Therefore, this book is not a standard macroeconomics textbook concerned with explaining the background to debates in macroeconomic theory. Rather, the intention is to provide general readers with a perspective for understanding the economic issues crucial to financial markets, and financial practitioners with a rigorous framework for analysis.

The core of this book is based on the manuscript of the first edition, and I wish to record here my gratitude to my wife Hilda, who helped considerably with the original text. For this second edition, Philippa Harrap of LGT Asset Management has done a great deal of work reorganizing the material, preparing the new text and helping with the production of charts and editing. Without her assistance, and in general without the support of LGT, this project could not have been completed. Margaret Sinnott also helped with the illustrative charts. The text and figures include material drawn from, or influenced by, research undertaken by present and former economists of LGT, with specific use made of research pieces by John Greenwood, Jon Mann and Alister Hibbert. I would like to note my thanks to Roger Yates for the support of LGT for this second edition.

My motivation to rework the original book for this new version has come largely from the encouragement of Simon and Schuster International Group and the very keen support given to the first edition by a number of economists and financial practitioners. In particular I would like to mention John Greenwood, Simon Ogus, Peter Eadon-Clarke, John Ricciardi and Connie Lutolf-Carroll, all of whose support for the first edition of *Economics for Professional Investors* was a great source of encouragement.

TIM LEE
SEPTEMBER 1997

MONEY, CREDIT AND INTEREST RATES   1

INTRODUCTION

The primary concern of this book is with the economic forces which shape the behavior of the financial markets. Monetary policy, whether expressed in terms of interest rates or liquidity conditions is a central aspect of all economic analysis of financial markets. Here, the analytical framework which is expounded is a consistent monetarist/classical framework, placing monetary policy as the key exogenous influence on financial and economic behavior, particularly with regard to the business cycle. Therefore, although this book is not intended primarily to be a treatise on monetary economics, an explanation of the basic monetary concepts makes an appropriate starting point. The second chapter expands on the concepts described, being an exposition of the monetary perspective of the behavior of financial markets and economic activity over the business cycle.

WHAT IS MONEY?

Definitions of money differ. However, generally, money is an asset of the nonbank private sector and a liability of the banking sector, including the commercial banks and the central bank. Money is distinguished from other assets held by the nonbank private sector because it is either directly a *means of payment* or is easily convertible into a means of payment without risk of capital loss in the process of conversion. An individual in a shop can pay for any purchase either with notes and coin or, possibly, with a check drawn on a demand deposit in a bank. She will not be able to pay by handing over other assets such as unit trusts, insurance or shares. Nor will she be able to pay directly with a noncheckable savings deposit held in a bank. However, unlike the unit trusts, insurance or shares, the savings deposit can very quickly be converted into cash currency or a checking deposit, which can then be used as a means of payment, without any risk of loss of capital. Although the shares and unit trusts could be sold for cash within a certain time, this could easily involve a capital loss. Unlike the savings deposit, there is no certainty regarding the value of these assets at any particular time.

Balance Sheets 1 and 2 place money within the context of the main components of the balance sheets of the relevant sectors of the economy. In these simplified balance sheets the items generally considered to constitute money – cash currency issued by the monetary authority and held by the nonbank private sector and the nonbank private sector's deposits in the banking system – are shown, capitalized, as both assets of the nonbank private sector and liabilities of the banking sector.

Balance Sheet 1

Banking Sector

Monetary authority		Commercial banks	
Assets	Liabilities	Assets	Liabilities
Net foreign assets	Currency held by banks	Cash currency	DEPOSITS OF NONBANK PRIVATE SECTOR
Government bonds	HELD BY NONBANK PRIVATE SECTOR	Deposits at monetary authority	Borrowings from monetary authority
Loans to financial institutions	Deposits of commercial banks	Government bonds	Bonds
	Deposits of government	Loans to nonbank sector	Equity
	Net worth	Net foreign assets	Net worth
		Real assets	

Balance Sheet 2

Nonbank Private Sector			
Nonfinancial corporate sector		Personal sector	
Assets	Liabilities	Assets	Liabilities
Real assets	Borrowings from commercial banks	Real assets (i.e. houses)	Borrowings from commercial banks
DEPOSITS AT COMMERCIAL BANKS	Bonds	CASH CURRENCY	Net worth
Insurance	Equity	DEPOSITS AT COMMERCIAL BANKS	
Net foreign assets	Net worth	Government bonds Corporate bonds Equity Unit trusts Insurance Net foreign assets	

In practice, because there is a large variety of monetary assets, each having differing degrees of ease or difficulty of conversion into a means of payment, economists use a number of different definitions of money. The most commonly used of these definitions are M1, M2 and M3. The exact composition of each of these 'monetary aggregates' varies from country to country, depending upon the institutional structure and the financial instruments available in the country. However, the basis for the inclusion of monetary assets in each of the measures of money is uniform, and depends upon how closely the monetary assets correspond with the notion of money as a means of payment.

M1, or 'narrow money', is the purest measure of money. It includes only assets of the nonbank private sector which directly constitute a means of payment, i.e. assets which can be used in their existing form to pay for goods and services. Thus M1 includes cash currency (notes and coin) held by the nonbank private sector and checking (demand) deposits at commercial banks held by the nonbank private sector. Travelers' checks are also usually included in M1.

M2 usually includes M1 plus assets of the nonbank private sector (liabilities of the banks) which can readily and immediately be converted into a means of payment without any loss or potential loss of capital or accrued interest being involved. For the most part this means savings, or call, deposits at banks. Thus, M2 usually includes M1 plus savings and call deposits at banks held by the nonbank private sector.

M3 is usually defined to include M2 plus other bank deposits held by the nonbank private sector which can be converted into a means of payment without risk of capital loss, but only after a short period of time has elapsed. This largely means time deposits or equivalents, although M3 generally does not include very long term (e.g. more than four years) time deposits.

Generally, definitions of money are restricted to include liabilities only of the banks. It could be argued that in practice there is little difference between the time deposits at banks included in M3 and certain other assets, such as short-term treasury bills, which are not liabilities of the banks (but in this case liabilities of the government). If a three-month treasury bill is bought on issue and held to maturity, there is no risk of capital loss at maturity, at which time the bill could be sold for money. There is a risk of capital loss if it is sold before maturity, when the value of the treasury bill could fall below the issue price if short-term interest rates rise sharply. However, there may in practice be little difference between holding a three-month treasury bill or a three-month time deposit at a bank. Often, the time deposit at the bank cannot be broken before maturity, or breaking the deposit involves a penalty.

Nevertheless, treasury bills or government savings bonds are not included in most national statistical definitions of M3, but are included in a still wider definition, termed L for 'liquidity'. This is the case, for instance, in the definitions of the monetary aggregates in the United States. In certain countries, short-term treasury bills are included in M3. In this book we assume that definitions of money embrace liabilities only of banks and not of the government or other entities.

Empirical evidence suggests that, for most economies, the narrower measures of money most closely corresponding to the definition of money as a means of payment bear a closer relationship to the business cycle than the broader measures. An example is given in Figures 1 and 2 showing, respectively, the (leading) relationship of real M2 (M2 deflated by the consumer price index) and real M3 to real

FIGURE 1 Spain: real M2 and domestic demand

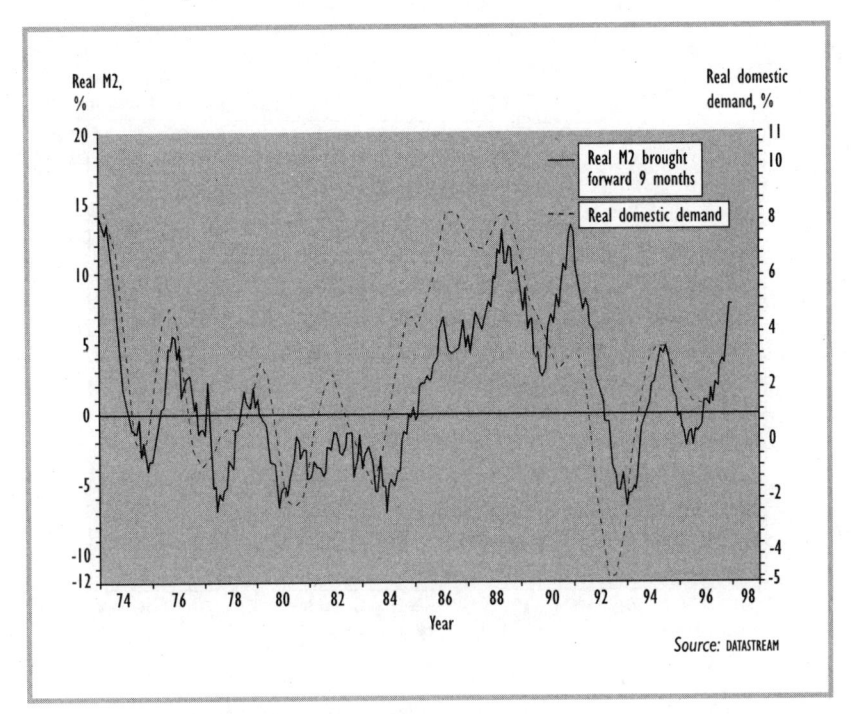

Source: DATASTREAM

domestic demand in the Spanish economy. The relationship of M2 to economic activity is much closer than for M3. In the United States, the attention paid by economic analysts to a relatively newly defined monetary aggregate, MZM (money of zero maturity), which incorporates the elements of M1 and M2 which genuinely have no holding period, is a further example of the greater significance of the definitions of money supply which come closer to the concept of money as a means of payment.

An analytical concept which has been used in econometric studies as a means of giving greater weight to forms of money which are held mostly for transactions purposes while still taking account of deposits which the holders may consider to be part of their savings (i.e. deposits, such as time deposits, which are mostly included in M2 and M3 or broader aggregates) is the concept of the Monetary Services Index or Divisia Money (named from the originator of the concept, François Divisia). The idea is to calculate a weighted average of each category of deposit or monetary asset, giving progressively higher

FIGURE 2 Spain: real M3 and domestic demand

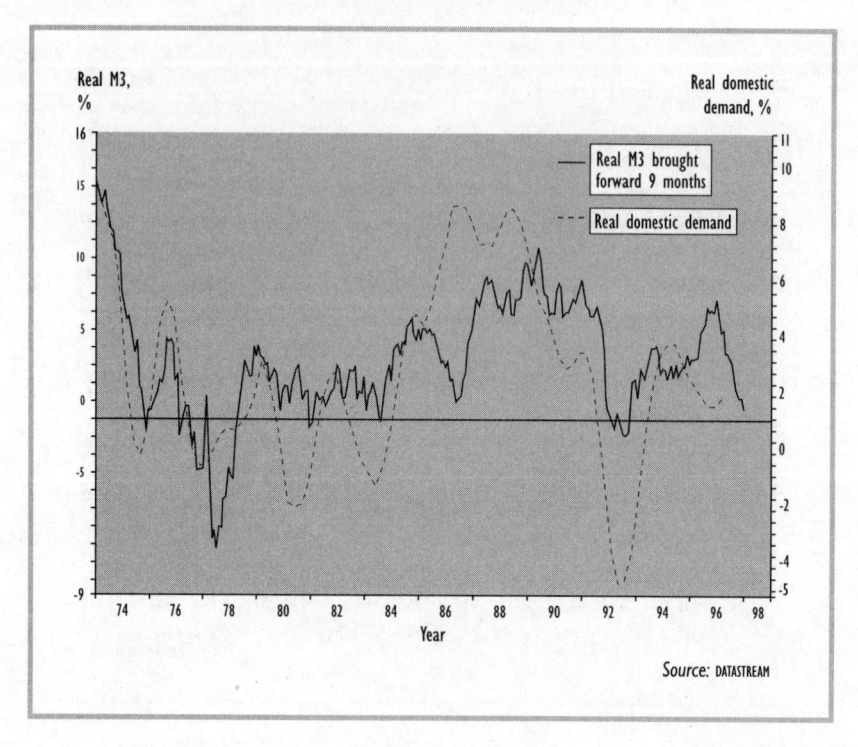

weights to those forms of money which are closer to pure transactions media (cash currency having the highest weight) and lower weights to monetary assets which are more savings media. The weights can be derived by making use of the reasonable assumption that deposits which pay interest at close to market levels are more likely to have a savings motivation for holding them, while monetary assets which pay interest rates lower than market levels or close to zero (for instance most checking accounts) are held largely for transactions purposes. Divisia money would usually be expected to provide a better fit to the business cycle than any of the discrete monetary aggregates considered alone, but it requires detailed data and involves fairly complex calculation and therefore is less practical. Combining the monetary aggregates with the structure of interest rates (the slope of the yield curve) can, in practice, capture much of the degree to which a varying proportion of the money stock is held for savings rather than transactions purposes, and this is discussed at the end of the chapter and in Chapter 2.

THE MONETARY BASE

The monetary base comprises two of the liability items on the balance sheet of the monetary authority, or central bank: cash currency (i.e. notes and coin) in circulation and the deposits of the commercial banks at the monetary authority. In Balance Sheet 3 the total of cash currency in circulation is separated into that part of currency in circulation held by the banks and that part held by the nonbank private sector. Only currency held by the nonbank private sector (capitalized) is part of the money supply, and so there is little overlap between the monetary base and any of the definitions of the money supply in terms of composition. Nevertheless, the monetary base is extremely important in determining the money supply, at least as a powerful constraint on the expansion of the money supply or at most as the absolute determinant of the money supply.

Cash currency in circulation represents notes and coin, which are the most acceptable means of payment for goods and services. In general, the greater is the total money supply the greater is the public's demand for notes and coin. A commercial bank requiring more notes and coin (to pay out to its depositors) has to pay the central bank for new notes by having its account at the central bank debited. A commercial bank requiring $10 million in notes will have its deposit at the central bank reduced by $10 million and in return the central bank will hand over $10 million in notes. For the whole banking system, therefore, in the first instance a rise in currency in

Balance Sheet 3

Monetary authority/central bank	
Assets	Liabilities
Net foreign assets	Currency held by banks
Government bonds	CURRENCY HELD BY NONBANK PRIVATE SECTOR[a]
Loans to financial institutions	Deposits of commercial banks
	Deposits of government
	Net worth

Currency held by banks, Currency held by nonbank private sector, and Deposits of commercial banks comprise the Monetary base.

[a] Part of the money supply

circulation is matched on the central bank balance sheet by an equivalent fall in the deposits of the commercial banks at the central bank.

Apart from being part of the mechanism through which new notes are paid for, in most monetary systems the commercial banks' deposits at the central bank also form the base of the bank clearing system. Imagine an example of an individual taking a bank loan in order to buy a car. The seller of the car ends up with a check from the purchaser which he deposits in his own bank. At this stage his bank has a liability (the deposit of the seller, representing part of the money supply) matched by an asset (the check, which is a claim on the bank of the purchaser). The purchaser's bank has an asset, which is the loan to the purchaser, and a corresponding liability which is the check, a liability to the bank of the seller. If the check is not offset by some other check in the opposite direction (i.e. drawn on the seller's bank and payable to the purchaser's bank), then it must be cleared through the purchaser's bank crediting the seller's bank with an interbank deposit. In theory, there are a number of ways this could be done. It could be that the seller's bank's account at the central bank is credited and the purchaser's bank's account at the central bank is correspondingly debited. Or it could be that a similar credit and debit is made to interbank deposits held not at the central bank but at a third bank. Or it could be that the purchaser's bank credits the seller's bank directly with a deposit with itself, replacing the check liability with an interbank deposit liability.

From this it can be seen that, for any one bank, deposits held at the central bank and at other, commercial, banks are substitutable. For the banking system as a whole they are not. Any one bank could transfer a deposit it holds at another commercial bank to the central bank and have its account at the central bank credited. However, the commercial bank losing the bank's deposit would now have a liability to the central bank in place of the original deposit liability, which would be 'settled' by a debit being made to its account at the central bank. The net result of the transfer of the deposit is merely a transfer of deposits held at the central bank from one commercial bank to the other, without any change in the total of banks' deposits at the central bank.

If any one bank, such as the car purchaser's bank above, expands its lending more rapidly than other banks, then it will continually be presented by other banks with checks for settlement, and ultimately its holdings of deposits at the central bank and at other banks will be run down. It could attempt to borrow from other banks, but ultimately there is a constraint on its lending and hence on the expansion of its balance sheet (and the money supply).

In monetary systems in which all interbank clearings have to be made via banks' accounts at the central bank, this constraint is much greater. An overlending bank will find its deposits at the central bank reduced, in the limit to zero. Other banks will find their accounts at the central bank correspondingly credited (because they will be receiving the checks drawn on the lending bank and presenting them for settlement). The overlending bank could begin to borrow from other banks, which would result in its account at the central bank being credited back and the other banks' accounts debited. However, this process could not continue for long, ultimately providing a constraint on the overlending bank.

If all banks simultaneously expand lending rapidly then checks presented for settlement by each bank to other banks are likely to balance out, meaning that the constraint to the growth of money supply provided by the deposits element of the monetary base is less binding. Then the constraint to the growth of the money supply hinges on the currency in circulation element of the monetary base. As the money supply expands, the demand for notes and coin naturally increases and so the banking system as a whole requires more notes and coin. Banks' deposits at the central bank are debited, in the limit being reduced to zero. Then the total money supply is only able to expand to the degree possible given the total of currency in circulation.

It must be emphasized that none of the processes described above alters the total size of the monetary base. When checks are cleared and settled with payments made from banks' accounts at the central bank, the result is that one bank's account at the central bank is debited and another's is credited by an equivalent amount. The total of banks' deposits at the central bank does not change, and the size of the monetary base does not change. When banks pay for new notes and coin by having their accounts at the central bank debited, then the total of banks' deposits at the central bank falls. However, the total amount of currency in circulation increases by the same amount. Again, the size of the monetary base does not change. In this second case, it is the composition of the monetary base that alters, to one of more currency in circulation and less banks' deposits.

It is an occasional misconception that the monetary base can be 'used up', in the sense of reduced, through increases in the money supply or economic growth. This is not the case. The monetary base can only be altered in size through actions of the authorities which result in changes in one or more of the other items on the central bank balance sheet – net foreign assets, government bond holdings of the central bank, loans to financial institutions or government deposits – which are matched by equivalent changes in the monetary base.

In a fractional reserve monetary system the monetary base is the direct determinant of the money supply. In this type of monetary system commercial banks are required by legislation to hold deposits at the central bank equal to a fixed, predetermined proportion of their total deposit liabilities (i.e. the deposits held with them by the nonbank private sector). If the predetermined ratio is 5 percent and a bank has deposit liabilities of $100 million, it is required to hold deposits at the central bank of $5 million to 'back' these deposits. The deposits at the central bank are known as *reserves* and the ratio of reserves to deposits is the *reserve ratio*.

In a fractional reserve system the size of the monetary base at any given time acts as a very binding constraint on the size of the total money supply. Banks are only able to increase lending, and hence deposits, to the extent that they have the reserves to back new deposits created. Any one bank can acquire reserves by borrowing from another bank (which results in its *reserve account* at the central bank being credited and the other bank's reserve account being debited), but the banking system as a whole cannot acquire reserves unless the central bank acts to change other elements of its own balance sheet. Thus, other things being equal, any one bank is only able to acquire reserves to the extent that other banks have more reserves than they need to back their own deposit liabilities. For the system as a whole, the total size of the deposit liabilities of the banks (or the money supply) is limited by the size of the monetary base.

The ratio of the money supply to the monetary base is known as the *money multiplier*. In practice this ratio is not fixed, even in a fractional reserve monetary system. A significant degree of flexibility arises from the currency in circulation element of the monetary base which bears no predetermined relationship to banks' deposit liabilities, but instead depends more on the whims of the public, in respect of the extent to which they wish to hold notes and coin. In a fractional reserve system, if the desire of the public to hold notes and coin for some reason increases substantially, and the central bank takes no offsetting action, then the money supply is forced to contract.

A numerical example may help to illustrate this. Suppose that the total of currency in circulation is $1,000 million, the total of banks' reserve deposits at the central bank is $500 million and the reserve ratio is 5 percent. Then, the total of banks' deposit liabilities can be up to $10,000 million ($10,000 \times 0.05 = 500$). (In practice, any cash currency held by the banking system – vault cash – would normally count towards reserves. Here, for simplicity, the vault cash element of reserves has been ignored.) The monetary base is $1,500 million ($1,000 million + $500 million). Then imagine that the nonbank public suddenly wishes to hold $200 million more money in the form of notes and coin, and equivalently less in the form of bank deposits (i.e. it draws down $200 million worth of bank deposits to obtain notes and coin). The banks have to go to the central bank to obtain the notes and coin, paying for the currency by having their reserve deposits debited by $200 million. Then their reserve deposits will total only $300 million ($500 million – $200 million). With a reserve ratio of 5 percent, reserves of this size are only capable of supporting deposit liabilities equal to $6,000 million. Bank deposits have to be contracted by $4,000 million ($10,000 million – $6,000 million), and, as currency in circulation has risen by only $200 million, the total money supply falls by $3,800 million. At the end of this process, the monetary base is still the same $1,500 million, but now made up of $1,200 million currency in circulation and only $300 million of reserve deposits. However, the money supply has fallen sharply and the monetary base now bears a much larger ratio to the money supply (i.e. the money multiplier has fallen sharply).

A second source of flexibility in the money multiplier arises from the fact that in nearly all fractional reserve systems the reserve ratio is not a standard, say, 5 percent, but is different for different types of deposit. Generally, M1-type deposits (checking accounts) have a higher reserve ratio applied to them than M2-type deposits (i.e. savings deposits). Often, for longer-term time deposits included in M3 the reserve ratio is zero. This means that shifts in funds by the nonbank private sector from one type of deposit to another can alter the money multiplier and have similar effects to changes in the desire of the public to hold notes and coin. For instance, if the public shifts much of its money in savings accounts (which bear a lower reserve ratio) to checking accounts (which carry a higher reserve ratio) the banks will require more reserves even though the broader measure of money supply – M2 – has not changed in total size (the composition has merely shifted). If the central bank does not act to increase the size of the monetary base, then total money supply will have to contract. Either way the money multiplier falls. If, on the other hand, the public shifts funds from checking accounts to savings accounts or time deposits, then generally the money multiplier will rise.

A third possible source of flexibility in the money multiplier is given by the extent to which banks may keep more reserves than they need. For instance, banks may have more deposits at the central bank than are required to back the current level of their deposit liabilities but they may decide not to increase lending. If, at a later date, they do increase lending, and as a result money supply expands, then the money multiplier will have increased. In most fractional reserve systems, reserve deposits at the central bank either do not pay interest or pay interest at below-market rates. Therefore, it is costly for banks to maintain more reserves than they need at any time and they are more likely to increase lending (and hence their own profits) to utilize fully their reserves.

Most countries have fractional reserve monetary systems with legislated reserve ratios for banks. The US monetary system represents the standard in this respect and in this book is treated as the standard for all 'floating exchange rate' monetary systems. Japan, Germany, France and many other countries have variants of the US-style fractional reserve monetary system. However, the UK and a number of its former colonies, including Australia and New Zealand, do not. The requirement to hold reserve deposits imposes a cost on the banking system, particularly if reserves are remunerated at below-market interest rates. Inevitably, therefore, innovation in banking and international competition between banking sectors in different locations can appear to undermine the legitimacy of reserve requirements. However, much of the criticism of fractional reserve monetary systems is based on a misunderstanding of the purpose of reserve requirements. Reserve ratios are not, as is commonly thought, a blunt instrument of monetary policy which are there to be varied in order to influence directly the rate of money growth. They are a lever which greatly enhances the effectiveness of the standard monetary policy instruments, such as open market operations (discussed in Chapter 7). Without them, monetary policy is likely to be more erratic and monetary stability more difficult to achieve.

An identity for the monetary base can be derived by equating the two sides of the balance sheet of the central bank, as shown in Balance Sheet 3. This identity is derived separately, and returned to a number of times throughout the course of this book. Taking Assets = Liabilities from Balance Sheet 3, and expressing the constituents in terms of changes, where Δ means 'increase in':

Δ Monetary authority's net foreign assets + Δ Monetary authority's holdings of government bonds + Δ Loans to financial institutions
= Δ Monetary base + Δ Government deposits + Δ Net worth

Because the government sector must finance its deficit (abbreviated to PSD) either by running down its deposits held at the monetary authority, or via net government bond sales to the monetary authority or domestic private sector, or by borrowing abroad, this identity can be stated in another way by substituting the terms involving the government sector (Δ Monetary authority's holdings of government bonds − Δ Government deposits at the monetary authority) with their counterparts from the PSD financing identity as follows:

Δ Monetary base = PSD − Δ Government bonds held by private sector − Δ Government external debt + Δ Loans to financial institutions + Δ Foreign reserves

In notation introduced in Chapters 4 and 5, this identity is abbreviated to:

$$\Delta M0 = PSD - \Delta B - \Delta ED + \Delta D + \Delta R$$

These ideas are developed and explained further in the rest of this book. For now, the key point to note is that although the PSD and government foreign borrowing are the result of actions of the government, the total of the right-hand side of the identity is within the control of the central bank. Therefore, the central bank is always able to control the monetary base if it wishes to do so. How it can and should undertake to do this is the issue of monetary policy, which is the subject of Chapters 6 and 7.

DIFFERENCE BETWEEN THE DEMAND FOR CREDIT AND THE DEMAND FOR MONEY

A common source of confusion is the distinction between money and credit or, more specifically, the demand for money and the demand for credit. Credit, in the sense of bank credit, refers to bank lending to the nonbank private sector. Bank credit is therefore on the opposite side of the balance sheet to money. Whereas money is an asset of the nonbank private sector and a liability of the banks, bank credit is a liability of the nonbank private sector and an asset of the banks.

The demand for credit refers to the extent to which the nonbank private sector desires to borrow. It may depend upon many factors, including interest rates, wealth, speculative opportunities or the strength of the economy. The demand for money, on the other hand, means the extent to which people and nonbank companies want to hold part of their assets in the form of money as opposed to (or in addition to) other possible assets they could hold such as bonds, equity, insurance and real assets. Therefore, the demand for money (or at least the demand for money to hold) means the demand for money as a form in which to hold assets.

The demand for money can also be affected by a number of factors. One very important factor is inflation. Because high inflation destroys the real value of money, in times of high inflation people generally wish to hold a lower proportion of their assets in the form of money and a greater proportion in forms which retain their real value such as real assets (e.g. houses) and equity. In extremes of hyperinflation the demand for money to hold drops to almost zero as people try to convert money they earn into other assets, or goods, as quickly as possible.

Given that the demand for credit and the demand for money are very different concepts, why is there often confusion between them? The source of the confusion is that an increase in the demand for credit is a necessary (but not normally sufficient) condition for an increase in the *supply of* money. In part, it is the concepts of the *demand for* money and the *supply of* money which are confused.

Returning to the car purchase example, when the bank increases its lending to the car buyer, other things being equal, the money supply increases. The bank credits the account of the buyer with the amount of the loan and he can then use the money to buy the car. The final result is an increase in the supply of money, with the new money 'created' in the hands of the seller.

It should be noted that only the actions of the banking sector can alter the supply of money in this way. Any transaction involving money between individuals or entities in the nonbank sector, whether it is the payment of wages by a company to its employees or an individual purchasing goods, does not affect the money supply. These types of transaction merely transfer a holding of money from one part of the nonbank private sector to another – from the purchaser to the seller – but do not actually alter the quantity of money in existence. Only actions involving the banking sector in an active role can potentially affect the money supply because money is defined as being a liability of the banking sector. Hence changes in the money supply impinge directly on the balance sheets of the banks.

This can be put into context by consideration of the asset counterparts to the money supply on the balance sheets of the banks. If we take Assets = Liabilities for the balance sheets of the commercial banks and monetary authority (presented at the beginning of the chapter) combined, we get the following identity (ignoring the net worth and real assets elements of the balance sheets, for simplicity):

Net foreign assets of banking sector (i.e. monetary authority plus commercial banks) + Banking sector's holdings of government bonds + *Monetary authority's loans to commercial banks* + *Cash currency held by commercial banks* + *Commercial banks' deposits at monetary authority* + Bank loans to nonbank sector = *Currency held by commercial banks* + CURRENCY HELD BY NON BANK PRIVATE SECTOR + *Deposits of commercial banks at monetary authority* + Government deposits at monetary authority + DEPOSITS OF NONBANK PRIVATE SECTOR + *Banks' borrowings from monetary authority* + (Bank bonds + Bank equity)

In the above identity the italicized items appear on both sides of the identity and can be taken out, and the capitalized items represent money M3. Thus the identity can be rewritten:

> Net foreign assets of banking sector + Banking sector's holdings of government bonds + Bank loans to nonbank sector = M3 + Government deposits at monetary authority + Commercial banks' nondeposit liabilities

where commercial banks' nondeposit liabilities refers to the items included within brackets at the end of the previous identity.

In the above identity, M3 will increase, and can only increase, if one or more of the terms on the left-hand side of the identity rises and/or one or more of the terms on the right-hand side of the identity, other than M3, falls. One of the terms on the left-hand side of the identity is bank loans to the nonbank sector.

The above identity is the basis of the 'monetary formation' approach to analyzing changes in the money supply. In this method of monetary analysis, financial economists analyze and forecast changes in the money supply by considering the changes, or likely changes, in the asset counterparts to the money supply. Written in the form of changes the above identity becomes:

> ΔM3 = Δ Bank loans to nonbank sector + Δ Banking sector's holdings of government bonds − Δ Government deposits at monetary authority + Δ Net foreign assets of banking sector − Δ Commercial banks' nondeposit liabilities

As with the monetary base identity, this can be restated by substituting the relevant terms with their counterparts from the PSD financing identity, bearing in mind that the PSD is equal to the increase in government bonds held by the banking sector and by the nonbank private sector, plus government foreign borrowing minus the increase in government deposits at the monetary authority.

Also, as explained later in Chapter 5, the current account surplus on the balance of payments is equal to the increase in net foreign assets held by the nonbank private sector minus any government foreign borrowing plus the increase in net foreign assets held by the banking sector. Therefore, the increase in the net foreign assets of the banking sector can also be substituted, by the current account surplus $(X - M)$ minus the increase in net foreign assets held by the nonbank private sector plus government foreign borrowing.

Substituting for these terms in the identity, government foreign borrowing 'drops out' and it becomes:

Increase in M3 = Increase in bank lending − Increase in non-deposit liabilities + PSD − Sales of bonds to the nonbank private sector + (X − M) − Capital outflows from the nonbank private sector

This is the identity that economists, particularly in the UK, often use to forecast changes in the money supply, by making predictions about each of the items on the right-hand side of the identity. The key term on the right-hand side is the first, the increase in bank lending, because bank lending is the major counterpart (i.e. the major item on the assets side of the banks' balance sheets) to the money supply (the liabilities side of banks' balance sheets).

The identity highlights the common notion of increases in money *supply* being associated with increases in loan *demand*. However, there is a big difference between the supply of money and the demand for *money*. Simply because the supply of money increases does not, in the first instance, mean that people wish to hold money in preference to other assets. In the example of the man borrowing money to purchase a car, the borrowing leads to the creation of money which ends up in the hands of the seller. The seller will not necessarily wish to hold this money: he may prefer to hold assets in other forms. If this is true for the economy as a whole, then there could be an attempt to switch out of money into other assets. In aggregate this switch cannot be achieved, and instead there will be other effects on asset prices, output and inflation in the economy.

INCOME VELOCITY OF CIRCULATION AND THE DEMAND FOR MONEY

Because the existence of money is a necessary requirement for spending, there must always be some relationship between money and expenditure, and hence output, in an economy. Nevertheless, this relationship is not completely straightforward. Money is a stock, whereas spending is a flow and so the measurement of spending has to have a time element, e.g. the quantity of expenditure over a one-year period (see Chapter 4). Moreover, for the economy as a whole, money can be spent more than once because, as noted earlier, spending does not destroy money but merely transfers it from the purchaser to the seller. What this means in practice is that any given quantity of money could support an infinite number of possible different spending totals for a given period, depending on how much of, and how often, the money is 'used' during the period. For instance, a broad money stock of $100 billion could support total spending over a year of $100 billion if the whole money stock was spent just once over the year, or $300 billion if it was spent three times. Or it could support spending of only $10 billion if $90 billion of the money was held as long-term time deposits by individuals holding part of their net worth in the form of money, and the remaining $10 billion was spent just once.

The notion of the degree to which the money stock is 'used' in spending over a given period is known in monetary economics as the *velocity of circulation* of money, abbreviated as V. If the quantity of money in existence in the economy is $100 billion and total spending over the year is $300 billion, then the velocity of circulation of money is said to be 3 ($300 billion/$100 billion). Velocity can be thought of as the turnover of money, in a sense. However, it should be noted that if velocity equals 3, there is no sense in which the whole money stock can be said to have 'turned over' three times during the year. It may be that, in the case of the example, $50 billion has not been spent at all and the remaining $50 billion of the money stock has been 'turned over' six times.

The concept of velocity can be defined (tautologically) as the ratio of expenditure to the money stock (i.e. total expenditure divided by the stock of money). As an identity we write:

$$MV = \text{Total spending}$$

where M is the money supply, and V is velocity. Total spending can be thought of as spending in real, or volume, terms (only measurable as an index) multiplied by the price level. Then the identity, which forms the basis of the quantity theory of money, can be written:

$$MV = PT$$

where T is spending in real terms and P is the price level.

Up until now we have not said what we mean by 'spending' or 'expenditure'. In economics, expenditure usually relates to gross national (or domestic) expenditure, which is identical to the gross national/domestic product (GNP/GDP) – see Chapter 9, page 183. However, GNP refers only to final output of goods and services, whereas money is spent on much more than final output, namely secondhand goods (e.g. used cars), existing real assets (e.g. old houses), and financial assets (stocks, bonds, etc.). In practice, because economists are more interested in output (i.e. GNP) than all spending (and because, in practice, spending on all goods and assets cannot be measured), the quantity identity is usually restated with T defined to include only spending on the GNP, in real terms. Then the identity becomes:

$$MV = PY$$

where Y is the real GNP and P is the GNP deflator (and so PY is the nominal GNP, or spending on the GNP in money terms). This, of course, changes the meaning of V, which is then the degree to which the money stock is turned over only in respect to spending on final output, or the income velocity of circulation of money. This V is smaller than the V in the previous identity (MV = PT), because PY (nominal GNP) is always smaller than PT (spending on all goods and assets, including the GNP). In effect, when money is 'turned over' in spending on, say, a secondhand car (not included in the GNP), this does not enter the measure of velocity in this definition.

The meaning of V is also altered if the definition of money is changed. If a broader definition of money (e.g. M3) is used, then V is smaller than if a narrower definition (e.g. M1) is used. Generally, different definitions of V (V1, V2, V3) are used to correspond with the different monetary aggregates. Thus,

$$M1V1 = PY$$
$$M2V2 = PY$$
$$M3V3 = PY$$

From this it could be concluded that velocity is a rather meaningless concept that becomes whatever is necessary for the quantity identity to work. The legitimacy of the quantity theory of money identity rests on whether or not V is an economic variable which bears a stable relationship to other economic variables and therefore can be forecast within a reasonable margin of error. Empirical evidence from many different economies strongly suggests that this is indeed the case.

From the previously given examples, velocity can be seen to comprise two basic elements. First is the degree to which money tends to change hands (often called the *transactions demand* for money). Economists believe that this is fairly stable and determined by institutional factors (e.g. the frequency with which people are paid their salary), the level of income and the distribution of income, which for any given economy do not change much in the short term.

The second, more important, element in velocity is the demand for money to hold. This concept was discussed earlier and relates primarily to what people, companies and institutions choose to do with their savings. The demand for money to hold (hereafter called simply the 'demand for money') is the extent to which money is desired, and held, as an investment in itself, an alternative or complementary investment to other assets such as stocks, real estate, precious metals, etc.

The velocity of money is inversely related to the demand for money. If the demand for money rises and the money stock remains unchanged, then as a greater proportion of the money supply is held as an investment, a lesser portion is available for transactions purposes. If the turnover of this money remains unchanged, then, by definition, spending must fall, i.e. nominal GNP must fall. In this case nominal GNP falls because velocity has fallen as the consequence of a rise in the demand for money. Alternatively, if nominal GNP is to remain unchanged, then the money supply must be expanded to meet the increased demand for money. Measured velocity will still fall because the money supply has grown while GNP has remained unchanged. Again, the fall in velocity reflects the increase in the demand for money.

A number of factors can affect the demand for money, but probably the two most important are inflation and interest rates. Low, or falling, inflation tends to increase the demand for money (i.e. reduce the velocity of circulation) because money retains its value in a low inflation environment and people feel comfortable holding a greater proportion of their net worth in the form of money. High inflation destroys the value of money and so, as inflation rises to very high rates, the demand for money to hold falls almost to zero. People tend to convert money as quickly as possible into assets which retain their value during inflation, e.g. real estate, precious metals. Therefore, at high, and rising, inflation rates, velocity tends to rise. In extremes of hyperinflation, velocity can rise extremely sharply as the normally stable, institutionally determined factors, which constitute the other element in velocity, also alter. Instead of being paid monthly, people are paid daily, or even hourly, to give them the chance to spend their income before it becomes valueless. Then, because the rate at which money changes hands is increased, velocity rises even more sharply.

The effect of interest rates on the velocity of money depends upon the monetary aggregate in question. Rising interest rates tend to raise the velocity of the narrow money aggregate, M1 (V1), i.e. lower the demand for M1. This is because cash currency and demand deposits included in M1 do not pay interest, or pay interest rates which are inflexible compared with market interest rates. As interest rates rise, depositors increasingly want to economize on holdings of money which do not pay interest in order to take advantage of the greater income-earning opportunities presented by the higher interest rates. Conversely, if interest rates fall, the demand for M1 tends to rise (i.e. velocity of M1 falls) because the interest rate factor becomes less important. Then people look more favorably on holding more of their money in the convenient form of demand deposits (i.e. checking accounts).

In general, this type of switching of deposits in response to interest rate movements should not have any effect on the broadest aggregates, e.g. M3. If, in response to a rise in interest rates, depositors move money not needed for spending from their checking accounts into time deposits, other things being equal this will reduce the quantity of M1 and raise the measured velocity of M1, but leave the quantity and velocity of M3 unaffected. Both the checking accounts and the time deposits are included in M3. Only the composition of M3 is altered in this example, not the total, and therefore, for a given GNP, the velocity is unaltered too.

The actual effect of changes in interest rates on the velocity of the broader monetary aggregates can depend on the institutional structure of the monetary system. If there are legislated interest rate ceilings on bank deposits, for example, as market interest rates (i.e. interest rates or yields on other, unregulated financial instruments, e.g. corporate bonds) rise towards and above the bank deposit ceiling levels, individuals may move funds out of the banking system and into other higher yielding financial instruments. This process, a form of disintermediation, results in more lending and borrowing taking place outside the banking system (i.e. without the banking system acting as the intermediary between lender and borrower) and would tend to raise the velocity of the broader monetary aggregates.

On the other hand, if bank deposit interest rates are determined freely (which is the case in most industrialized economies today), then it is arguable that a rise in short-term interest rates not fully matched by a rise in long-term rates (i.e. a flattening or inverting of the *yield curve* – see subsequent section of this chapter) might reduce the velocity of circulation of the broadest monetary aggregates. This is because bank deposit rates are largely tied, along with banks' prime lending rates, to the shorter-term market interest rates. If these rates rise relative to long-term interest rates, a bank deposit might appear to become a more attractive investment than alternative financial instruments, raising the demand for M3. This phenomenon is discussed in greater depth in the following section, and also in Chapter 2.

Chapter 2 also describes how *measured* velocity fluctuates over the course of the business cycle. These cyclical fluctuations in the *measured* demand for money reflect not sustainable (*ex ante*) changes in the demand for money to hold, but temporary disequilibria which occur as economic agents attempt to adjust to monetary expansions or contractions. They are therefore (*ex post*) changes in money demand which reflect the time lags between monetary developments and economic activity and inflation, as discussed in the next chapter.

INTEREST RATES AND THE YIELD CURVE

The interest rate (there are actually many different interest rates) is often mistakenly referred to as the 'price of money'. In fact, it is not, either in strict economic terminology or even in everyday language, the price of money. Price implies the cost of buying something, whereas the interest rate is the return from holding money, at least if held in the form of a savings or time deposit. The interest rate is also the cost of credit – the price that has to be paid for borrowing.

In so far as there is a 'price' of money, it is the cost of having money in that this involves giving up the opportunity of having other things that the money could buy. The cost of these other things, if they are goods and services, is their price level. Therefore the 'price' of money is the inverse of the price level, i.e. $1/P$. Because, in the long run, the exchange rate tends towards its purchasing power parity value (see Chapter 3), the exchange rate equates to the inverse of the price level, at least as long as price levels in other countries remain constant. Therefore, in a relative sense, the exchange rate and not the interest rate best represents the concept of the 'price of money'. (This makes perfect sense. If you are a British resident and wish to buy US dollars, the price you pay for that money is the exchange rate for the dollar in terms of the pound, not the interest rate.)

The interest rate, then, is the cost of credit or the return from holding money or bonds, also known as the *yield*. There are many different interest rates, depending on: (1) the maturity of the asset involved, (2) the currency in which the investment/borrowing takes place, and (3) the risk (of bankruptcy of the borrower) involved. Interest rates are usually expressed on an annualized percentage basis, i.e. the return, or cost of credit, over a year, expressed as a percentage.

Long-term interest rates

The long-term interest rate is usually taken to be the yield on long-term bonds. For government bonds in Japan or continental Europe the most widely quoted are the yields on the ten-year government bond, in the UK, the fifteen- or twenty-year, and in the United States the twenty- or thirty-year government bond. The point to note is that, as long as the borrower or investor holds the bond until maturity, the interest rate or return on a conventional bond is fixed for the whole life of the bond at the time of issue or purchase. If the investor buys $100 worth of twenty-year government bonds yielding 9 percent, he receives annual income of $9 each year for the next twenty years until the bond matures, when he also receives his $100 back.

Over the life of the bond the price of the bond can fluctuate. If after two years the capital value of the bonds has fallen by half, to only $50, and the investor sells the bonds, he will take a capital loss greater than the income he has received over the two years. His total return will have been negative. The investor who buys the bonds from him for $50 still receives a coupon of $9 and so the simple interest rate that she earns is double that of the initial owner, at 18 percent $((9/50) \times 100)$. For the issuer of the bond (the borrower) the fluctuations in the price of the bond do not matter as he is committed only to paying income (the coupon) of $9 each year and the original $100 back in twenty years' time, when the bonds mature.

Note that the holder of the bonds receives not only the annual coupon, or income – in this case $9 – but also the initial investment – in this case $100 – back when the bonds mature. That means the total return, or yield to maturity, is higher than the 'interest rate' quoted in this example. The investor who buys the bonds for $50 after the price has halved not only receives the simple interest rate of 18 percent per annum, but also a capital gain of $50 on the maturity of the bonds.

The determination of risk-free, long-term interest rates is discussed at length in Chapter 3. In essence, any long-term interest rate, i, can be seen as composed of three parts: the real interest rate, r, the expected inflation rate over the life of the investment, $\dot{P}$, and the risk premium, K, i.e.

$$i(A, 1) = r + \dot{P}(A) + K(1)$$

where $i(A, 1)$ is the nominal interest rate for a borrowing in the currency of country A by borrower 1. The higher is the credit standing of the borrower, the lower is the risk premium in the interest rate. Thus, the debt of a major blue chip company commands a low risk premium, whereas the debt of a company undergoing bankruptcy proceedings would command a very high risk premium. The debt of governments of major industrial countries (e.g. the United States, Japan) commands risk premia close to zero because there is no chance of such governments becoming bankrupt, particularly as they always have the ability to raise taxes if necessary.

From the above it is evident that the risk premium in any given interest rate is specific to the borrower, the inflation component is specific to the currency in which the borrowing takes place, and the real interest rate should be the same for any currency of an open economy (see Chapter 3). This holds true as long as we assume that exchange rates tend back towards purchasing power parity levels in the long run. Then the depreciation of country B's currency against the currency of country A depends only upon the extent to which inflation in country B exceeds that in country A. This is examined in Chapter 3, where it is also shown that, as a consequence, the only factor which can affect a specific long-term interest rate for a given (or zero) risk premium, other than a change in the savings/investment balance for the whole world (assuming free international capital flows), is a change in inflationary expectations.

Short-term interest rates

The shortest-term interbank interest rate is the 24-hour, or overnight, rate. This is the rate at which banks lend to, and borrow from, each other to meet temporary liquidity, or reserve, needs. In a fractional reserve banking system, funds lent and borrowed are either reserves or substitutable for reserves. In the United States, because it is the Federal Reserve ('Fed'), the US monetary authority, which regulates the quantity of reserves available to the banking system, the overnight interbank interest rate is known as the Federal funds rate. (For further discussion of the reasons that banks borrow in the interbank market and the way in which the Fed controls the amount of reserves available, and other issues raised in this section, see Chapter 7 on monetary policy.)

The important point to note here is that, unlike the long-term interest rate, the interest rate at which funds are lent and borrowed for a period as short as twenty-four hours is little influenced by savings and investment, or expectations for inflation. Instead, the most important determinants of the overnight interest rate are the availability of interbank funds and the demand for them. In a fractional reserve banking system the availability, or supply, of reserves is controlled by the central bank. In the United States, if the Fed acts to reduce the supply of reserves to the banking system, then, other things being equal, the Federal funds rate tends to rise. Reserves are needed to back bank deposits, and so the demand for reserves by the banks depends in the first instance upon the quantity of deposits in the banks, i.e. the money supply. Money supply tends to be under pressure to grow more rapidly if credit demand is strong. Therefore, ultimately, the demand for reserves by the banking system is a function of the demand for credit by the nonbank public. If the central bank's policy remains unchanged, stronger credit demand tends to lead to higher interbank interest rates.

In general, the shorter is the interest rate the greater is the direct influence of the central bank's actions to restrict or increase reserve availability in the determination of the rate. The longer the term of the interest rate the greater is the importance of inflationary expectations and the level of the real interest rate as determining factors of the rate.

The yield curve

Even if we consider only risk-free interest rates (i.e. government bond and bill rates) in one given currency, at any time there is still a variety of interest rates available to the lender depending on the term, or length of time, for which he is prepared to lend. These range from the interest rate for overnight lending and borrowing through three-month, six-month and one-year treasury bill rates, out to twenty- or thirty-year long-term government bond rates. The relationship between these interest rates at any one time can be depicted by a yield curve, which is a curve plotting the interest rates against the maturity.

The yield curve is positively sloped, or upward sloping, if longer-term interest rates are higher than shorter-term interest rates. Some degree of upward sloping of the yield curve is 'normal' because savers prepared to commit savings for a longer period, facing an uncertain return if they sell before maturity, expect to receive a higher annual return to compensate for uncertainty and/or loss of liquidity.

If short-term interest rates are higher than long-term interest rates, then the yield curve is inverted. In this case, the longer the saver initially commits his funds the lower is the annual return he receives. How can this happen? Generally, an inverted yield curve indicates that the central bank is following a tight monetary policy, restricting the availability of reserves to the banking system. The restriction of the supply of reserves pushes up the short-term interest rate. If people perceive that the tight money policy, leading to lower money supply growth, will eventually reduce inflation, then long-term interest rates may fall. This is because the important determinant of any individual economy's long-term interest rate is the expectation for inflation.

An inverted yield curve also means that people believe interest rates themselves will fall in the future, following inflation. If individuals and economic entities have neutral expectations for interest rates (i.e. they believe that interest rates will remain unchanged in the future), then, facing an inverted yield curve, they would choose to borrow long-term (at lower rates) and lend short-term (at higher rates). However, their actions in so doing, in raising the demand for long-term funds and increasing the supply of short-term funds, would raise long-term interest rates and reduce short-term interest rates. The yield curve would then cease to be inverted. The fact that a yield curve is inverted means that economic agents expect interest rates to fall. Then borrowing long-term and lending short-term is not an attractive proposition, because it means locking in a borrowing for a long time at a rate which will soon appear to have been unattractive (if rates fall as expected) and lending funds for a short time, which will not be renewable at such a favorable rate on maturity (again, if rates have fallen).

The shape of the yield curve, then, denotes a market expectation for interest rates. It is also generally the best single long leading indicator of an economy's growth rate over the cycle. The difference between the long-term and short-term interest rates is often a more accurate indicator of monetary conditions than is the growth of money supply, which can be distorted by regulatory or institutional change or other shifts in the demand for money function. In addition, because a shift in the central bank's policy towards reserve provision has an immediate impact upon short-term interest rates, but usually leads money growth by three or more months (see Chapter 7), the slope of the yield curve is a longer leading indicator than money growth itself. In industrialized economies with well developed financial markets, the difference between long-term and short-term interest rates is often an excellent leading indicator for real domestic demand and GDP, with a leadtime of 12–18 months. A good example is given in Figure 3, which overlays the long bond yield minus the three-month interest rate, brought forward by one year, upon real GDP growth for Germany.

A complication is that, in today's global capital market, long-term interest rates and hence the slope of the yield curve, can become divorced (at least for a period) from domestic monetary policy influences. The next chapter explains how this can occur as a result of business cycle divergences. More fundamentally, the yield curve may give a somewhat ambiguous message about monetary conditions within an economy if foreign investors are dominant in the bond market and form their inflation expectations differently from residents. The inflation expectations of residents of an economy (people and companies) tend to be highly influenced by the actual inflation rate over the previous few years – see Chapter 3. Foreign investors, on the other hand, can attach more credibility to the central bank's statements of policy intent, and be more influenced by the shorter-term behavior of the actual inflation rate, and also by international factors. Therefore, the implicit inflation expectations

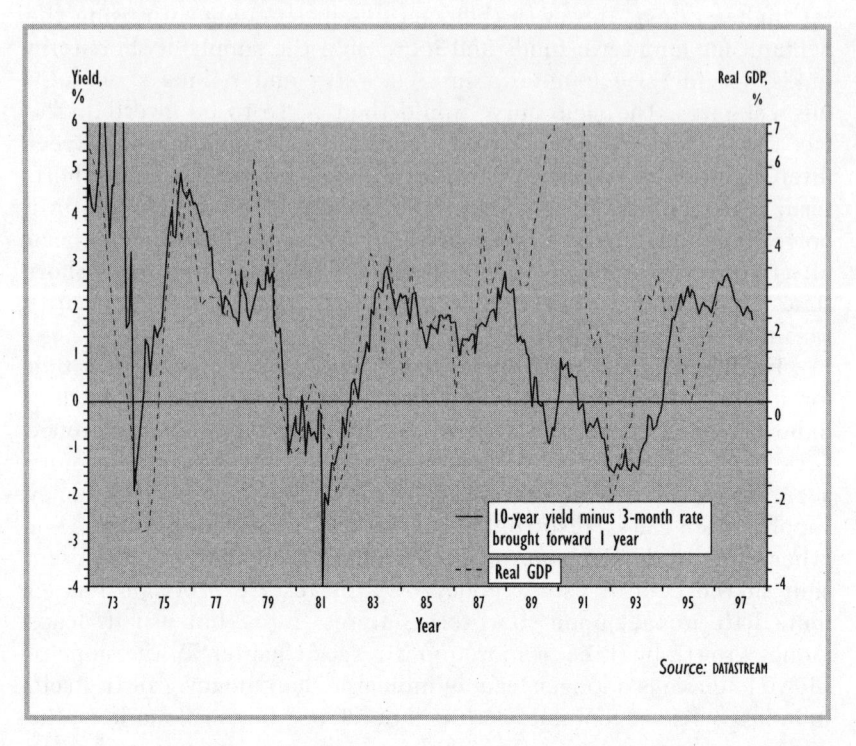

FIGURE 3 Germany: slope of the yield curve and GDP

Source: DATASTREAM

of foreign (largely institutional) investors can differ from those of residents, resulting in a 'distorted' yield curve if foreigners are dominant. An example occurred in 1993 when certain higher-yielding peripheral bond markets were the recipients of heavy foreign inflows, and again in 1996/97 when anticipation of European economic and monetary union (EMU) encouraged heavy buying of formerly higher-yielding European bond markets by both domestic and foreign institutions in the respective markets. In 1993 the Spanish financial markets, as an example, saw portfolio capital inflow totalling over US$25 billion, or over 5 percent of GDP, financed mostly by short-term borrowing in Spanish pesetas. In both cases, yield curves ended up flatter, or less positively sloped, than might otherwise have been the case.

The yield curve can then become as much, or more, an influence on the demand for money than an indicator of the monetary stance, for if the yield curve, and the assets which are priced off the yield curve, no longer reflects the profile of interest rate expectations of residents, residents are likely to respond by adjusting their own asset holdings, including money. If the yield curve becomes too flat, or inverted, residents may respond by attempting to shift savings from long-term financial instruments into shorter-term assets, including money. In the example of Spain in 1993, Spanish residents could sell their bonds to foreign investors and retain the proceeds in bank deposits, interest rates on which began to look attractive relative to 'artificially depressed' (from the perspective of Spanish residents) yields on bonds.

The conclusion is that, particularly in an environment of unrestricted capital flows, it is necessary to consider both the slope of the yield curve and the growth of monetary aggregates, in order to assess monetary conditions in an economy. An illustration of this is provided in the following chapter.

MONETARY EXPLANATION OF THE BUSINESS CYCLE

2

THE BUSINESS CYCLE

Over time, the natural state of affairs is for economies to grow in real terms as a result of labor force growth, investment in new capital stock and associated increases in productivity, in particular deriving from technological progress. Over periods of many years most economies tend to grow at an average rate which remains fairly constant. However, these trend rates of growth differ between economies. Given the right conditions – the rule of law, stable government, an open and free market economy – less developed countries ('emerging economies') can grow more rapidly for prolonged periods than developed economies, as they benefit from inward investment and transfer of technology. Conversely, for the richest economies, the long-term trend rate of growth can gradually fall away as productivity advances become more difficult to achieve. It is also conceivable that the trend growth rate of an economy could fall if its efficient workings become hindered by increased government intervention or an increasingly excessive tax burden. Figure 4, comparing the ten-year moving average of French GDP growth with the share of total government revenue in GDP, offers a suggestion that France's trend growth rate may have been falling as the tax burden has risen to the 50 percent of GDP level.

Any economy will tend to experience growth in an irregular cycle around the long-run trend, with periods of recovery and expansion – possibly lasting up to ten years – during which the growth rate of demand and output equals or exceeds the trend rate, and shorter periods, not usually more than one or two years long, of slowdown or recession when growth is less than trend or, indeed, negative.

Figure 5 shows GDP for the UK, with a fitted 'trend', both expressed in log form so that the constant growth trend is shown as a

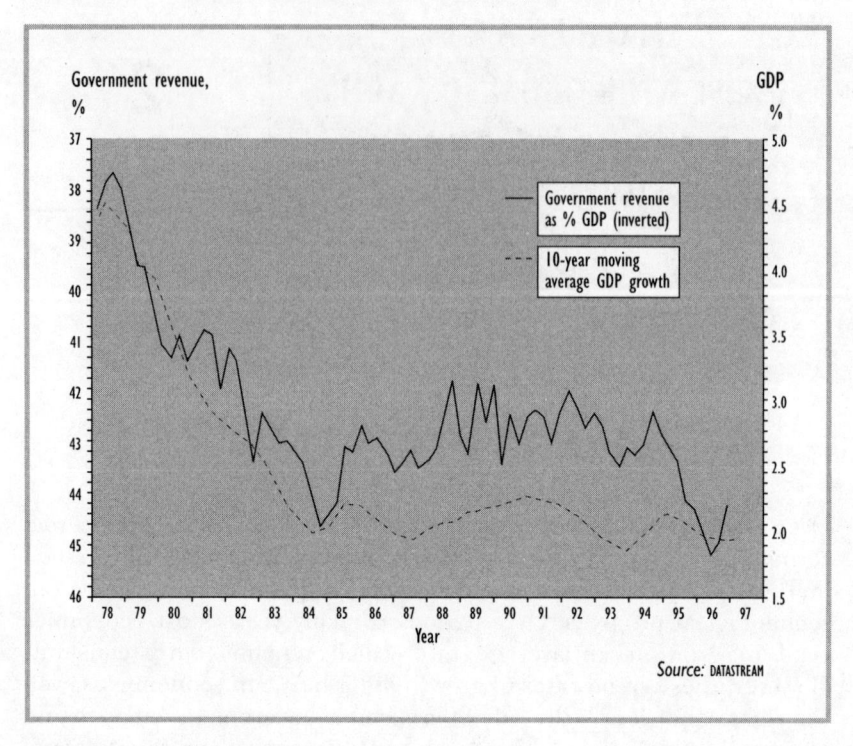

FIGURE 4 France: tax burden and trend growth rate

straight line. The periods of slowdown and recession (1974/75, 1980/81, 1990/92) show up as the drop in log GDP beneath the trend line. The amount by which GDP exceeds or falls beneath trend is often termed the *output gap*, and many financial economists explain inflation or inflationary pressures in the economy in terms of the degree to which demand, and therefore output, is exceeding the long-run trend. Figure 6 shows the output gap for the UK in terms of the difference between the two lines in Figure 5 (i.e. the deviation of GDP from its trend) and compares this with retail price inflation in the UK.

One problem with output gap analysis is that the economist cannot be certain that the trend growth rate has not changed in recent years. In the case of France, for instance, it was suggested earlier that the trend growth rate might be declining gradually under the burden of a ballooning tax take. If this proves ultimately to be the case – and accurate judgements can only be made with the benefit of long hindsight – then current estimates of the output gap will understate the degree to which output exceeds trend or possibly suggest a negative output gap when actually it is positive.

FIGURE 5 UK: GDP and trend

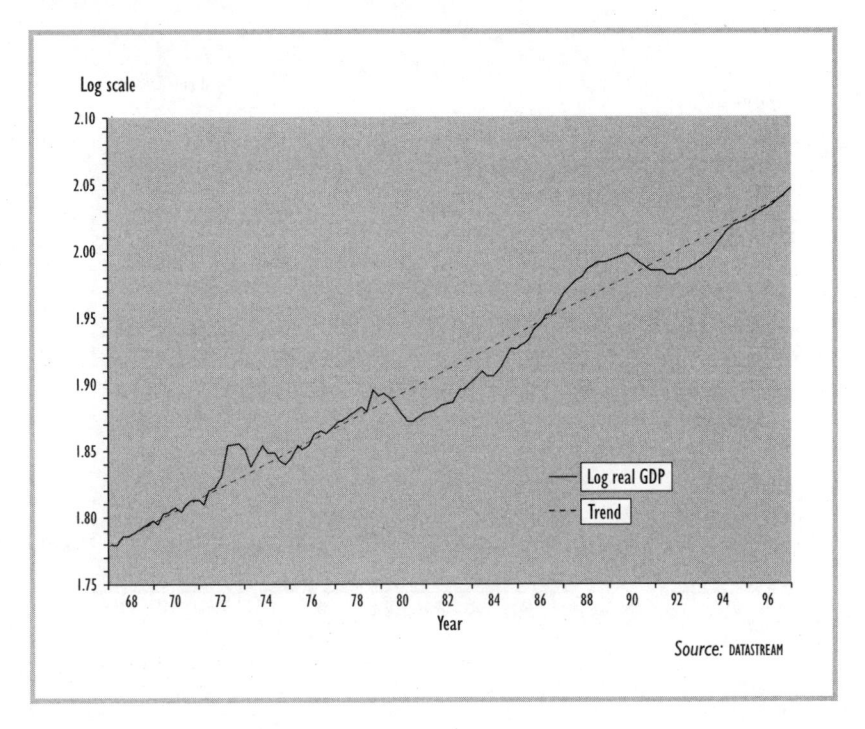

A better way to analyze the business cycle is to look directly at the cause of medium-term fluctuations in demand and output, which are cycles in monetary conditions. Within a monetary framework, a rate of growth of the money supply in excess of the rate of growth of money demand, if it persists, will give rise to higher than trend growth in demand for goods and services for a period, and ultimately inflation. We can consider the identity $MV = PY$, discussed in Chapter 1, in terms of changes, approximating it to $\dot{M} + \dot{V} = \dot{P} + \dot{Y}$ (where $\dot{M}$ equals the change in the money supply, $\dot{P}$ equals the change in the price level, etc.). Over the long run, $\dot{Y}$, the growth of real GNP, will be the trend growth rate given by the growth of the labor force and of labor productivity, which will be associated with trend growth in the transactions demand for money. $\dot{V}$, the increase in the income velocity of circulation of money, is the inverse of the change in the demand for money to hold. Over the long term, $\dot{V}$ could be influenced by the institutional development of the financial system and changes in its structure brought about by, for instance, financial deregulation, or by persistent high inflation. (Over shorter periods it could be greatly

MONETARY EXPLANATION OF THE BUSINESS CYCLE

FIGURE 6 UK: output gap and inflation

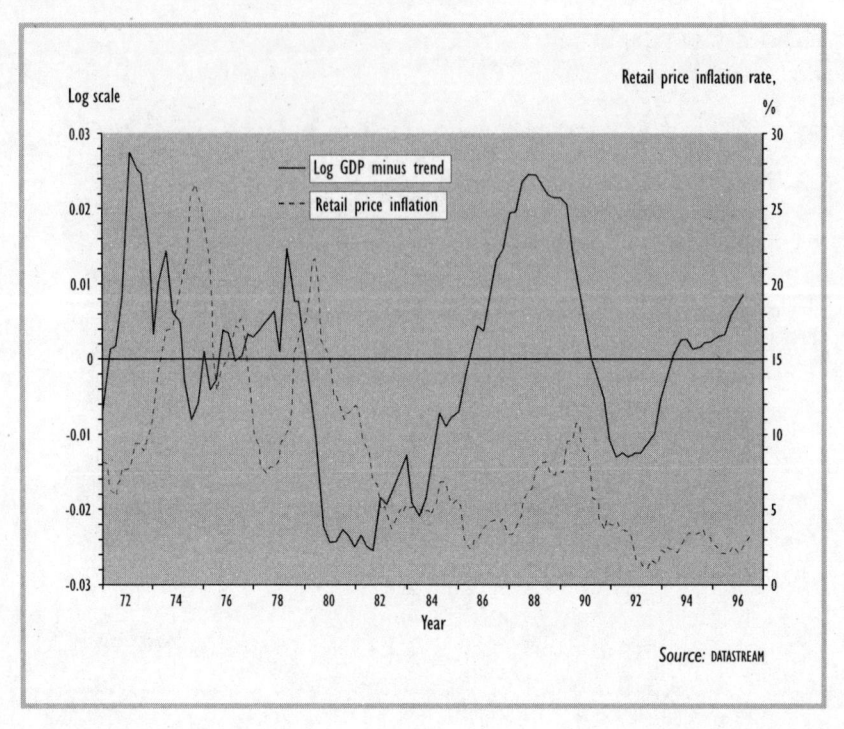

affected by shifts in the structure of interest rates, as discussed in Chapter 1 and expanded upon later.) If $\dot{M}$, the growth of money supply, is persistently higher than $\dot{Y} - \dot{V}$, the growth of money demand, then the longer term result can only be inflation, $\dot{P}$.

In the shorter term, the real economic growth rate is not immune to changes in the rate of money supply growth. If money supply is expanded more rapidly, the consequent higher rate of growth of demand can for a time stimulate a higher growth rate, as unemployment or underemployment is reduced or higher demand results in higher labor productivity. In addition there is the problem that GNP captures only part of the total 'spending' of money. If additional spending which results from more rapid growth of the money supply is not spending on the GNP but on assets or secondhand goods not included in the GNP, then measured velocity will tend to fall as money supply growth rises.

Now consider what actually happens when the rate of money supply growth in an economy is increased sharply. If the demand to hold money has not risen (i.e. the factors which affect velocity are unchanged) then, by definition, people and economic entities will find themselves holding 'excess' money. It is possible in these circumstances that they will spend the extra money on goods and services. It is far more likely, however, that, at least initially, they will seek to diversify their assets by putting the extra money into other assets such as stocks and shares or other financial assets, or perhaps putting the money down as a deposit on a new house. As a result, prices of these other assets will rise because the demand for them has increased. However, the 'excess' money does not disappear. For every buyer of an asset there must be a seller, and so the sellers of the assets are now holding the money. In the case of stocks and shares it may be that higher prices will encourage companies to issue more equity. In this case, at least a part of the additional money will then come into the hands of companies issuing new stock.

As long as this process continues, the measured velocity of money must be declining. Although, as we have assumed, money supply growth is rising sharply, demand for the GNP has not changed. Excess money is instead being spent on assets not included in the GNP. Therefore, by definition, in the identity $\dot{M} + \dot{V} = \dot{P} + \dot{Y}$ the change in measured velocity $\dot{V}$ must be negative.

As money is not actually destroyed by the purchase of assets but merely changes hands, how long might this process continue? It is possible that a new equilibrium could be reached when stock, property and other asset prices reach such levels that people are no longer prepared to buy more. They may then choose to hold extra money as an investment because money now appears to be a good investment relative to stocks and property, the prices of which are 'too high'. In this case, the demand for money to hold rises and the fall in velocity will have become a permanent one. However, it is more likely that people will start to increase spending on goods and services included in the GNP, for not only do they still have, in aggregate, more money than they started with, but also they are wealthier because the prices of their assets – stocks and property – have risen.

Initially, because of increased demand the output of goods and services tends to increase rapidly. Ultimately, the pressure of demand leads to rising wages and prices. Higher inflation may reduce the demand for money to hold, raising velocity, and for a while increase demand in the economy further. However, higher prices also mean that the need for money for transactions purposes is higher. Eventually, a new equilibrium will be reached with a higher level of prices and stable velocity.

To summarize, this process can be set out in four stages (with arrows signifying the directions of change at each stage of the process):

Stage 1: $\dot{M}\uparrow +\dot{V}\downarrow \quad = \dot{P} + \dot{Y}$
Stage 2: $\dot{M}\uparrow +\dot{V}\downarrow\uparrow \quad = \dot{P} + \dot{Y}\uparrow$
Stage 3: $\dot{M}\uparrow +\dot{V}\downarrow\uparrow\uparrow \quad = \dot{P}\uparrow + \dot{Y}\uparrow$
Stage 4: $\dot{M}\uparrow +\dot{V}\downarrow\uparrow\uparrow\downarrow \quad = \dot{P}\uparrow + \dot{Y}\uparrow\downarrow$
i.e. $\dot{M}\uparrow +\dot{V} \quad = \dot{P}\uparrow + \dot{Y}$

This tells us that the only lasting result of the increase in money supply growth is a rise in inflation.

Figure 7 shows a stylized diagram of the business cycle. The lags between the different stages of the cycle are variable and differ significantly between economies and over time. As a generalization, economic activity tends to accelerate between six months and one year after the initial rise in the money growth rate in excess of money demand. An illustration comparing real M2 growth brought forward by nine months with GDP growth for the US economy is given in Figure 8. The lag between money growth and inflation is much longer, usually between two and three years but sometimes, including historically for some continental European countries, up to as long as four years. A good example of the relationship between money growth and inflation is given in Figure 9 for the Swedish economy.

The simple monetary analysis of the business cycle cannot tell us much about the composition of GNP over the cycle. The description of the process whereby excess money translates into higher demand for goods and services via higher asset prices would suggest an acceleration of domestic demand, particularly consumer spending, leading the first stage of the upswing. Although this might often be the

FIGURE 7 Stylized business cycle

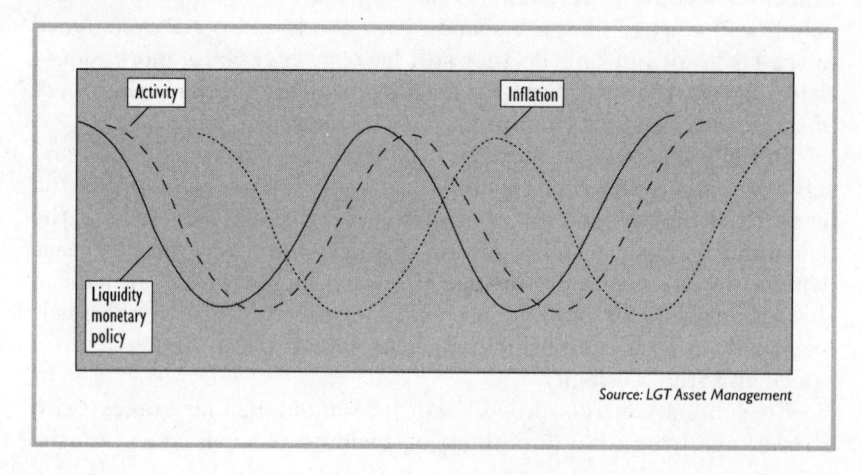

Source: LGT Asset Management

FIGURE 8 United States: real M2 and GDP

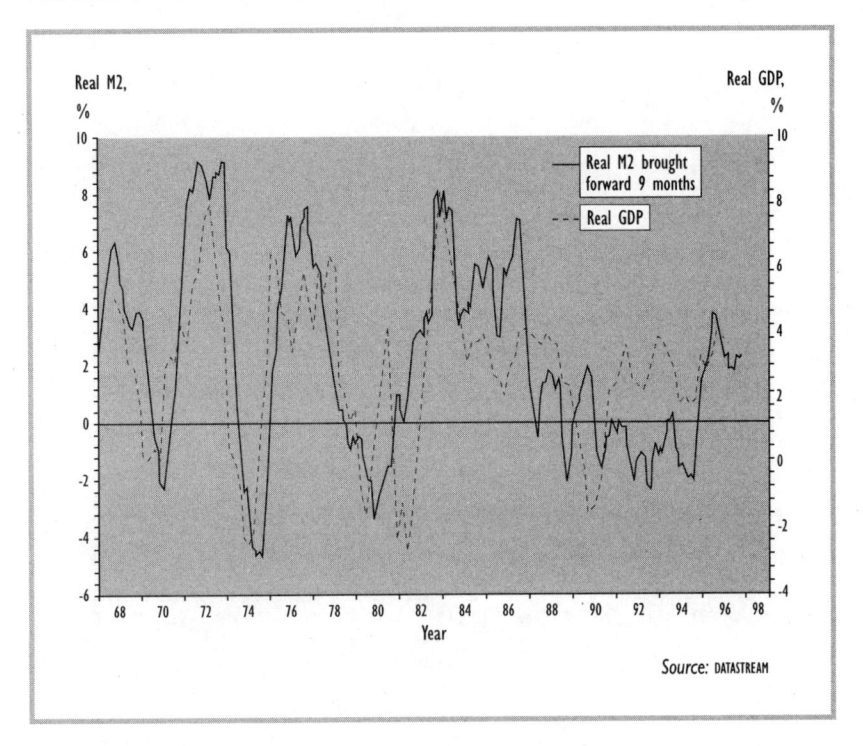

case, the initial monetary stimulus might also tend to weaken the exchange rate, giving a boost to export growth. The increased demand for assets that occurs in stage 1 of the cycle (above) will likely include foreign assets, meaning that the monetary expansion will be associated with capital outflows and a weaker currency. Stronger domestic demand growth, in itself, tends to support the real exchange rate, which is a concept explored in Chapter 3. Therefore, the less responsive domestic demand is to the monetary stimulus, the weaker will be the currency (other things being equal), and the greater will be the role of net export growth in the economic recovery. The more responsive is domestic demand, the more the exchange rate will tend to be supported, reducing the net export component of growth in the upswing or even turning it negative as imports recover.

Fiscal policy is a factor which has an important effect on the composition of growth over the cycle but, contrary to popular belief, its impact on the course of GNP as a whole is limited. An expansive fiscal policy will tend to 'crowd out' other components of spending, in particular investment or net exports, through its impact on the real interest rate and the real exchange rate (see Chapter 3). An example is

FIGURE 9 Sweden: money and inflation

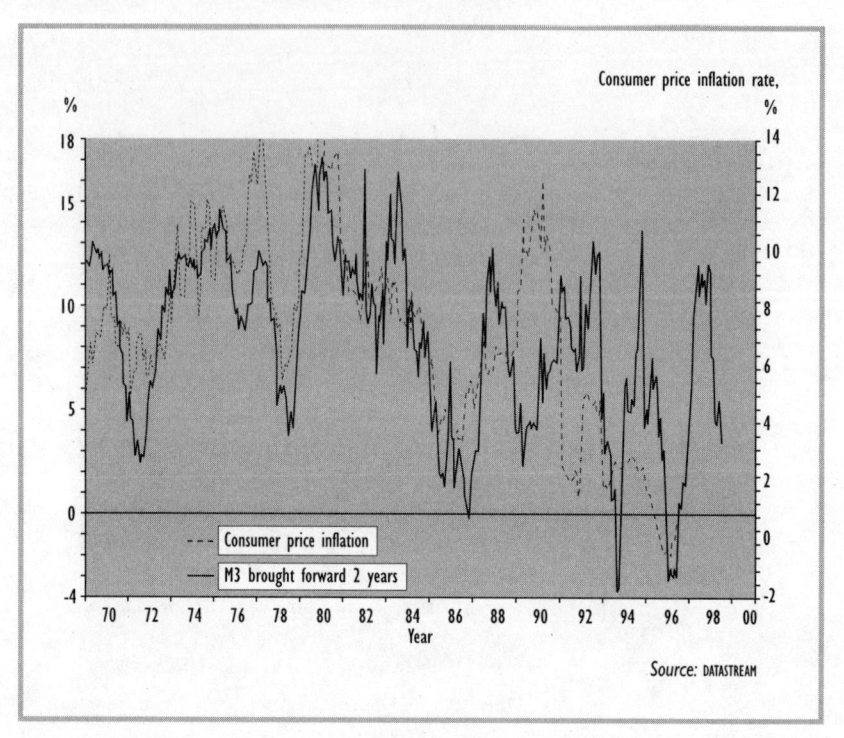

the recovery of the German economy from the slowdown of 1995/96, which followed from the German central bank's (the Bundesbank) aggressive easing of monetary policy in late 1995. Figure 10 shows a *composite liquidity indicator*, which is a combination of real money supply growth and the slope of the yield curve – which in Germany has an important effect on the demand for money (see the following section of this chapter) – and relates this to consumption.

The chart shows how in previous cycles an upturn in the monetary cycle (composite liquidity indicator) was invariably followed by an acceleration of consumption, but in the 1996 recovery this was not the case. Consumer spending was constrained by the government's fiscal efforts to meet the criteria for European economic and monetary union (EMU) and to correct the excessive rise in wage costs which had followed German unification, the result of which was zero or very low growth in real wages and disposable incomes. Nevertheless, an acceleration of overall economic activity still took place over 1996/97. The failure of domestic demand to recover adequately enhanced the tendency for excess liquidity to translate into currency weakness. The sharp weakening of the Deutschmark was not an

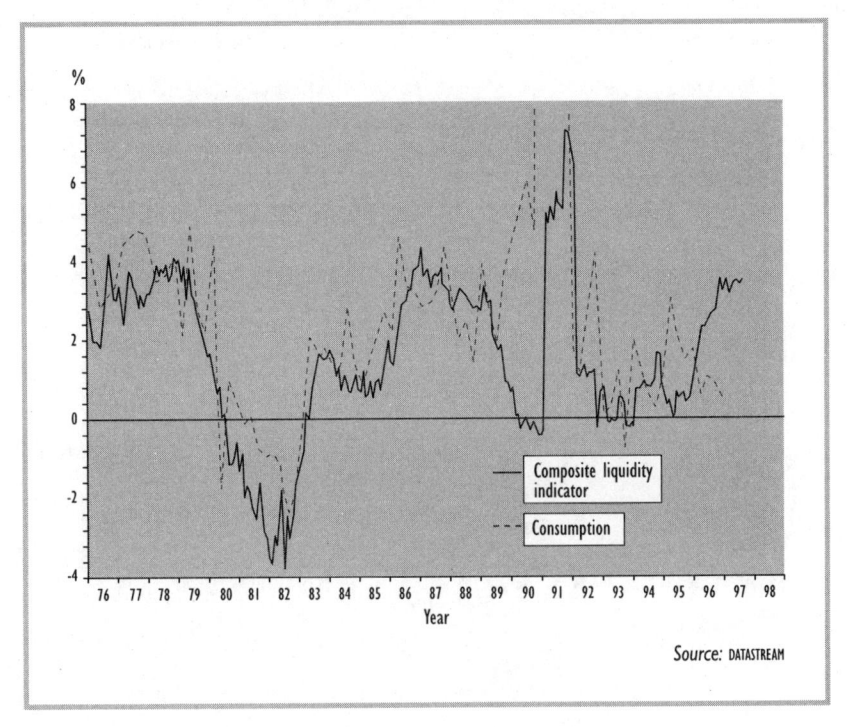

FIGURE 10   Germany: composite liquidity indicator and consumption

exogenous factor that appeared 'out of the blue', but the transmission mechanism through which the monetary easing translated into an acceleration of economic activity.

Figure 11 shows that the composite liquidity indicator appears to have a particularly long lead to inflation in Germany, of around four years. Four years is a long time, particularly in financial markets where data are scrutinized on a daily basis. Therefore, despite the experience of history, it is easy for financial analysts and investors to become complacent that a given episode of easy monetary policy is not having any negative effect for inflation. In the latter part of the 1990s, when most of the world economy is still seeing the benefit of tight monetary policies during the first half of the decade, it has become fashionable to believe that the increase in global competition (the globalization of the world economy) has eliminated for ever the threat of inflation in the developed economies. This argument is wrong. Increased competition within certain industries can certainly result in reduced output prices for those industries, and changes in the structure of the economy, but of itself it has no bearing on either the supply of money

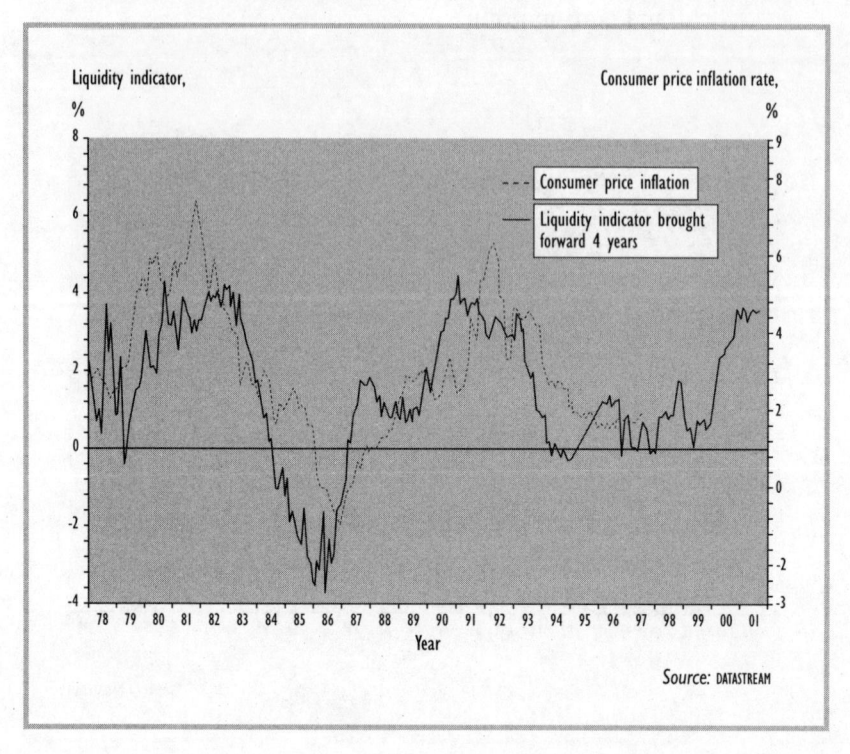

FIGURE 11 Germany: composite liquidity indicator and inflation

or the demand for money and therefore, over the medium to longer term, no consequence for the general price level. The impact, if any, will rather be on relative prices.

For instance, imagine if a developing country, e.g. China, suddenly appears as a major low cost competitor for developed nations in certain industries. For the developed countries, imports from China will be associated with downward pressure on real wages in the competitor industries and lower prices to consumers for the affected products. However, for a given amount of spending, consumers' purchasing power will now have been freed up for other goods and services, demand for which will consequently be greater. Also, for China itself, exports cannot permanently exceed imports (see Chapter 4) and therefore exports of these new products will be matched by greater imports of, possibly higher value added, goods and services. China, in the example, may be a source of greater supply in the world economy, but it is also a source of greater demand. The impact will be on the structure of the world economy and relative prices for different goods and services but not on overall prices.

We can always look around the world and find examples of countries which have very high inflation, however open they may be to the forces of global competition. Invariably this very high inflation will be associated with a very high rate of money growth.

ASSET PRICE MOVEMENTS OVER THE BUSINESS CYCLE

The monetary explanation of the business cycle given above leads naturally to an explanation of cyclical movements in financial asset prices. The first impact of monetary stimulus is seen in asset markets, as holders of excess money balances attempt to dispose of them by shifting deposits into other assets. Financial assets – stocks and bonds – being the most liquid alternative investment form are the obvious candidates, meaning that the demand for equities, in particular, tends to rise fairly coincidentally with the upturn of the monetary cycle. The impact of monetary stimulus on stock prices will potentially be at its most potent during stage 1 of the cycle (explanation given earlier) when money supply is expanding more rapidly than the demand for money and there is as yet no impact on real GDP. By definition, the measured income velocity of circulation of money is falling as money balances are being pushed around in the financial markets rather than spent on goods and services output. Therefore it is quite common, in financial analyses or models, for cycles in the equity markets to be related not to money supply growth alone but to money supply relative to nominal GDP. If money supply is rising relative to nominal GDP (or GNP), i.e. the measured income velocity of circulation of money is falling, then the stock market will tend to be performing well.

A schematic diagram of the cycle in monetary conditions (not the cycle of economic activity, which lags the monetary cycle) is shown in Figure 12. The panels give the key economic characteristics of the different phases of the monetary cycle and point to the asset classes likely to be performing absolutely or relatively well at each phase. In this simplified diagram the major movements of both short-term and long-term interest rates are identified with the same phases of the cycle. Actually, bond prices might be expected to move ahead of short rates as they respond earlier to the cycle and anticipate actions by the central bank. During the downswing of the monetary cycle, equities will be in the midst of a bear market, but bond yields will stabilize and then begin to fall (i.e. bond prices rise) as economic activity first peaks and then begins to weaken. In the classic cycle, by stage 4 as the

40 • MONETARY EXPLANATION OF THE BUSINESS CYCLE

FIGURE 12 Stylized monetary cycle

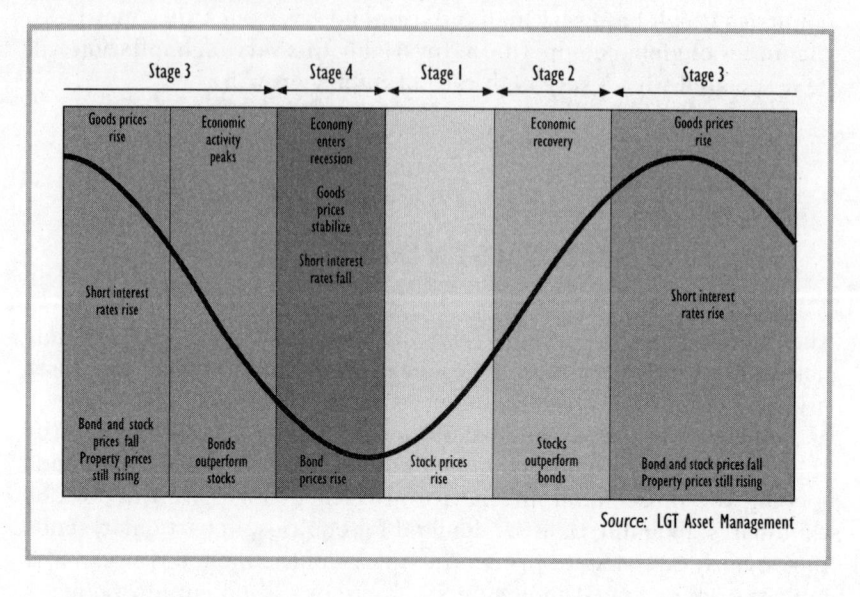

Stage 3	Stage 4	Stage 1	Stage 2	Stage 3
Goods prices rise	Economic activity peaks	Economy enters recession / Goods prices stabilize / Short interest rates fall	Economic recovery	Goods prices rise
Short interest rates rise				Short interest rates rise
Bond and stock prices fall / Property prices still rising	Bonds outperform stocks	Bond prices rise	Stock prices rise / Stocks outperform bonds	Bond and stock prices fall / Property prices still rising

Source: LGT Asset Management

economy enters recession, bonds will be well into a bull market by the time that measured inflation peaks and the central bank begins to reduce short rates. Therefore, in stage 4, long-term rates are still falling more quickly than short-term rates, i.e. the yield curve is inverting further.

At this stage, although short rates are being reduced, credit demand is weakening and inflationary expectations are beginning to fall, so that the reduction of short rates is not yet enough to be associated with a restimulation of money growth. The point when this occurs is, by definition, the turn of the monetary cycle into stage 1. Bonds are likely to continue to rise into the upturn of the monetary cycle as, like stocks, although to a lesser extent, they benefit from liquidity conditions turning expansionary. However, during stage 1 short rates will be falling faster than long rates, with long rates eventually stabilizing some time into the economic recovery in stage 2. By the top of the cycle, in stage 3, monetary conditions will eventually begin to tighten when short rates are being pushed up more quickly than bond yields are rising, i.e. the yield curve is beginning to flatten or invert. Hence the classic monetary cycle is actually a cycle in the slope of the yield curve, explaining the notion of the central bank being 'behind the curve' or 'ahead of the curve' in the implementation of its monetary policy.

The yield curve is the earliest monetary indicator of the cycle, usually leading economic activity by about twelve to eighteen months. Private credit demand is generally a lagging indicator as it tends to pick up sometime after economic activity and may still be strong after economic activity begins to weaken in the downswing, as corporate productivity falls away but wages and input prices are still rising. This is the point (the second panel of stage 3), when monetary conditions are tightening sharply, that stresses in the financial system become most intense, and historically in many of the developed economies, a major bankruptcy or financial crisis has persuaded the central bank to cut short rates sharply, heralding Stage 4 of the cycle. In Figure 13 this is illustrated for the United States.

At the bottom of the monetary cycle private credit demand will still tend to be weak and therefore the increase in banks' assets which corresponds to the growth of the money supply as the cycle turns upwards is likely to be concentrated in banks' securities holdings, including government bonds. Banks are able to take advantage of the easier and cheaper availability of short-term funds associated with the

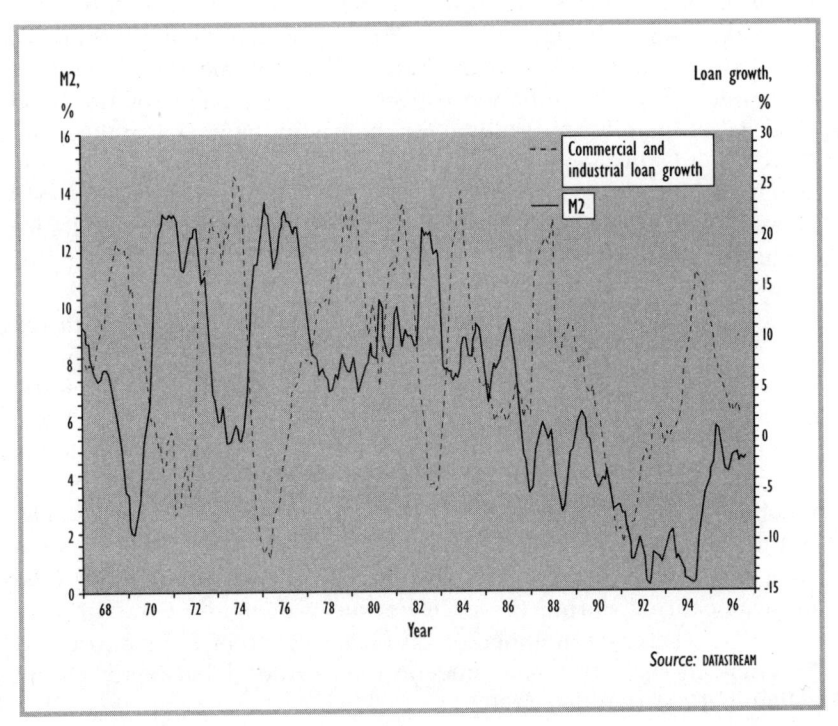

FIGURE 13 United States: money and credit cycle

fall in short rates to lock in higher yields on longer-term investments, playing the yield curve. Bank share prices may reflect this improved environment, meaning that bank and other financial shares tend to outperform during the late stages of the monetary downswing and early phase of the upswing. Obviously, it might be expected that cyclical stocks would outperform during the economic recovery phase of stage 2 of the cycle, first consumer and light cyclicals (e.g. retailers, autos, consumer goods, etc.) then heavier cyclicals (e.g. chemicals, steel), followed by inflation beneficiaries in stage 3 (e.g. real estate, commodity producers). However, although the broad movements of asset prices tend to be influenced by the pattern of the cycle, successive cycles are never identical and it is impossible to be definitive about very specific asset categories. The development of financial markets is an evolutionary as well as a cyclical process and the behavior of markets in each cycle in part reflects the accumulated experience of past cycles as well as financial conditions at the time.

Furthermore, in today's global financial markets the behavior of the financial markets in any one open economy will often reflect global financial conditions as much as the domestic liquidity cycle. The real long-term interest rate (i.e. interest rate adjusted for inflation expectations – see Chapter 3) embodied in bond yields and the valuation of equities is largely determined in a 'world capital market' which represents the aggregate of all the open capital markets and to this extent is at least partly independent of any one country's economic cycle. The inflation expectations component of the bond yield is ultimately determined by domestic monetary policy and therefore it is this component of the yield which is likely to provide the strongest link to the domestic business cycle in the manner described above. Nevertheless, in the early stage of the upswing of the cycle, for example, inflation is still falling and therefore inflation expectations may well be slow to respond to the upturn of the cycle.

If an economy is experiencing an upswing out of phase with the rest of the world then it is conceivable that bonds may continue to perform well into the economic upturn for longer than domestic economic conditions would suggest reasonable, because of a background of a falling global real interest rate. This raises the possibility that the yield curve could, for instance, flatten or even invert at a much earlier point in the recovery than described for the classic cycle. In the converse case, global influences might cause the yield curve to steepen ahead of the bottom of the monetary cycle. An example of the former occurred during the acceleration of demand in the UK over 1996/97, whereas a number of European economies, in particular, experienced the latter phenomenon during the global bond market selloff of 1994 (Sweden, Italy).

The tendency of real interest rates to converge on a global level involves capital flows, and therefore instances of divergence between business cycles in different economies are likely to result in, sometimes sharp, real exchange rate adjustments. If an economy is experiencing an 'out of synch' upswing then capital inflows will act to equalize the real interest rate – which would otherwise be tending to rise – with the rest of the world. This implies real exchange rate appreciation, such as experienced by the UK over 1996/97. The converse case of an out-of-synch downswing will be associated with depreciation of the real exchange rate. This relationship between the real interest rate and real exchange rate is discussed in the following chapter.

A further complication is that the partial divorcing of the behavior of financial asset prices from the domestic economic cycle can have implications for the demand for money. For instance, if international influences cause bond yields in an economy to be lower than would normally be consistent with domestic economic circumstances, inverting or flattening the yield curve beyond the degree usually experienced, residents may find bank deposits a more attractive haven for savings than bonds or related financial assets, yields on which would appear too low. This would not change the rate of money growth (unless there was a corresponding impact on the demand for bank credit) but it could mean that future nominal GDP growth would be lower for a given rate of money growth, as the money supply would contain a greater element of desired savings relative to transactions balances. This would represent a rise in the demand for money, and is an example of how the yield curve can be an influence on money demand as well as, or instead of, an important measure of the factors determining the supply of money, i.e. the stance of monetary policy. This was discussed in Chapter 1, and a practical implication is that a measure of the monetary cycle which combines both money supply growth and the slope of the yield curve, such as the composite liquidity indicator for Germany shown in Figure 10 on page 37, is generally superior to considering only measures of money supply growth or the yield curve alone.

REAL INTEREST RATE AND REAL EXCHANGE RATE   3

REAL INTEREST RATES

The real long-term interest rate is the long-term interest rate adjusted for the annualized rate of inflation expected until maturity. It is a risk-free concept and therefore best represented by the expected real return on government bonds, usually of ten years or greater maturity. Higher real returns apparently available from bonds or other instruments with a lower credit rating include a *risk premium*, or compensation to the investor for taking the risk that the issuer may go bankrupt. Strictly, the risk premium is a separate component of any nominal interest rate and not part of the real interest rate. In practice it is difficult to distinguish the return that savers expect from postponing consumption of goods and services (i.e. the notion that an individual will require greater consumption in the future to compensate him for sacrificing consumption now – which lies behind the real interest rate) from the return that reflects uncertainty. In particular, if the inflation rate is high there might be a great deal of uncertainty with regard to the prospective inflation rate. The investor might expect an annualized inflation rate of, say, 50 percent, but with a wide range of variability of possible outcomes. The 'real' interest rate on government debt is then likely to be higher than if the inflation rate were expected to be 2 percent with equivalently less uncertainty about the outcome. A high observed real interest rate is one of the economic costs of persistent high inflation, as the risk represented in the 'real' rate cannot be recouped within the prospective return on capital projects, thereby resulting in lower investment and economic growth.

The real interest rate is usually calculated as the annualized yield to maturity on long-term government debt minus expected annualized inflation. This is a slight approximation of a true real return which would be equal to the return on the bond divided by the appreciation of the general price level. For instance, if the ten-year government bond yield is 10 percent and the saver purchases $100 of the government bond today and reinvests all the interest receipts from the bond also at 10 percent, at the end of ten years she will have

$$100 \times 1.1^{10} = \$259.37$$

If inflation is expected to average 6 percent annually over the ten years, at the end of the ten years the price level will have risen by 79.1 percent ($1.06^{10} = 1.7908$) and hence it will require $179 to buy a basket of goods that cost only $100 today. Thus the saver will be able to buy 44.8 percent more goods with the proceeds of her savings in ten years' time than she can today ($259.37/179.08 = 1.4483$). This represents an annual rate of return of 3.77 percent ($\sqrt[10]{1.4483} = 1.0377$) which can be calculated more simply as $1.1/1.06 = 1.0377$. Usually, however, the real interest rate in this example would be given as 4 percent (10 percent − 6 percent).

In calculating the real interest rate it is very difficult to know what the inflation rate is expected to be in the future. Therefore, studies involving calculations of the real interest rate usually use some measure of past inflation, perhaps the inflation rate over the past year, as a proxy for future inflation. Often, an average of inflation rates over the past three to five years works as a better proxy than the current annual inflation rate, as people's awareness of the inflation rate is formed over a period of time. Even then it should be noted that this approach gives only a guide, and a rough one at that, to the real interest rate. In reality, to the prospective saver the rate of inflation over a period in the past is an irrelevance, or at least is only relevant to the extent that it gives a rough guide to what inflation could be in the future. What matters to the saver is what inflation will be over the life of the investment that he is thinking of making.

Index-linked government debt provides a direct market measure of the real interest rate. With an index-linked bond the investor receives separate compensation for inflation over the life of the bond through the direct linking of both the coupon and principal to an index of the price level such as the consumer price index. With future inflation therefore removed as a factor in the saver's decision, the yield to maturity of the index-linked government bond will be the real interest rate. For the time being, a practical problem is that there have been relatively few issues of index-linked debt by only a small number of governments, and the markets in the instruments are generally not liquid enough to give confidence that their yields are an accurate measure of the real rate as embodied in the valuation of other assets. The UK has a relatively long history of index-linked issuance (since 1981), and the market is fairly large. However, even in the UK it appears that only comparatively recently has the yield on index-linked gilts become a good guide to the real interest rate as it reveals itself in the valuation of financial assets over the economic cycle. Therefore historical studies or comparisons will generally still need to rely on a calculated real rate, obtained using some proxy for inflation expectations.

We might expect that, for a given level of income, the saver will save more of his income the higher is the real interest rate or real return that he anticipates. This gives rise to an upward sloping relationship between savings and the real interest rate for the economy, as indicated in Figure 14.

For a given level of national income, if the real interest rate is at r_1, then the savings of the economy will total S_1. If the real interest rate rises to r_2 then savings rise to S_2. For all the possible real interest rates between r_1 and r_2 there will be resulting levels of savings between S_1 and S_2. These points can be joined together to form the savings curve, S, depicting the relationship between real interest rates and savings for a given level of national income. (At this point, we assume away the problem posed by the government sector, for which savings

FIGURE 14 Savings curve

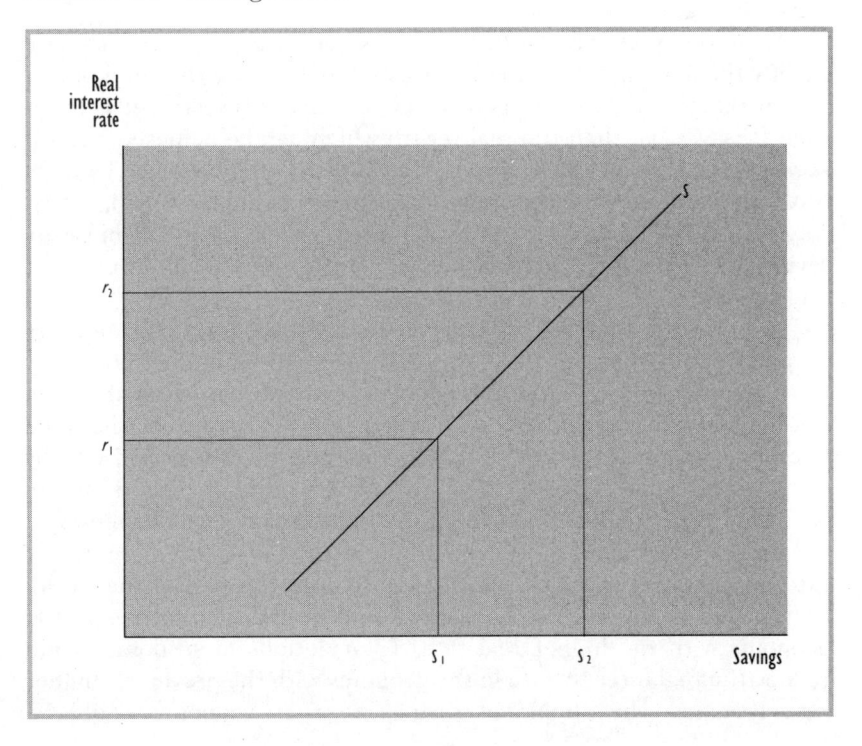

do not necessarily respond to market forces). Of course, this S curve will not be stable because national income does not remain at a given level for very long. Over time, economies grow (or possibly contract) and hence the quantity of savings for any given real interest rate will increase (or decrease) as people's incomes rise (or fall). Economic growth will tend to shift curve S to the right as the quantity of savings increases in line with income growth.

Looking at the private investment side of the savings/investment balance, for a given level of income the more savings that are invested the lower the real interest rate is likely to be. This is because the savings have ultimately to be invested in real assets to generate the real return in terms of goods and services. For a given level of GNP, the more investment undertaken the lower the return is likely to be as investment projects with the highest potential return will be undertaken first, and those with increasingly lower potential returns thereafter. Thus, the investment function is downward sloping from left to right. For a given level of national income, the greater is the level of investment the lower is the real return, or real interest rate.

In full long-run 'equilibrium' the level of savings is equal to the level of investment. At this equilibrium the real interest rate is that which equates the level of savings with the level of investment. This is shown in Figure 15.

With the real interest rate at r_e savers are persuaded to save exactly the amount which can be invested to generate this level of real return (i.e. r_e) in terms of goods and services. If investment is lower than I_e, say at I_2, then the real return which can be achieved, r_2, will persuade savers to save too much, S_2, to finance that level of investment. If, on the other hand, investment is higher than I_e, at I_1, then only a low return, r_1, can be achieved, which will result in savers saving too little, S_1, to finance the large amount of investment undertaken.

At any given time for any given economy this equivalence of gross national savings and gross national investment is unlikely to apply (although it will be a long-run tendency). This is because, for the open economies of the world, the real interest rate will tend to be the same in every economy. In the short to medium term there is no reason why this 'world' real interest rate will be one which results in an equivalence between savings and investment in any given economy.

To see why this is so we have to consider that if the real interest rate in any given economy was higher than in the rest of the world, then savers in the rest of the world would invest their savings in the economy with the higher real rate. Their actions in so doing would reduce the real interest rate in the economy with the previously higher rate (because the supply of savings to that economy would be

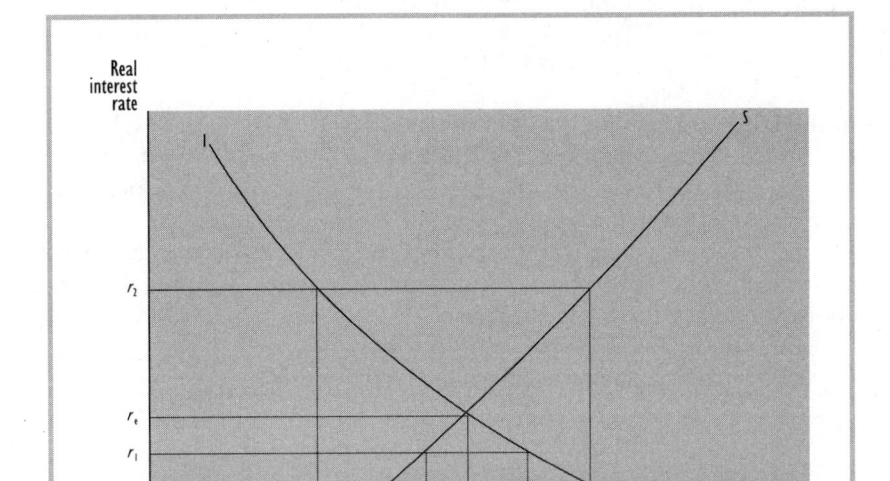

FIGURE 15 Savings/investment equilibrium

[Figure: Savings/investment equilibrium diagram with real interest rate on vertical axis and savings on horizontal axis. Downward-sloping investment curve I-I and upward-sloping savings curve S-S intersect at equilibrium rate r_e with corresponding savings S/I_e. At rate r_2 (above equilibrium), savings S_2 exceed investment I_2. At rate r_1 (below equilibrium), investment I_1 exceeds savings S_1.]

increased) and increase it for the rest of the world, until the real interest rate in every country was brought into line.

If we imagine two countries, A and B, then a saver in country B has two choices: either he can invest his savings in his home country, B, or in the foreign country, A. He will consider where he expects to obtain the greatest nominal, or money, return. Considering comparative risk-free returns, the risk-free return he can obtain in his home country B is the nominal interest rate, $i(B)$ (i.e. the real interest rate, $r(B)$, plus the expected inflation rate, $\dot{P}(B)$). The return he can obtain from investing in country A is the nominal interest rate in country A, $i(A)$, plus the expected appreciation of A's currency against B's currency, i.e. $i(A) + E\dot{R}(B/A)$. He will invest in country A – the foreign country – as long as:

$$i(A) + E\dot{R}(B/A) > i(B)$$

If the reverse is true, that is if:

$$i(A) + E\dot{R}(B/A) < i(B)$$

then he will invest at home, in country B.

Because savers across the world are prepared to shift funds in this manner, in equilibrium it must be true that:

$$i(A) + E\dot{R}(B/A) = i(B)$$

In the following section it will be shown that, over time, the exchange rate must keep returning to the purchasing power parity level, $PPP(A)_T$, where T refers to the time of measurement. Therefore, the best expectation for the appreciation of the exchange rate is the change in the purchasing power parity rate, $P\dot{P}P(A)$. This depends only upon the relative inflation rates in countries A and B, and approximates to $\dot{P}(B) - \dot{P}(A)$. Thus,

$$\text{expected } E\dot{R}(B/A) = \dot{P}(B) - \dot{P}(A)$$

The previous equality then amounts to:

$$i(A) + \dot{P}(B) - \dot{P}(A) = i(B)$$

or

$$i(A) - \dot{P}(A) = i(B) - \dot{P}(B)$$

or

$$r(A) = r(B)$$

The nominal interest rate minus inflationary expectations, or the real interest rate, should be the same for both countries. Extending this to the world as a whole, it implies that the real interest rate, at least adjusted for risk, should be the same in all economies open to free capital movement.

The previous chapter explained how bond yields rise and fall over the business cycle. Bond yields tend to fluctuate fairly coincidentally with economic activity, i.e. with some delay to the monetary cycle shown in Figure 12 on page 40, and this is particularly true of the real interest rate component of the yield. This follows from the explanation of the determination of the real interest rate from desired savings and investment given above. As economic activity picks up in the upturn of the business cycle (stage 2 of the monetary cycle in Figure 12), investment opportunities are likely to become apparent more quickly than the supply of savings readily available to fund them, i.e. the investment schedule as depicted in Figure 15 moves to the right more quickly than the savings schedule, as real national income rises, tending to push up the equilibrium real interest rate. Therefore, the 'world' real interest rate – the real rate which tends to be equalized for all open economies – might be expected to be pro-cyclical. Figure 16 confirms this, showing a definite correlation between the cycle in industrial production growth for the OECD countries (all developed economies) and a measure of the world real interest rate calculated as a GDP weighted average of real rates for the G5 countries, where each individual G5 member country's real rate is proxied by the ten-year government bond yield minus a three-year moving average of the annual inflation rate.

The previous chapter touched upon how any tendency for real interest rates to diverge in two economies with diverging business cycles would be likely to manifest itself not in different real interest rates but in an adjustment of the real exchange rate between the currencies of the two countries. This is explored more fully in the final section of this chapter, as is the influence of government finances, which represent another potential source of funds demand in an economy and therefore a further potential influence on the real interest rate.

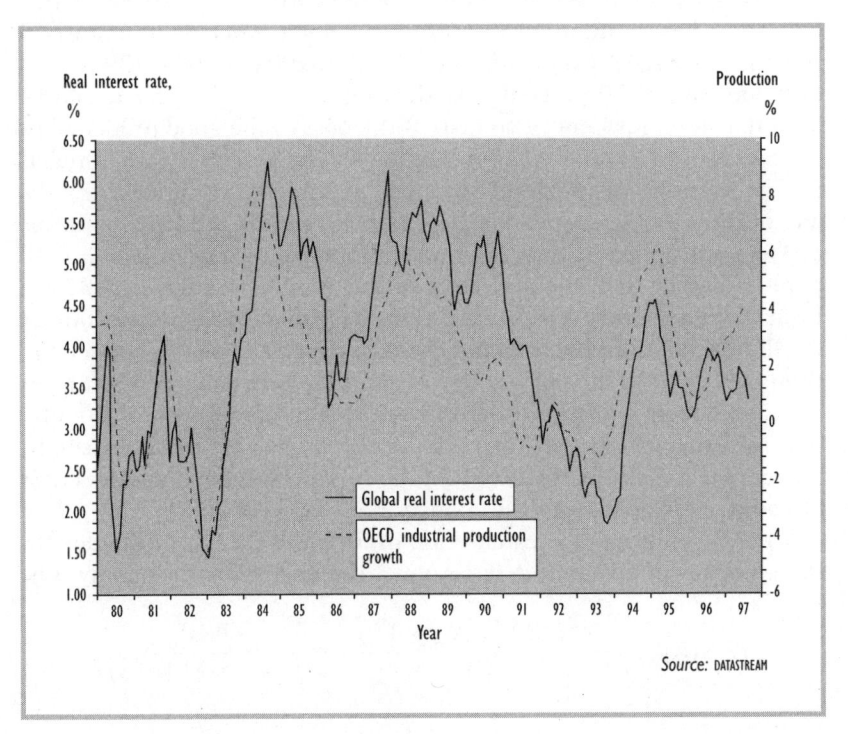

FIGURE 16 OECD industrial production and global real rate

Source: DATASTREAM

PURCHASING POWER PARITY AND REAL EXCHANGE RATE

This section explores more fully the concept of the real exchange rate, which is closely related to the notion of purchasing power parity (PPP).

Economists use the idea of the real exchange rate, or inflation-adjusted exchange rate, to distinguish movements in exchange rates that alter a country's competitiveness from those which merely reflect inflation. A fall in the real exchange rate for a currency in terms of another nation's currency implies a genuine increase in competitiveness for the first economy relative to the second. It should, over time, lead the first economy's current account balance with the second to improve. Conversely, a rise in the real exchange rate means a deterioration in competitiveness.

Consider two countries, A and B. Country A's dollar is initially worth five of country B's dollars (i.e. A$1 = B$5). Country A has a current account deficit, and over a year the value of its currency falls to being worth only B$4. At the same time, however, the price of an average good produced by country A rises from A$20 to A$33 (i.e. country A has an inflation rate of 65 percent), whereas in country B the same average good rises in price from B$100 to only B$120 (i.e. an inflation rate of 20 percent). At the beginning of the year it can be seen that for a resident of country B the cost of the good produced by country A is B$100 (i.e. A$20 multiplied by the exchange rate, which is 5), the same as for the good produced within country B itself. By the end of the year the cost of the good has risen to B$132 (the new price of A$33 multiplied by the new, lower, exchange rate of 4), which is 10 percent higher than the new price of the good in country B (B$120). Even though country A's exchange rate has fallen, residents of country B will now be more likely than before to purchase goods produced in their own country than in country A, and therefore country A's current account deficit is likely to deteriorate rather than improve. Country A's real exchange rate against country B can be said to have risen by 10 percent, reflecting the extent of the relative loss of competitiveness of country A's goods against country B's.

The formula for the calculation of a real exchange rate index for the currency of economy A in terms of the currency of economy B is:

$$\text{RER}(A)_T = \frac{100 \times \text{ER}(B/A)_T \times P(A)_T}{P(B)_T} \times \frac{P(B)_B}{P(A)_B \times \text{ER}(B/A)_B}$$

where $ER(B/A)$ is the exchange rate for economy A's currency in terms of how many units of B's currency one unit of A's currency is worth; P is a representative index of the prices of traded goods (perhaps the wholesale price index); subscript B indicates some chosen base year for which the value of the index is to be set to 100, and subscript T indicates the time (year, month or day) for which the current value of the real exchange rate index is being calculated.

For the above example, using the formula and taking the beginning of the year as the base period, the real exchange rate for country A at the beginning (beg) of the year would be:

$$RER(A)_{beg} = \frac{100 \times 5_{beg} \times 20_{beg}}{100_{beg}} \times \frac{100_{beg}}{20_{beg} \times 5_{beg}}$$
$$= 100$$

which must be the case because the beginning of the year has been chosen as the base period, at which the index is set to 100. (It should be noted that the second part of the formula merely acts to index the real exchange rate to 100 at the base period. In this example it is not necessary because the price of goods for country B was already equal to 100 at the beginning of the year.)

At the end of the year, A's real exchange rate is calculated from the formula:

$$RER(A)_{end} = \frac{100 \times 4_{end} \times 33_{end}}{120_{end}} \times \frac{100_{beg}}{20_{beg} \times 5_{beg}}$$
$$= \frac{100 \times 132}{120} \times \frac{100}{100}$$
$$= 110$$

A's real exchange rate has risen from 100 to 110 over the year, or by 10 percent, reflecting the 10 percent loss in competitiveness to B.

In reality it is not always the case that merely because country A's real exchange rate relative to country B has risen, country A's overall trade position will worsen. In the above example country A's real exchange rate has risen because its inflation rate is higher than B's. However, it may be that in other economies inflation is equally as high as in A. If A's currency has fallen relative to these other currencies as well as relative to B's, economy A is becoming more competitive relative to the rest of the world apart from B. Although its trade position with B might be deteriorating, it may be improving with the rest of the world by more than enough to offset this, at least for a time.

Simple exchange rates are concerned with only two countries. The yen/dollar rate, for instance, tells how many yen a dollar is worth, but nothing about either Japan's or the United States's relationship to third countries. To get around this, and to approach an estimate for an economy's overall competitiveness, economists use the concept of the real effective exchange rate. A real effective exchange rate for any country is the average of the real exchange rates against the currencies of each of its trading partners. It is usually a weighted average in which the weight attributed to each of the real exchange rates reflects the relative importance of each of the trading partners to the economy. (The weights are usually the share of each trading partner's trade with the economy expressed as a percentage of the economy's total trade.)

To calculate a real effective exchange rate for country A, above, we first need to calculate the real exchange rates with its other trading partners, countries C, D, E, etc. Then we calculate the average of all the real exchange rates, weighting each real exchange rate by a factor which represents the importance of each of B, C, D, E, etc. as a trading partner to country A. An appropriate weight would be the sum of A's exports to and imports from each country as a fraction of A's total exports and imports. The formula is:

$$\text{REER(A)}_T = 100 \times \sum_{I=1}^{n} \frac{\text{ER(I/A)}_T \times P(A)_T}{P(I)_T} \times \frac{P(I)_B}{P(A)_B \times \text{ER(I/A)}_B} \times W_I$$

The formula is similar to the previous one for the real exchange rate. The main difference is that country B has now become country I, where I represents, in turn, each of country A's trading partners numbered from 1 to n. The real exchange rate is calculated for each of the I, and for each multiplied by the appropriate weight, W. The numbers resulting are then summed to give the final real effective exchange rate for country A at time T.

The real effective exchange rate is a measure of overall trade competitiveness. If an economy starts from a position of current account balance (i.e. its underlying current account balance is zero) and its real effective exchange rate rises (i.e. it loses competitiveness), other things being equal it should then move into deficit on current account. At a later stage, when its real effective exchange rate falls back, the current account deficit should disappear as competitiveness is regained.

The theory of purchasing power parity suggests that at some exchange rate between two countries' currencies, relative competitiveness will be restored to the level of some former time when trade for the two countries was in balance. At this level of the exchange rate, trade should then be in balance again. In its most extreme form, purchasing power parity is taken to mean that, at this exchange rate for which trade is in balance, an identical good produced in both countries will cost the same in each country. A simple version of this is the not entirely serious notion of the 'hamburger standard', developed by the *Economist* magazine. If a 'Big Mac' costs £1.00 in England and costs ¥400 in Japan, then the appropriate, or equilibrium, exchange rate between the pound and the yen is said to be £1 = ¥400, because this is the exchange rate which would equalize the price of a hamburger in both countries for residents of either country. The *purchasing power* of £1.00 in England would be equal to, or at *parity* with, the purchasing power of £1.00 in Japan.

In practice, it is not necessarily true that the exchange rate which balances the current account for any two countries will be one that results in the price of any particular good, or even basket of goods, sold in the two countries being the same. In the case of the 'Big Mac' example, the fast-food hamburger is more a service than a traded good. If wage levels for hamburger cooks and servers in Japan are higher than in England, or property prices are higher, then the price of a hamburger in Japan could be higher than in England even at a long-run equilibrium exchange rate between the yen and the pound. In a world in which there were a free market in resources (including land, labour, capital), wage levels might eventually be equalized by hamburger cooks and servers leaving England to work in Japan to earn more money (reducing the labour supply and raising wages in England and increasing the labour supply and depressing wages in Japan), and property prices in Japan would be reduced through increased supply of property. In practice, the real world of language barriers, immigration controls and regulation of land use presents obstacles to these economic adjustments.

Although it is easier to conceive of a purchasing power parity exchange rate as one which would equalize the cost of some basket of *traded* goods (i.e. goods which, unlike hamburgers, are actually exported and imported) produced by two economies, in practice this is difficult to measure. Therefore, purchasing power parity is usually measured as a relative, rather than absolute, concept. A purchasing power parity exchange rate is calculated as being the exchange rate that would restore competitiveness between the two countries to the level it was at some previous base date. The base date is usually chosen as one when trade was in balance (the base year may be not one year, but an average), then price indices are taken to give the rate of inflation each country has experienced since the base year. The purchasing power parity exchange rate (PPP) between the two countries' currencies is calculated so that if the exchange rate were at the PPP level, the exchange rate movement would offset the effect of inflation to leave the relative competitiveness between the two countries the same as at the base date.

Returning to the original example of countries A and B, country A had an inflation rate of 65 percent and B an inflation rate of 20 percent. If we assume that, at the beginning of the year, trade was in balance, we can set price indices to 100 at the beginning of the year for each country. At the end of the period the price index for A will be 165 and for B, 120. At the base period (i.e. the beginning of the year) the exchange rate was A$1 = B$5. The exchange rate which would leave competitiveness the same at the end of the year as it was at the base period (i.e. the beginning) is:

$$PPP(A) = \frac{120}{165} \times 5 = 3.6363$$

that is:

$$A\$1 = B\$3.6363$$

Hence A$1 = B$3.6363 is the PPP value for A's currency at the end of the year. If A's currency depreciated against B's to this level, the depreciation of the exchange rate would just offset the fact that A's inflation rate has been higher than B's, to mean that A's products remain equally as competitive with B's as they were at the base period.

The full formula for the PPP level of country A's currency in terms of country B's is:

$$PPP(A)_T = \frac{P(B)_T}{P(A)_T} \times \frac{P(A)_B}{P(B)_B} \times ER(B/A)_B$$

The second part of this formula is the adjustment factor, which sets the price indices for both countries to 100 at the base period if they are not already 100.

It should be noted that the PPP level for the exchange rate is completely independent of the current exchange rate: $ER(B/A)_T$ does not enter into the above formula. The PPP depends only upon the exchange rate at the base period and the inflation rates since that time.

The practical calculation of accurate PPP exchange rates depends on the availability of suitable price indices. The ideal price index would be one which contained a negligible nontraded good (including services) component but which included the broad spectrum of the economy's traded goods output. In practice, export price, producer price or wholesale price indices (in that order of preference) usually suffice. A consumer price index may give misleading results for an economy, particularly if the prices of services are changing relative to the prices of traded goods. It was explained, for the example of hamburgers, that the lack of a free market in resources means that significant differences between nations in the prices of services and nontraded goods can be sustained more or less indefinitely. If the price of services in an economy is tending to rise relative to the price of goods, then the rate of increase of consumer prices, which usually include a large services element, will be faster than the rate of traded goods price inflation. Because the higher service price inflation does not have implications for trade competitiveness, use of the consumer price index in the purchasing power parity calculation would give a misleading result.

The most common economic cause of a persistent rise in the relative price of services is structural change resulting from a rapid rate of economic development. In an economy that is industrializing rapidly, a high rate of productivity growth in manufacturing results in increasing real wages for manufacturing workers. Higher real wages attract workers from the other sectors of the economy, causing real wages in those sectors to rise similarly. In the service sector the productivity growth being experienced in manufacturing cannot be achieved. Instead, higher wages translate directly into higher prices, with the result that the prices of services keep rising relative to the prices of manufactured output. This pattern has been noticeable in Japan over the 1940s, 1950s and 1960s, the other dynamic east Asian economies subsequently, and more recently in Spain, since that country joined the European Community in 1986.

There is a direct relationship between the current exchange rate, the PPP exchange rate and the real exchange rate. In our example the actual exchange rate at the end of the year was A\$1 = B\$4. This is $4/3.6363 = 1.1$, or 10 percent, higher than the PPP level of the exchange rate. Therefore, it can be said that A's currency is 10 percent 'overvalued' relative to what it would need to be to achieve current account balance. In the previous calculation of the real exchange rate for A it was shown that the real exchange rate at the end of the year was 110, having risen by 10 percent during the year. If the base period for the real exchange rate calculation is set at a time when trade is judged to have been balanced (as in the PPP calculation), then the real exchange rate merely shows the degree to which the current exchange rate is over- or undervalued relative to its PPP level. A real exchange rate of 110 denotes a 10 percent overvaluation relative to PPP and a real exchange rate of 90, a 10 percent undervaluation. This is easily seen from the fact that if we take the current exchange rate, $ER(B/A)_T$ and divide it by $PPP(A)_T$ we get:

$$\frac{ER(B/A)_T}{PPP(A)_T} = \frac{ER(B/A)_T \times P(A)_T \times P(B)_B}{P(B)_T \times P(A)_B \times ER(B/A)_B}$$

which is the same formula as derived for the real exchange rate.

Similarly, if the base period for the real effective exchange rate calculation is set to the year, or period, at which the current account is judged to have been in balance, then the real effective exchange rate will give the degree of over- or undervaluation of the currency, except on a multilateral (i.e. relative to many countries, or all the trading partners) basis, rather than just relative to one other currency.

In the next chapter it is explained how the current account for any country must ultimately return to balance. Foreigners will not be prepared to continue to accumulate exposure to a deficit country's currency indefinitely and, in the case of a surplus country, residents will not wish to increase exposure to the currencies of the rest of the world without limit. Combining this with the notion that the PPP level of the currency is the level at which competitiveness is restored such that the current account returns to balance, suggests that any currency must ultimately return to its PPP level. This gives rise to the theory that, over time, exchange rates will fluctuate around their PPP levels. A typical example is given in Figure 17 showing the Swedish krona/Deutschmark exchange rate and its PPP level.

TWO-COUNTRY MODEL OF REAL INTEREST RATE AND REAL EXCHANGE RATE DETERMINATION

From here we can move on to develop a simplified example of the relationship between the world's two major economies – the United States and Japan – during the 1980s. To simplify the analysis, let us imagine that the United States and Japan are the only two economies in the world. The real interest rate for the world is then determined as the equilibrium between savings for the United States plus savings for Japan and investment for the United States plus investment for Japan. We must also introduce the existence of a government sector in each of the economies. Savings and investment of the government sector are less responsive to market forces than those of the private sector,

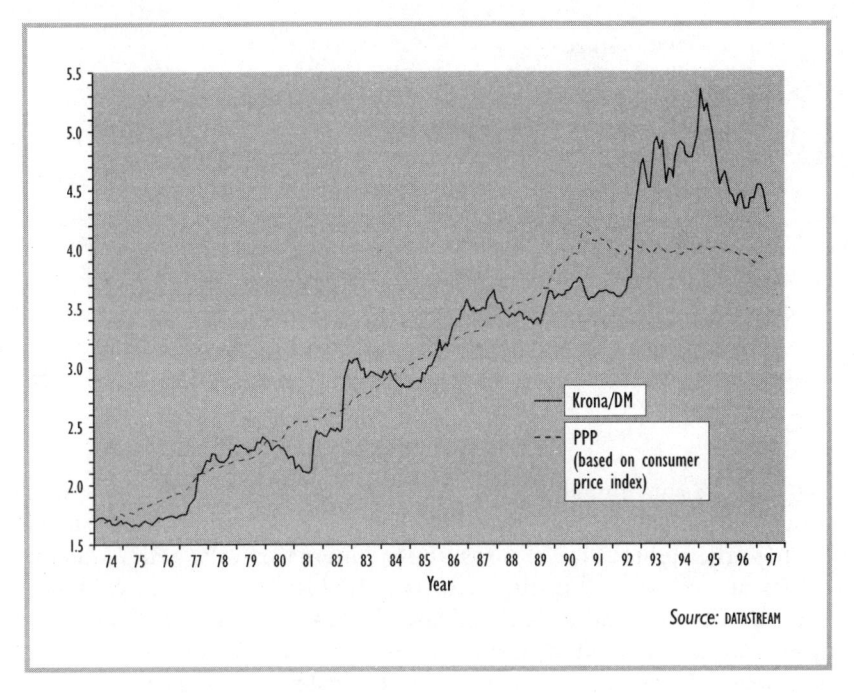

FIGURE 17 Sweden: krona/Deutschmark rate versus purchasing power parity

and hence it is reasonable to exclude government savings from the savings (S) curve, which then represents only private savings. To compensate, we have also to subtract government savings from the investment (I) curve, which then represents private investment plus government investment minus government savings, or private investment plus the PSD (public sector deficit), i.e. the two domestic uses of savings.

We can imagine a long-run equilibrium in which the real interest rate is determined by the equality of savings and investment for the world (United States plus Japan) and this same real interest rate also equalizes savings and investment in each of the countries. At this long-run equilibrium the exchange rate between the US and Japanese currencies would be at the purchasing power parity level.

In Figure 18 the real interest rate, r_e, is determined by the intersection of the savings and investment plus PSD schedules for the world (i.e. the savings and investment plus PSD schedules for the United States and Japan added together). This real interest rate also happens to equate savings with investment and the government deficit in each of Japan and the United States considered separately.

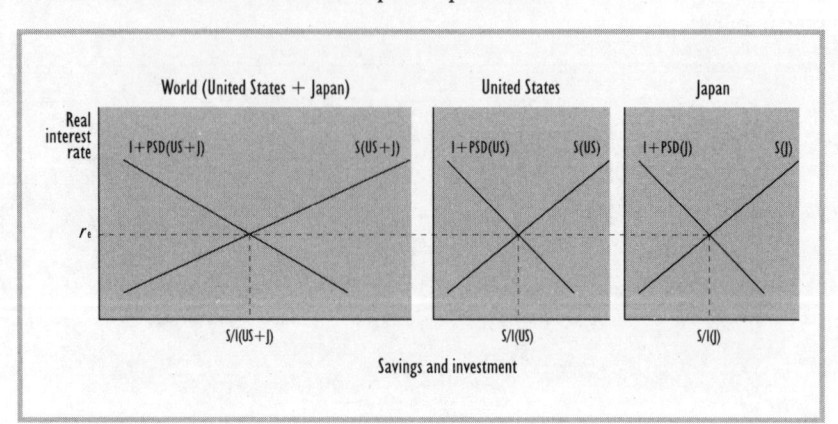

FIGURE 18 United States/Japan equilibrium

Now, let us imagine that the investment schedule (or, more properly, the investment plus PSD schedule) for the United States drifts to the right, either as a result of an increase in the budget deficit (PSD) or an increase in the returns available to private investment, because of more favorable tax laws for investment, or both. This approximates to what occurred in the United States between 1981 and 1985. The rise in the I + PSD schedule for the United States is reflected in an equivalent rise in the I + PSD schedule for the world.

In Figure 19 the I + PSD schedule for the United States drifts to the right to a new position I' + PSD' as a result of a larger budget deficit and an overall higher return becoming available to investment because of favorable tax changes. The I + PSD schedule for the world as a whole therefore moves to the right by the same amount, to position I' + PSD'(W). The world real interest rate rises to the new position r', the real interest rate which is now necessary to equalize the supply of savings with the demand for them for investment purposes. In essence, the rise in the I + PSD(W) schedule signals that a higher return is now available at each level of investment. The real interest rate rises to the new level which will call forth a new, higher, amount of savings to match a new, higher level of investment which can achieve that real return. As a result, at the new equilibrium S'/I' + PSD'(W), both savings and investment (more correctly investment plus the government deficit) are higher.

Considering the situation for the United States and Japan separately, the new equilibrium real interest rate, r', is below the real interest rate which would be necessary to balance savings and

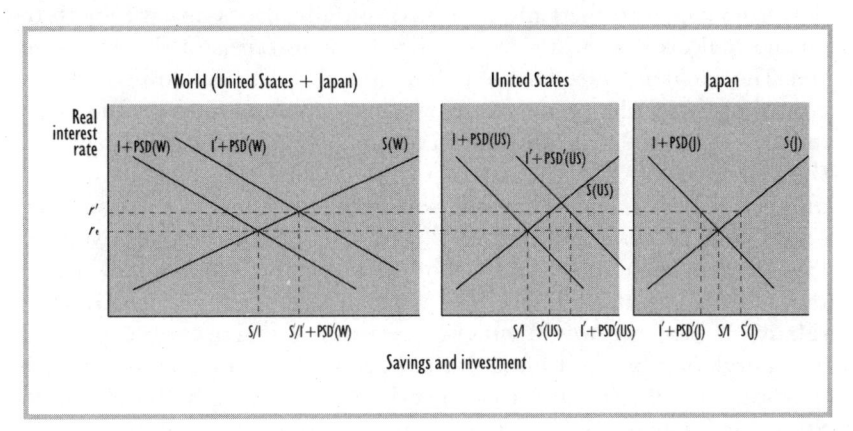

FIGURE 19 US public sector deficit increases

investment for the United States alone and above the level necessary to balance savings and investment for Japan. Consequently, at this real interest rate investment, at I' + PSD' (US) exceeds savings, S'(US), in the United States, whereas in Japan savings, at S'(J), exceed investment plus the budget deficit at I' + PSD'(J). Savings for Japan exceed investment in Japan because part of the Japanese savings is now going to finance investment and the budget deficit for the United States. This 'excess' of savings in Japan and 'deficiency' of savings in the United States at the new world equilibrium real interest rate is matched by Japan running an equivalent current account surplus with the United States (because S − I − PSD = X − M; see Chapter 4). The sharp deterioration of the US public sector finances in the early 1980s was followed by an equivalent deterioration of the US current account balance.

How is this current account imbalance generated? Intuitively, what occurs is that a rise in the demand for savings in the United States places upward pressure on real interest rates there. The tendency towards higher real interest rates not only raises savings in the United States but also attracts funds from Japan seeking the higher real return now available. At the new equilibrium, higher investment in the United States is financed partly by increased US savings and partly by Japanese savings. To some extent the attraction of Japanese savings to the United States displaces investment in Japan (the extent to which the new quantity of investment, I' + PSD'(J) is below the old quantity, S/I + PSD(J)) and to some extent it raises the overall level of savings in Japan (the extent to which the new quantity of savings, S'(J), exceeds the old quantity S/I + PSD(J)).

The movement of funds from Japan to the United States (a capital flow from Japan to the United States) initially places upward pressure on the real exchange rate for the US dollar in terms of the Japanese yen. The exchange rate for the dollar rises above its PPP level, and this contributes to the generation of the matching current account imbalance between the United States and Japan. (This occurred over the period 1982–85.) The extent of the dollar's rise depends upon a number of factors, including the sensitivity of changes in demand for goods and services internationally to changes in competitiveness. Free-market economists would tend to argue that only a small rise in the dollar above its PPP level (i.e. a small loss of US competitiveness relative to Japan) would quickly generate an appropriate current account deficit for the United States because the demand for Japanese goods and services relative to US goods and services in both the United States and Japan would respond very quickly to the change in price competitiveness. Unfortunately, the history of floating exchange rates has been one in which it has appeared that large movements of real exchange rates tend to be necessary to generate appropriate current account responses. The rise and fall of the real value of the dollar over the period 1982–87 is a classic example of this.

The equilibrium reached at this point is not a final, long-term equilibrium. If sustained, it would require Japanese residents to continue accumulating net claims on US residents (reflecting the current account imbalance) and therefore continually increasing net exposure to the dollar (except to the extent that US residents are willing to accumulate yen liabilities). These concepts are explored in the next chapter, and are illustrated in Figure 20, in which the actual build-up of the debt/credit imbalance between the United States and Japan during the 1980s is shown. Interest payments on external debt in themselves contribute to a further deterioration of the current account, which means that the situation illustrated in Figure 20 is ultimately unsustainable.

At some point this means that the dollar has to fall back to its PPP level, and probably below it for a time, in order to bring the current account back into balance. (This occurred over 1985–87.) The effect that this process has on savings and investment in both the United States and Japan determines the final, long-run equilibrium. In practice, in a dynamic world economy, it is unlikely that the long-run equilibrium would be reached before another exogenous shock impacted on the economic system. Nevertheless, market forces will ensure that there will always be a tendency to the equality of real interest rates in each economy, exchange rates at PPP levels, and current accounts in balance.

FIGURE 20 United States and Japan: debtor and creditor nations

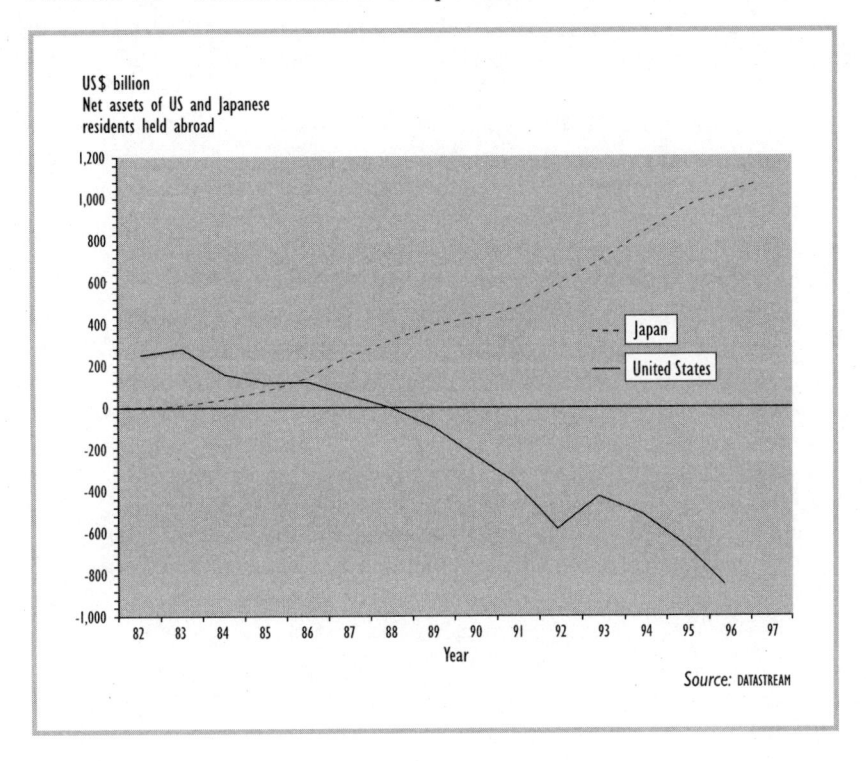

Source: DATASTREAM

SAVINGS, INVESTMENT AND FLOWS OF FUNDS

4

EQUIVALENCE OF SAVINGS AND INVESTMENT

The previous chapter showed how, in a closed economy or for the world economy (which is one big closed economy), the real interest rate can act as an equilibriating mechanism between *desired* savings and *desired* investment. In a single open economy this equilibrium is more likely to come about through capital inflow or outflow, i.e. drawing on, or providing, savings from or to the rest of the world. In an accounting framework actual achieved savings and investment are essentially the same thing and therefore *ex post*, in a closed economy (or an economy with current account balance), savings and investment for the whole economy are necessarily identical. This is true by virtue of the fact that, for the closed economy as a whole, *income* can only be spent on consumption or saved, whereas *spending* can only be consumption spending or investment spending. As total income is derived from, and equal to, total expenditure on the economy's output, saving and investment must be the same.

A small example may help to illustrate this. Consider two people, Ms X and Ms Y. Ms X spends half of her annual income of 100, and places the other 50 in the bank. The bank in turn lends this 50 to Ms Y, who, for the sake of simplicity, we shall assume has no income. Ms Y then spends this 50 on a new automobile. If we make the assumption that Ms X and Ms Y represent a whole economy, we can then see what the savings investment balance looks like:

Ms X's income = 100 and consumption = 50, and therefore
Ms X's savings = 100 − 50 = 50
Ms Y's income = 0 and consumption = 50, and therefore
Ms Y's savings = 0 − 50 = −50, i.e. Ms Y is 'dissaving'

For Ms X and Ms Y together, therefore:

total income = 100 + 0 = 100
savings = 50 − 50 = 0
investment = 0. Therefore,
savings = investment = 0

Now let us assume that Ms Y is actually the sole proprietor of a car rental company and buys the automobile to add to her fleet. In this case the purchase is classified as an investment and not as consumption, because it is an equipment purchase by a company. Now, Ms X's income = 100, consumption = 50, savings = 50 as before, but,

Ms Y's income = 0 and consumption = 0, therefore
Ms Y's savings = income − consumption = 0.

However, investment by Ms Y's company = 50. For Ms X and Ms Y together then:

income = 100 + 0 = 100
saving = 50 + 0 = 50
investment = 50
i.e. savings = investment = 50.

This example helps to illustrate that, because savings and investment are equivalent by definition, the measured amount of savings for an economy is to some extent dependent upon the definition of investment. Economists in the past have used this argument to explain the low rate of savings in the US economy. They argue that a high proportion of consumer spending in the United States is spending on durable goods, i.e. goods expected to have a life of longer than three years, and that if spending on these durable goods were reclassified as investment, the US savings rate would no longer appear low on an international comparison.

For an open economy, savings must always be invested, but the investment does not have to be within the domestic economy itself. However, only domestic investment, in the first instance, contributes to national income. Furthermore, the only other way in which income can be 'generated' domestically is from consumption spending, which is the inverse of saving. With some thought it can be seen that the only way in which savings can exceed domestic investment for an economy (i.e. the only way in which there can be net investment overseas) is if the income from which the 'excess' savings derive is generated externally, i.e. from net foreign spending on domestic goods and services, or exports minus imports. This is stated in the following identity:

$$S(\text{Total}) = I(\text{Total}) + X - M$$

where X and M are exports and imports of goods and services and $X - M$ is therefore the current account balance.

This identity can be derived easily from the simple national income accounting identities. National income accounting principles and concepts are discussed in Chapter 9, but at this point it is sufficient to note the identities for the sources and uses of income. Income represents the proceeds from spending on the final output of the economy as paid out or retained by the entities (e.g. firms) responsible for producing that output. As such, the total income, Y, of the economy (GNP) will be equivalent to the sum of private consumer spending (C), private investment spending (I), government spending (G), and net foreign spending $(X - M)$ on final goods and services output. That is:

$$Y = C + I + G + X - M$$

Income may be paid to the government as tax, or spent (i.e. consumer spending). If it is used in neither of these ways, then it is defined as being saved, or becoming saving (S), i.e.:

$$Y = C + S + T$$

where T here is taxes net of transfers paid back by the government in the form of welfare benefits, etc.

Equating the right-hand sides of these identities, which are both equal to Y, or the GNP, gives:

$$I + G + X - M = S + T$$

or

$$S = I + \text{PSD} + (X - M)$$

where PSD, the public sector deficit, is the excess of government sector spending on goods and services output over taxes net of transfers, or $G - T$ in the previous identity (see Chapter 8).

The public sector deficit, PSD, is also equivalent to the difference between the government's own investment and savings. The government's net tax revenue (T) is either spent as government consumption (CG) or, by definition, must be saved (SG), i.e.

$$T = CG + SG$$

Similarly, government spending on final output comprises government consumption spending (CG) and government investment spending (IG):

$$G = CG + IG$$

Therefore:

$$PSD = G - T = IG - SG$$

or the excess of government investment over government savings. The previous identity,

$$S = I + PSD + (X - M),$$

can then be restated to incorporate private and government sector savings and investment as S(Total) and I(Total), respectively:

$$S(Total) = I(Total) + (X - M),$$

as before, where:

$$S(Total) = S + SG \text{ and } I(Total) = I + IG$$

For the world economy considered as a whole there can be no possibility of access to outside savings. Total world exports equal total world imports $(X - M = 0)$ and therefore the identity is:

$$S(World) = I(World) + PSD(World)$$

That is, the world's total private savings must finance the world's total private investment plus the sum of the world's governments' deficits, or savings deficiency of the world's governments.

The example given in the previous chapter of the relationship between the US and Japanese economies in the 1980s can be seen in the context of these identities. They lie at the root of the concept of 'crowding out'. If the available 'supply' of savings is assumed to be fixed, then in the event of any of the terms on the right-hand side of the identity rising, one or both of the other variables will have to fall. Traditional economics tended to assume that individual economies are 'closed' (i.e. trade and, more importantly, flows of capital between countries are restricted). This led economists to argue that a rise in the government deficit (PSD) tends to lead to a fall in private domestic investment (I). As the government deficit rises, less of the private sector's savings than before are available to finance private investment. Thus, at the previously existing level of real interest rates, demand for savings outweighs the supply. There is upward pressure on real interest rates until people have been encouraged to save more because of the possibility of earning a higher return and/or the marginal investment projects (i.e. investment projects which were only just profitable at the previously existing level of real interest rates) have been squeezed, or crowded, out.

In an open world economy, flows of capital between the major economies are largely unrestricted by regulations, and as was shown in Chapter 3, real interest rates in any one country cannot exceed those in another country for long because savings would be drawn from the lower real interest rate country to the higher. Similarly, it makes little sense to consider the supply of savings available for investment in any one economy to be fixed, because investment in any one economy can be financed through drawing on the savings of the rest of the world, and need not be restricted to financing from the savings of the economy in which the investment is taking place.

As has been seen, in this situation it is far more likely that a rise in the government deficit for any one country will lead to a fall in the trade surplus, or a larger trade deficit if imports already exceed exports. A rise in the government deficit in country A will attract capital from the rest of the world (i.e. will be financed from the rest of the world's savings). If, for simplicity, we assume that trade was previously balanced (i.e. $X = M$, or $X - M = 0$), there will then be a growing tendency for savings to exceed investment in the rest of the world – because part of the rest of the world's savings is invested in country A. Conversely, in country A there will be a shortfall of savings relative to domestic investment, or savings investment gap, reflecting the government deficit. The income which sustains this savings investment imbalance must be generated through the rest of the world running a trade surplus with country A.

For country A, if private savings are assumed fixed and private investment remains unchanged, then a rise in the government deficit must be accompanied by a fall in the trade surplus (or larger trade deficit). That is,

$$S_A = I_A + PSD_A \uparrow + (X - M)_A \downarrow$$

For the rest of the world $(X - M)$ must rise. If we assume that private saving for the rest of the world is also fixed, and that the sum of the government deficits for the rest of the world remains unchanged, then private investment in the rest of the world must fall. Because part of the rest of the world's savings is financing investment in country A, less is left to finance domestic investment. That is:

$$S_{row} = I_{row} \downarrow + PSD_{row} + (X - M)_{row} \uparrow$$

Under these conditions private investment is still crowded out by a larger government deficit, but not necessarily within the country in which the larger government deficit is incurred. For the world as a whole it remains true that:

$$S(World) = I(World) + PSD(World)$$

or that the total private savings of the world must finance the world's total private investment plus the sum of the world's governments' deficits. If S(World) is assumed fixed, then if PSD(World) rises, I(World) must fall. In reality, the extent to which private investment falls in the country in which the larger government deficit is incurred will depend to some degree upon the size of that country in relation to the world as a whole, as well as the rate of return to private investment, and other factors.

In practice, of course, total world private savings are not fixed, but grow in line with world economic growth as well as changes in the gross national savings ratios for each country.

SAVINGS AS A FLOW, ASSETS AS A STOCK

In economic terminology, savings, whether for an individual, entity or whole economy, are that part of income for a given time period which are not spent on consumption. Thus, if an individual's total post-tax income is $20,000 a year and he spends $12,000 on consumer goods and services, his savings will be $8,000 for that year. It should be noted that this is a rather different meaning of the word 'savings' from that used in common practice, when it is often used to denote an individual's total holdings of (usually financial) assets, as in 'life savings'.

As has been noted, what actually constitutes 'consumer' goods is largely a matter of definition. As far as individual, or personal, spending is concerned, consumption is by convention defined as spending on all goods and services apart from houses. What is left out of income, i.e. savings, also by definition, represents the acquisition of assets. In the case of an individual or individual entity, the assets acquired could be real assets (for an individual, houses; for a corporation, plant and equipment or buildings) or they could be financial assets. However, as explained below, a financial asset for one individual or entity must be a financial liability for another. Therefore, if savings for all the individuals and entities which make up the economy are totalled, these financial assets and their counterpart liabilities cancel out (except where the liabilities are liabilities of foreign resident entities) and so, as already shown, savings for the whole economy equal only investment in real assets (i.e. housing, buildings, plant and equipment) and overseas assets.

It should be noted that the key distinction between savings and assets is that savings are a flow, whereas assets are a stock. In economics, a flow statistic is one that has a time dimension, whereas a stock statistic is one that does not. National income statistics, including savings, are flow statistics. If I say, for example, that my income is $2,000, this is a fairly meaningless statement unless I also include the time period over which I earn this income. (Is it my weekly, monthly or annual income?) However, if I say that my total assets are $500,000, then this statement stands alone without any mention of a time period. Assets are therefore stock statistics. It should be clear that the flow of savings represents an addition to the stock of assets, or strictly assets net of liabilities, i.e. the stock of assets minus liabilities, because assets can be acquired through incurring liabilities (borrowing) as well as through saving. An individual or entity can borrow funds to purchase an asset instead of, or as well as, saving to make the asset purchase.

In terms of one analogy, savings are like the flow of water from the tap into the bath and assets are like the pool of water in the bath. In reality it should be noted that there is one significant difference between stocks of financial assets and water in the bath in the analogy. This is that assets, and financial assets in particular, can change in value as a result of movements in their market price. It is not necessarily the case that if my total assets net of liabilities are $500,000 at the beginning of the year and I save $10,000 during the year, my total net assets (i.e. assets minus liabilities) will be $510,000 at the end of the year. If my assets are all common stocks they could decrease in value so that my total net assets at the end of the year are less than $500,000 despite my savings out of income. In economic statistics, this problem is usually avoided by considering the value of assets and liabilities at cost of purchase, or value when they are incurred, rather than at market value. This means that net assets at the beginning of a period plus savings over the period always equal net assets at the end of the period.

Therefore, savings equal the accumulation of assets minus the accumulation of liabilities. As a simple equation this could be written:

$$\text{Savings} = \Delta \text{ Assets} - \Delta \text{ Liabilities}$$

where Δ means 'increase in'. Another way of writing this is:

$$\Delta \text{ Assets} = \text{Savings} + \Delta \text{ Liabilities}$$

That is to say, assets can be accumulated either by saving or by incurring liabilities (i.e. borrowing to purchase the asset). Assets accumulated are either real assets or financial assets. The accumulation of real assets is investment in a national income accounting sense. A further distinction between real assets and financial assets is that a financial asset always has a corresponding financial liability, whereas a real asset does not. In essence, if I purchase a financial asset I am lending funds to another person or entity. I am making my savings available for their use, and they will owe me those funds, i.e. they will have a liability to me. Thus a government bond is a liability of the government, a corporate bond or common stock a liability of a corporation, and a bank deposit, in the first instance, a liability of the bank. A real asset such as a house, on the other hand, has no corresponding liability.

ASSETS AND LIABILITIES FOR THE ECONOMY

Assets and liabilities for any entity, or sector, or the economy as a whole can be presented as separate sides of a balance sheet. It is commonly said, in this balance sheet sense, that assets always equal liabilities. However, this is only true by definition because the amount by which assets for any entity exceed liabilities is presented as a liability item, so that the sum of the assets side of the balance sheet then equals the sum of the liabilities side of the balance sheet.

Above it was explained that the increase in assets minus the increase in liabilities for any period is equal to an entity's savings over that period, i.e.

$$\Delta \text{Assets} - \Delta \text{Liabilities} = \text{Savings}$$

From this it can be seen that, at least when measured on a cost of purchase, or value when incurred, basis (to eliminate the effects of changes in the value of assets and liabilities) the entity's total assets minus total liabilities at any time will be equivalent to the entity's accumulated savings for the whole period of the entity's existence until that time, i.e.

$$\text{Assets} - \text{Liabilities} = \text{Cumulative savings}$$

This statement is, of course, a tautology. It is true by definition because cumulative savings and net assets, measured at cost of purchase, are the same thing.

Another term for the difference between assets and liabilities, i.e. net assets, is *net worth*. In general, though, net worth is measured with assets and liabilities taken at market value rather than cost of purchase and so differs from cumulative savings to the extent that assets and liabilities acquired change in value via movements in their market price. (Hereafter, we will ignore this problem and treat net worth and cumulative savings as identical.) For an individual, net worth is what everyone understands to be his or her wealth. For a corporation, the net worth can be seen as being actually 'owned' by the company's shareholders and so, strictly, might be considered a liability to the shareholders.

Simplified balance sheets for all the key sectors of the economy can be presented to include the main items shown in Balance Sheet 4. (This is not an exhaustive list and some items have been netted out, for simplicity.) Note that, in this balance sheet, individual liability items are considered to represent only liabilities to domestic entities. Liabilities to foreign entities are assumed to be included as a negative component of the 'net foreign assets'.

In most presentations of assets, liabilities and flows of funds data, commercial banks and other financial institutions are lumped together as financial institutions. Here they have been separated because of the special monetary significance of the banks. In many presentations also, nationalized industries would constitute a separate sector, but for simplicity here we have ignored public sector corporations.

If the balance sheets of the government and monetary authority are consolidated, the government's deposits at the monetary authority, marked (A) in the balance sheet, can be cancelled out. The item appears on both the assets and liabilities sides of the consolidated balance sheet and hence can be netted out. Similarly, government bonds held by the monetary authority can be subtracted from the total government bonds liability of the government. This leaves the total government sector balance sheet as illustrated in Balance Sheet 5.

In a consolidation of the total private sector balance sheet the items marked with corresponding numbers (1) to (6) are both assets and liabilities of the private sector and hence can be cancelled out. In most cases, a proportion of the assets corresponding to any liability – say, equity – would be held by overseas residents. To this extent it would be a liability of the domestic private sector, but not an asset of the domestic private sector. To get around this problem here, we have assumed this to be offset as a liability item in the 'net foreign assets' item.

Balance Sheet 4

Government sector

Government

Assets	Liabilities
Real assets	Government bonds
	Foreign debt
Deposits at monetary authority (A)	Net worth

Monetary authority

Assets	Liabilities
Net foreign assets	Currency in circulation
Government bonds	Deposits of commercial banks
Loans to financial institutions	Deposits of government (A)
	Net worth

Private sector

Commercial banks

Assets	Liabilities
Cash currency	Deposits of nonbank private sector (4)
Deposits at monetary authority	Borrowings from monetary authority
Government bonds	Bonds (3)
Loans to nonbank sector (1)	Equity (2)
Net foreign assets	Net worth
Real assets	

Other financial institutions

Assets	Liabilities
Equity (2)	Insurance (5)
Government bonds	Unit trusts (6)
Corporate bonds (3)	Net worth
Real assets	

Balance Sheet 4 continued opposite

ASSETS AND LIABILITIES FOR THE ECONOMY • 75

Nonfinancial corporate sector		Personal sector	
Assets	Liabilities	Assets	Liabilities
Real assets	Borrowings from commercial banks (1)	Real assets (i.e. houses)	Borrowings from commercial banks (1)
Deposits at commercial banks (4)		Cash currency	
	Bonds (3)		Net worth
Insurance (5)		Deposits at commercial banks (4)	
	Equity (2)		
Net foreign assets	Net worth	Government bonds (3) Corporate bonds (2) Equity (6) Unit trusts (5) Insurance Net foreign assets	

Balance Sheet 5

Consolidated government sector	
Assets	Liabilities
Real assets	Government bonds (held outside the monetary authority) (9)
Net[a] foreign assets	
Loans to financial institutions (7)	Currency in circulation ⎱ Monetary base (8) Deposits of commercial banks ⎰
	Net worth

[a]Net of any government or central bank foreign debt

The bracketed items of cash currency in circulation and the commercial banks' deposits at the monetary authority in Balance Sheet 6 together constitute the monetary base which was explained in Chapter 1.

Finally, in a consolidation of the government sector and private sector (i.e. the whole economy), items (7) to (9) could be cancelled, leaving the whole economy's balance sheet as shown in Balance Sheet 7. (Note again that government bonds held overseas are taken as a liability to be accounted for within the *net* foreign assets' component.)

As all financial assets have corresponding liabilities, for the whole economy the only net assets are real assets and net foreign assets. On a cost of purchase/incurrence basis, the total of real assets and net foreign assets is equivalent to the economy's accumulated savings and is a measure of the total wealth of the economy.

Balance Sheet 6

Consolidated private sector	
Assets	Liabilities
Monetary base (8) { Cash currency; Commercial banks' deposits at monetary authority	Commercial banks' borrowings from monetary authority (7)
	Net worth
Government bonds (9)	
Net foreign assets	
Real assets	

Balance Sheet 7

Consolidated whole economy	
Assets	Liabilities
Real assets	Net worth
Net foreign assets	

FLOWS OF FUNDS

Flows of funds analysis is concerned with *changes* in assets and liabilities, and specifically the changes in net financial assets which correspond to the 'savings/investment gaps' for each of the sectors of the economy.

It was explained earlier that:

$$\text{Savings} = \Delta \text{ Net worth} = \Delta \text{ Assets} - \Delta \text{ Liabilities}$$

Applying this simple identity to the balance sheet for the whole economy above, it can be seen that:

$$\text{Savings} = \Delta \text{ Real assets} + \Delta \text{ Net foreign assets}$$

Δ real assets, i.e. the increase in real assets, is, by definition, investment in the national income accounting sense. Therefore, this identity can be written:

$$S(\text{Total}) = I(\text{Total}) + \Delta \text{ Net foreign assets}$$

or

$$S(\text{Total}) - I(\text{Total}) = \Delta \text{ Net foreign assets}$$

Previously, it was also shown that:

$$S(\text{Total}) - I(\text{Total}) = X - M$$

These are identities describing the savings/investment gap for the economy, and the equivalent (inverse) gap for the rest of the world. In a similar fashion, the savings/investment gap for any individual sector of the economy can be described in terms of the acquisition of financial assets minus financial liabilities. As savings represent the acquisition of net financial assets and real assets, the latter being investment, savings minus investment for any sector equals the sector's acquisition of net financial assets. The acquisition of net financial assets can be seen, in a sense, as the extent to which the sector has savings above its own investment needs. These 'excess' savings go to finance investment in sectors which have a 'deficiency' of savings relative to investment. It is this relationship which is shown in flows of funds tables.

Two examples help to illustrate this. Returning to the nonfinancial corporate sector's balance sheet, shown in Balance Sheet 2 on page 3, we can see that:

Net worth = Real assets + Deposits at commercial banks
+ Insurance + Net foreign assets − Borrowing from
commercial banks − Corporate bonds − Equity

Putting this in terms of changes, and bearing in mind that the change in real assets is equal to investment, we have:

Δ Net worth = Savings = Investment + Δ Bank deposits
+ Δ Insurance + Δ Net foreign assets − Δ Bank borrowings
− Δ Bonds − Δ Equity

The savings/investment gap for the corporate sector then comprises:

Savings − Investment = Δ Bank deposits + Δ Insurance
+ Δ Net foreign assets − Δ Bank borrowings − New bonds
and equity issued

This is likely to sum to a negative number, as investment by the corporate sector tends to exceed the corporate sector's savings. (This is in part because of the definition of investment employed in national income accounting.)

During the first half of the 1980s there was a sharp increase in the savings/investment gap, or financial surplus, of Japan's corporate and personal sector, which more than doubled (from an annual ¥13 trillion to over ¥30 trillion) over the period. More than the whole of the large increase in the personal sector's financial surplus which took place at that time was in the form of insurance. Other net financial assets of the personal sector actually declined. The personal sector's growing holdings of insurance policies and products did not, of course, have their counterpart in a growing financial institutions' deficit, but rather a rest-of-the-world deficit as the insurance companies channelled personal sector savings into foreign assets.

We can understand this type of process more clearly by considering the flows of funds identities for the consolidated private sector and consolidated public sector balance sheets for which were derived in Balance Sheets 5 and 6 above. For the private sector, from the balance sheet derived earlier, the savings/investment gap is given by:

Savings = Δ Net worth = Δ Real assets + Δ Monetary base
+ Δ Government bonds + Δ Net foreign assets − Δ Commercial
bank borrowings from monetary authority

That is,

Saving/investment gap = Δ Monetary base + Δ Government bonds
+ Δ Net foreign assets − Δ Bank borrowing from monetary authority

In the case of Japan during the 1980s, a growing excess of savings of the private sector corresponded to an accumulation of foreign assets (by the financial institutions). In another example, that of Taiwan, a growing private sector financial surplus in the late 1980s was reflected in a rapidly increasing monetary base. This interesting example is explored further in Chapter 7.

Useful abbreviations for the terms in the identity (the first two of which have already been used) are:

S   Private sector savings
I   Private sector investment
M0 Monetary base
B   Government bonds held by private sector
K   *Increase in* private net foreign assets
D   Bank borrowings from the monetary authority

Thus, the identity can be written:

$$S - I = \Delta M0 + \Delta B + K - \Delta D$$

Turning to the government sector, we have (from the consolidated government sector balance sheet):

Government savings − Government investment
= Δ Net foreign assets + Δ Loans to financial institutions
− Δ Government bonds − Δ Monetary base

Denoting total government net foreign assets as NFR, this identity can be written:

Government savings − Government investment
= ΔNFR + ΔD − ΔB − ΔM0

The details of government financing are discussed more thoroughly in Chapter 8. For the time being, it has already been shown that government investment minus government savings is equivalent to the government deficit. Therefore, the above identity can be rewritten negatively as:

Government investment − Government savings
= PSD
= ΔM0 + ΔB − ΔD − ΔNFR

The government can finance a deficit either through increasing the monetary base (i.e. 'printing' money), increasing government bonds held by the private sector (i.e. selling bonds), reducing loans of the monetary authority outstanding, or running down net foreign reserves.

Adding the savings/investment gaps of the government sector and private sector together, to return to the savings investment gap for the whole economy gives:

$$(S - I) + (-PSD) = S(Total) - I(Total)$$
$$= (\Delta M0 + \Delta B + K - \Delta D) + (\Delta NFR + \Delta D - \Delta B - \Delta M0)$$
$$= K + \Delta NFR$$

That is, the increase in the private sector's net foreign assets plus the increase in the government sector's net foreign assets. This is the 'rest of the world financial deficit' (or surplus if the economy has a deficiency of savings relative to investment). The identity simply states that if savings are not invested domestically then they must be invested overseas. It was also derived earlier from the consolidated whole economy balance sheet.

Furthermore:

$$S(Total) - I(Total) = X - M$$

From this it is clear that:

$$X - M = K + \Delta NFR$$

If the economy is exporting more to the rest of the world than it is importing from the rest of the world, then it must be acquiring investments in, or financial claims on, the rest of the world (see Chapter 5).

DIFFERENCE BETWEEN SAVINGS AND MONEY

To conclude this chapter it is worthwhile to derive a link between savings and money, or at least the change in money supply, as confusion occasionally arises between the concept of money and the concept of savings.

At its most basic level this confusion stems from the fact that many people view their savings as being the amount of money they

DIFFERENCE BETWEEN SAVINGS AND MONEY • 81

hold. In economics, 'savings' and 'money' have very different meanings. A basic difference is that savings is a flow, as discussed, whereas money is a stock.

By considering the consolidated balance sheet of the personal sector, nonfinancial corporate sector and other financial institutions sector, i.e. the total nonbank private sector, we can derive an identity for the savings of the nonbank private sector as follows:

Nonbank private sector's savings = Δ Net worth of nonbank private sector = Δ Real Assets + Δ DEPOSITS AT COMMERCIAL BANKS + Δ *Insurance* + Δ Net foreign assets + Δ CASH CURRENCY + Δ Government bonds + Δ *Nonbank corporate bonds* + Δ Bank bonds + Δ *Nonbank equity* + Δ Bank equity + Δ *Unit trusts* − Δ Borrowings from commercial banks − Δ *Nonbank corporate bonds* − Δ *Nonbank equity* − Δ *Insurance* − Δ *Unit trusts*

In this identity the capitalized items represent the increase in the money supply (i.e. broad money M3). The italicized items cancel out. Given that 'Δ real assets' is the same as 'investment', the identity reduces to:

> Nonbank private sector's savings = Investment + Δ Money (M3) + Δ Net foreign assets + Δ Government bonds + Δ Bank bonds (i.e. bank debentures) + Δ Bank equity − Δ Borrowings from commercial banks (i.e. bank lending to the private sector)

If we make the, admittedly unrealistic, assumption that all the nonbank private sector's borrowing is to finance investment (i.e. in houses, plant and equipment) and that, further, all investment is financed by borrowing from the banks, we can cancel out the items 'bank lending to the private sector' and 'investment' in the above identity. It then reduces further to the following equation:

> Savings = Δ Money (M3) + Δ Net foreign assets + Δ Government bonds + Δ Bank bonds + Δ Bank equity

This is a relatively simple equation in which there is apparently a relationship between the savings of the nonbank private sector and the increase in the money supply. Unfortunately, in practice it is not the case that investment and bank lending can be cancelled out in this manner. If all of the increase in bank lending is to finance consumption (e.g. purchases of cars and other durable goods), for instance, then the increase in bank lending could massively exceed investment in the original identity. The missing term in the reduced equation above (Investment − Δ Borrowings from commercial banks) would then be a large negative item. In this case the increase in money M3 would likely be far larger than the savings of the nonbank private sector (assuming that the other items in the identity are relatively small). In other words, it can never be assumed that a large increase in the money supply implies a high savings rate of the nonbank private sector. It may be that bank borrowings of the nonbank private sector to finance consumption have also increased by a large amount.

BALANCE OF PAYMENTS AND EXCHANGE RATE   5

INTRODUCTION TO THE BALANCE OF PAYMENTS

The balance of payments for an economy is a summary of all transactions between residents of the country and nonresidents. Sales and purchases of all physical goods by resident entities to and from nonresidents (i.e. exports and imports) make up the merchandise trade balance. Sales and purchases of services and also transfers of income between residents and nonresidents are included in the balance of services, or invisible trade balance. Together, the trade balance and balance of services sum to the current account of the balance of payments. Purchases and sales of assets and incurrence of liabilities comprise the capital account of the balance of payments. Often, the capital account is separated into the accumulation of net foreign assets/liabilities by the nonbank sector, the commercial bank sector and the central bank, or monetary authority. In this case the sum of the current account balance and the capital account of the nonbank sector is often termed the basic balance, or in some countries' statistics the overall balance, of payments.

The balance of payments is a flow of funds concept. Indeed, as Chapter 4 demonstrated, the current account surplus is identically equal to gross national savings minus gross capital formation (i.e. the sum of the savings/investment gaps for all of the sectors of the economy) and also equal to the increase in net foreign assets for the whole economy, i.e.:

$$S(\text{Total}) - I(\text{Total}) = X - M = K + \Delta NFR$$

X and M here refer respectively to exports and imports of goods and services plus also receipts and payments of factor incomes, or net property income. That is, the current account surplus is equivalent to the surplus of the nation in the GNE/GNP, not the GDE/GDP (see Chapter 9).

In balance of payments statistics no differentiation is made between earnings from nonfactor services and receipts of factor incomes (see Chapter 9), both of which are components of the invisibles/services balance. This is because the balance of payments is more concerned with flows of funds, in which the important concept is flows of savings out of total income, and the accumulation of assets or liabilities. In contrast, in the measurement of gross *domestic* product a very important distinction is between income/spending flows which arise from, or constitute, a direct demand for final output, and other flows or transfers of income which do not. For example, income from overseas investments is not part of the external component of GDP because it does not represent a direct demand for goods and services output. However, it does represent income to those entities or individuals in the economy which receive it, and for the aggregate economy it can be used to purchase imports or saved and used to acquire (overseas) assets. Therefore, this *factor income* from abroad is included in exports of goods and invisibles on the current account, and similarly payments of investment income and other factor income are included with imports.

Chapter 9, on national income accounting, includes a more thorough discussion on income transfers. It should be noted that the term 'transfers' in the balance of payments has a somewhat different meaning from the word as used in national income accounts. Specifically, transfers in the balance of payments include remittances of funds which are of a capital nature but which do not represent the acquisition of claims on or liabilities to the overseas sector. They are therefore usually included in the current account, rather than the capital account, of the balance of payments. These include such items as grants of aid, including government aid, and funds brought in (exports) or taken out (imports) by immigrants and emigrants who are changing their country of residence.

Exports of goods and invisibles plus incoming transfers, minus imports of goods and invisibles and outgoing transfers are equal to the current account balance. The current account balance, in turn, equals the net increase in foreign assets or liabilities, that is:

$$X - M = K + \Delta NFR$$

The easiest intuitive way to understand this balance of payments identity is that if a country is exporting more than it is importing, then it must be receiving something in return. This 'something in return' is an increase in net claims on the rest of the world, i.e. net foreign assets, or a decrease in net liabilities to the rest of the world. Similarly, if the country is importing more than it is exporting, then the rest of the world is acquiring claims on it. The country is incurring net foreign liabilities or experiencing a decrease in its net foreign assets. These foreign assets could be deposits in a foreign bank, loans, investments in foreign stocks or bonds. They could also be real assets, such as real estate, factories, plant or machinery.

It is worthwhile to note that a savings/investment gap is often thought of purely in terms of financial assets. For instance, the difference between total private sector savings and investment (S − I in our notation) is often referred to as the 'private sector's net acquisition of *financial* assets'. This is a misnomer because the assets acquired could be real assets abroad as well as financial assets. The I in the S − I calculation refers to investment in real assets in the domestic economy only, because it is a component of gross domestic expenditure. In the balance of payments, therefore, the savings/investment gap for the whole economy includes investment in foreign real assets. (This problem was glossed over in Chapter 4, in which foreign real assets were implicitly included as a component of 'foreign assets', separate from (domestic) real assets.)

The overall change in the *net* foreign asset/liability position of an economy represents the outcome of many *gross* purchases and sales of assets and liabilities. To put it fully (using the terms 'purchases' and 'sales' for what should more correctly be 'acquisitions of' and 'reductions in'):

> Increase in net foreign assets
> $= K + \Delta NFR$
> $=$ Gross purchases of foreign assets − Gross sales of (1)
> foreign assets − Foreign gross purchases of domestic
> assets + Foreign gross sales of domestic assets

Gross purchases of foreign assets and foreign gross sales of domestic assets are each (gross) capital outflows. Gross sales of foreign assets and foreign gross purchases of domestic assets are capital inflows.

Often, in summary balance of payments statistics, only the net capital flows are presented. That is, the right-hand side of the above identity is implicitly reduced to:

> Net purchases of foreign assets − Foreign *net* purchases
> of domestic assets

or possibly to the overall net position, divided by the class of asset. The shortcoming of this type of presentation when used for analytical purposes is that time series of the overall change in net foreign assets, even when divided by the class of assets, can sometimes mask significant swings in the constituent *gross* capital flows. For example, over the two years prior to the world stock market crash of October 1987, growing Japanese purchases of US bonds and stocks played a large role in financing the US current account deficit. During and immediately after the crash, net figures show that overall net capital flows in the form of bond and stock transactions out of Japan and into the United States actually rose sharply. At first sight this appears strange because the problems of the US trade deficit were widely perceived as being a major cause of the stock market crash. The net figures hide the fact that it was not Japanese purchases of US bonds and stocks that increased during the crash, but *foreign sales* of Japanese stocks, particularly sales by US institutions, which sought to repatriate funds to their home markets in response to the uncertainty engendered by the crash. In terms of the full components of the change in net foreign assets listed in identity (1), as far as Japan was concerned the net capital outflow had temporarily switched from comprising mainly gross purchases of foreign assets to comprising mainly foreign gross sales of domestic assets.

Transactions between residents and nonresidents involving financial assets such as stocks and bonds are often lumped together as *portfolio investment* in capital account statistics. In detailed statistics showing a breakdown of portfolio investment there can be categories of capital flow in addition to the four categories listed in identity (1). Specifically, the increase in domestic liabilities to foreigners can be considered separately from foreign purchases of domestic assets. An increase in domestic (portfolio) liabilities to foreigners occurs when a domestic company issues a bond in a foreign bond market, whereas foreign purchases of domestic assets include, among others, the case of a foreign entity purchasing the bond of a domestic company (or the government) in the domestic market. In an accounting sense, there is no difference between these two cases because both involve an increase in domestic bond liabilities to foreigners. In a practical sense, a difference can be discerned in that in the first case the transaction is initiated by the domestic company, whereas in the second case it is initiated by the foreign entity. In this respect the former instance is borrowing, and is conceptually difficult to distinguish from borrowing by a domestic entity from a foreign bank. However, bank borrowing would not normally be considered as portfolio investment, but would constitute a separate category of the capital account.

Apart from portfolio investment, the other important elements of the capital account of the balance of payments are transactions involving real assets, termed *direct investment* (including, for instance, companies establishing plant overseas or foreign companies establishing plant domestically and transactions in real estate, etc.), borrowing by domestic nonbank entities from foreign banks, net lending to or borrowing from foreign entities by domestic banks, and net foreign lending/increase in foreign assets of the monetary authority. The overall balance of payments can therefore be arranged as in Balance Sheet 8.

Up to now we have said little about the capital account transactions of the central government, which are not explicitly differentiated from those of the private sector in this type of balance of payments layout. The key point to note is that in balance of payments accounting, capital inflows arising as a result of foreign borrowing by the central government (an increase in government foreign debt) are considered separately from the change in the central bank's holdings of foreign assets. This issue is discussed in more detail in Chapter 7.

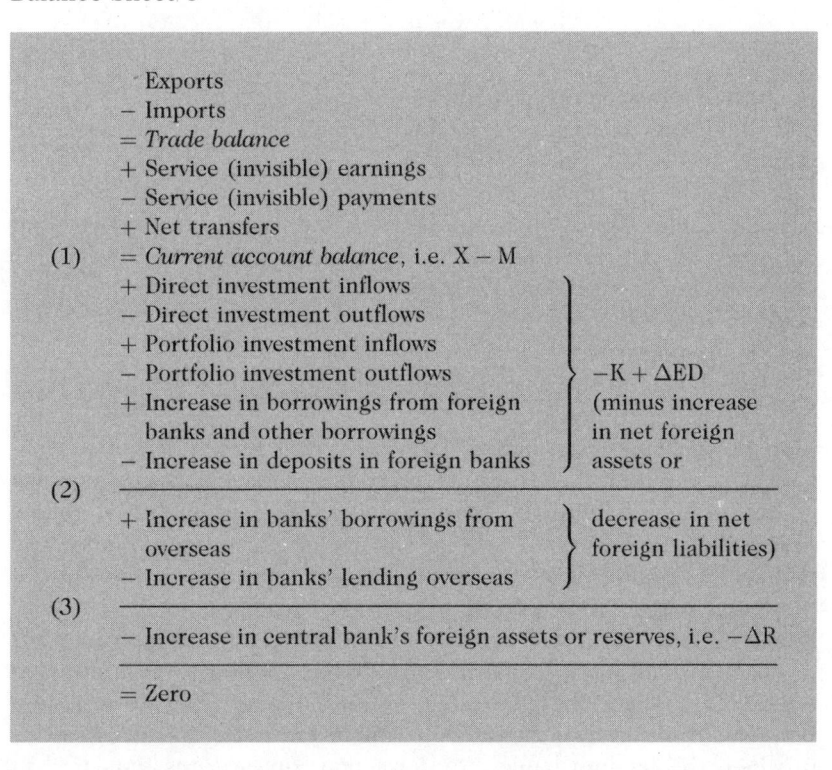

Balance Sheet 8

```
           Exports
         − Imports
         = Trade balance
         + Service (invisible) earnings
         − Service (invisible) payments
         + Net transfers
    (1)  = Current account balance, i.e. X − M
         + Direct investment inflows        ⎫
         − Direct investment outflows       ⎪
         + Portfolio investment inflows     ⎪
         − Portfolio investment outflows    ⎬  −K + ΔED
         + Increase in borrowings from foreign  ⎪  (minus increase
           banks and other borrowings          ⎪   in net foreign
         − Increase in deposits in foreign banks ⎭  assets or
    (2)  ─────────────────────────────────────
         + Increase in banks' borrowings from   ⎫  decrease in net
           overseas                             ⎬  foreign liabilities)
         − Increase in banks' lending overseas  ⎭
    (3)  ─────────────────────────────────────
         − Increase in central bank's foreign assets or reserves, i.e. −ΔR
         ─────────────────────────────────────
         = Zero
```

88 ● BALANCE OF PAYMENTS AND EXCHANGE RATE

It is useful to introduce a notation to separate the increase in the total official (i.e. government) sector's net foreign assets (ΔNFR in Chapter 4) into the increase in the central bank's foreign reserves (ΔR) minus the increase in central government foreign debt (ΔED), i.e.:

$$\Delta NFR = \Delta R - \Delta ED$$

In the above type of balance of payments presentation, the increase in the central government's external debt (ΔED) is included within portfolio investment inflows and the increase in borrowings from foreign banks.

Because

$$X - M = K + \Delta R - \Delta ED$$

or

$$X - M - K + \Delta ED - \Delta R = 0$$

the sum of all the items in the balance of payments necessarily is zero. It is sometimes said that the balance of payments always balances. In practice, we talk of the overall balance of payments surplus or deficit, reflecting the fact that a cutoff point is usually made, at either point 2 or point 3. The sum of the items above the chosen dividing line is then defined to constitute the 'overall balance of payments'. The items below the line, with the sign changed (because, for instance, at cutoff point 3, if $X - M - K + \Delta ED - \Delta R = 0$ then $X - M - K + \Delta ED = \Delta R$) are then considered to be 'financing' items.

The change in the commercial banking sector's net foreign asset position is sometimes known as the monetary capital outflow (for an increase in net foreign assets/decrease in net foreign liabilities), or monetary capital inflow (for a decrease in net foreign assets/increase in net foreign liabilities). In some balance of payments statistics presentations, borrowings by nonbanks from foreign banks are included as capital flows 'above the line', whereas the changes in the domestic banks' net foreign assets are taken as 'below-the-line' financing items (i.e. the cutoff point is point 2). This treatment is inconsistent in so far as if universally applied the nonbanks' borrowings taken above the line would appear as below-the-line financing items in the balance of payments statistics for the countries in which the lending banks are domiciled. However, as indicated in

Chapter 1, there may be some justification for this because of the monetary significance of monetary capital flows.

It may be helpful at this point to consider some simple balance sheet examples to illustrate how the balance of payments 'always balances'. Let us consider an exporter exporting a good worth 100 currency units to an importer overseas, and the balance sheets for each of them, together with their respective banks.

In stage 1 (Balance Sheet 9), the exporter exports 100 worth of goods to the importer in the foreign country. The importer pays for these goods by drawing a check/draft on his local bank, payable to the exporter.

At this stage the balance of payments for the country of the exporter will be:

Current balance	+ 100	(i.e. the export)
Capital flows	− 100	(increase in claims/deposits in foreign banks)
	0	

In stage 2 (Balance Sheet 10), the exporter deposits the check/draft in his own local bank, which credits him with a deposit in local

Balance Sheet 9

Domestic			
Exporter		Exporter's bank	
Assets	Liabilities	Assets	Liabilities
Claims on foreign banks +100			

Overseas			
Importer		Importer's bank	
Assets	Liabilities	Assets	Liabilities
Deposit at local bank −100			Deposit of importer −100 Liability to foreign exporter +100

Balance Sheet 10

Domestic			
Exporter		**Exporter's bank**	
Assets	Liabilities	Assets	Liabilities
Claims on foreign banks 0		Claims on foreign banks +100	Deposit of local exporter +100
Deposits in local banks +100			
Net foreign assets = 0		Net foreign assets = +100	

Overseas			
Importer		**Importer's bank**	
Assets	Liabilities	Assets	Liabilities
Deposit at local bank −100			Deposits of importer −100
			Liability to foreign banks +100
Net foreign liabilities = 0		Net foreign liabilities = +100	

currency. If the balance of payments for the domestic economy is compiled at this stage, it will be as follows:

Current balance	+100	(the export)
Capital flows	−100	(monetary capital outflow represents
	0	the net claim on the importer's bank by the exporter's bank)

If at the same time a domestic resident wished to buy, say, a foreign bond, she might pay for the bond by drawing a check or draft on her local bank. A similar set of changes in assets/liabilities – the reverse of those illustrated above – would take place. The net result in balance of payments terms would be that part, or the whole, of the current account surplus would then be financed by portfolio investment outflows rather than merely monetary capital outflows. Simple balance sheets, as above, can be drawn to illustrate conceivable transactions. Always, the balance of payments can be shown 'to balance'.

When it comes to 'drawing the line' in the balance of payments, all three dividing lines noted in Balance Sheet 8 have significance. Cutoff point 2 has significance because the below-the-line financing items are assets of the domestic banking system and hence counterparts to the liabilities of the banking system, most importantly including the money supply. (In the example illustrated above, it can be noted that the increase of 100 in the domestic exporter's deposits in the local banking system amounts to an increase in the money supply). Cut-off point 3 is even more significant in a monetary sense because the remaining below-the-line item is the increase in the central bank's foreign reserves, which is a counterpart to the change in the monetary base. (In Chapter 4 it was shown that $PSD = \Delta M0 + \Delta B + \Delta ED - \Delta D - \Delta R$ (substituting $\Delta ED - \Delta R$ for $-\Delta NFR$). The rearrangement of this identity into the monetary base identity $\Delta M0 = PSD - \Delta B - \Delta ED + \Delta D + \Delta R$ highlights the significance of ΔR, the change in the foreign reserves.) These considerations are explored in the chapters on monetary policy.

The importance of cutoff point 1, the current balance itself, is that a current account surplus implies an increase in residents' net exposure to foreign currencies (and hence to movement in the exchange rates for those currencies) or, alternatively, a decrease in nonresidents' exposure to the domestic currency or possibly an increasing 'short' position in the domestic currency. For a current account deficit, the reverse possibilities hold (i.e. a decrease in residents' net exposure to foreign currencies, etc.). These concepts, which are important in the understanding of currency movements, are discussed in the remainder of this chapter.

CURRENT ACCOUNT BALANCE, CURRENCY EXPOSURE AND FORWARD EXCHANGE MARKET

It has been shown above that a current account surplus is equivalent to an increase in the economy's net foreign assets, or net claims on the rest of the world, or a decrease in net foreign liabilities. A current account deficit is equivalent to a decrease in net foreign assets or increase in net foreign liabilities. These changes in net foreign assets/liabilities also imply equivalent changes in the net exposure of residents to foreign currencies and/or the net exposure of residents of foreign countries to the domestic currency.

Export and import transactions, and also capital transactions, can be denominated and paid for in any currency. Perhaps this will be the currency of the exporting country, or the currency of the importing country, or the currency of a third country such as the US dollar. Nevertheless, if exports exceed imports (or vice versa) there will be a change in the exposure of residents of the exporting country to foreign currencies or the exposure of foreign residents to the domestic currency. For instance, in the example above, at stage 1 the exporter, having exported 100 worth of goods, has a claim of 100 on an overseas bank. This could be a claim in foreign currencies (perhaps the currency of the importing country), or it could be a claim denominated in the domestic currency. In the former case the exporter has exposure to foreign currencies, and is exposed to risk in the sense that he will lose money, in terms of his home currency, if his home currency rises in value relative to foreign currencies (i.e. foreign currencies fall in value). In the latter case the overseas bank is exposed to the risk of the exporter's home currency rising in value, because it has a liability (i.e. borrowing) denominated in that currency.

Any individual can easily *hedge* currency risk, whether they are an exporter, importer or simply a holder of foreign assets or liabilities. All methods of doing this involve contracting to buy or sell one currency for another currency at an agreed rate at some given time in the future, thus fixing the exchange rate until that time. However, while any one individual can hedge in this manner, for the world as a whole the currency risk cannot be eliminated because there must be someone else to 'take the other side' of the forward currency contract. For instance, the exporter might hedge his own currency risk by contracting to sell the foreign currency he is exposed to and buy his home currency at a given rate at some given time in the future. Although he will then have neutralized his currency risk, the individual or entity which agrees to buy his foreign currency and sell him his home currency at a fixed rate in the future will now have taken on the risk. The currency risk represented by the original export has not been eliminated by the hedging but merely transferred to another holder.

Often, the entity which in the first place 'takes the other side' of a hedging contract is a bank. In general, banks do not assume large currency risks themselves and so will take offsetting measures on their balance sheets. If the bank is not able to match a forward currency contract with an opposite one, then it can neutralize the foreign exchange rate risk by borrowing the currency it is exposed to and then selling it for its domestic currency. In this case, the initial hedge leads to a transaction which is represented in the balance of payments. (Forward currency contracts are not in themselves part of the balance of payments when they are initiated because they are contracts and not realized transactions.)

It is worthwhile considering an example to illustrate this. Suppose that the holder of a foreign asset, such as a foreign bond or stock, wishes to hedge the foreign currency risk implicit in the asset. He therefore contracts with his bank to sell the foreign currency to the bank for domestic currency one year in the future (which is when he envisages selling the foreign asset), but at an exchange rate agreed now. The bank is now exposed to the foreign currency risk. If the foreign currency falls in value over the course of the year it has to buy, at the end of the year, the foreign currency from the asset holder for more than it is then worth in terms of domestic currency. One way it can neutralize this risk is by borrowing foreign currency for a year, but immediately selling the borrowed foreign currency for domestic currency. Then at the end of the year it can use the foreign currency it buys from the asset holder to repay its foreign currency borrowing. This would involve no currency transaction, and hence the bank would be left unexposed to foreign exchange movements.

If the asset holder's foreign asset is worth 100, then the bank's balance sheet would be as in Balance Sheet 11.

Balance Sheet 11

Assets	Liabilities
Domestic asset (100) (purchased with the foreign currency borrowed)	Foreign liability (100) (foreign currency borrowed)
	Total net foreign liabilities = 100
Off balance sheet item: Agreement to buy 100 of foreign currency for domestic currency = 100	
Total foreign exchange risk = 0	

The bank has net foreign liabilities of 100, which represents a monetary capital inflow on the balance of payments. (The borrowing of foreign currency will likely be a capital inflow. The forward contract to buy foreign currency is neither an increase in foreign assets nor a capital outflow because it is a contract and not a realized transaction. In this example the forward contract is anyway with a domestic resident, not a foreign resident.) It also has no exchange rate risk. However, the original currency risk represented by the asset holder's foreign asset has not disappeared. It has now been acquired by whoever has purchased the borrowed foreign currency from the bank with domestic currency.

A point worth noting is the year-ahead exchange rate for foreign currency in terms of domestic currency at which the bank will be willing to contract with the asset holder, or hedger. In this example the bank has no exchange rate risk, but it has a potential cost (or profit) represented by the difference between the interest rate it has to pay on its one-year foreign currency borrowing and the interest it earns on its domestic asset over the year. If the interest it has to pay is higher than the interest it will earn, it will offset this cost by agreeing to a forward exchange rate which values the foreign currency below the current or 'spot' value by enough to offset the interest rate cost. That is, it will make a profit on the difference between the price at which it sells the foreign currency it borrows for domestic currency (the spot, or current exchange rate) and the price at which it buys the foreign currency back from the hedger in a year's time. This 'profit' will equal and offset the interest rate cost. Similarly, if the interest rate on the foreign currency is lower than on the domestic currency, then the forward currency rate will value the foreign currency above the spot value, such that the interest rate gain from borrowing the foreign currency is offset by the cost of buying the currency forward to hedge into domestic currency.

The differential between the forward exchange rate and the spot exchange rate is known in foreign exchange market jargon as the *swap*. In percentage terms it must be the same as the interest rate differential between the two currencies for the relevant time period. If it differed then there would be an opportunity to profit by *arbitraging* the difference.

Because the opportunity to arbitrage always keeps the swap and the interest rate differential in line, the swap rate between two currencies always implies an interest rate differential, and an interest rate differential between two currencies implies a swap rate. Currencies carrying a relatively high interest rate (relative to domestic currency) are always 'cheap' to buy forward and 'expensive' to sell forward (i.e. the forward rate will be below – weaker than – the spot

CURRENT ACCOUNT BALANCE, EXPOSURE AND FORWARD EXCHANGE MARKET

rate). Currencies with a low interest rate are 'expensive' to buy forward and 'cheap' to sell forward (i.e. the forward rate is above – stronger than – the spot rate).

The above discussion and examples serve to illustrate that the hedging of currency risk only transfers risk but does not eliminate it. If a country has net foreign assets, then because these net claims are necessarily denominated in a currency, there is an implied currency exposure and associated currency risk. Either net foreign claims are denominated in foreign currency, in which case residents have net exposure to foreign currencies, or they are denominated in domestic currency, in which case they represent a net liability of foreigners in the domestic currency. More likely it will be a mixture of both of these. In either case the currency risk is a risk that the domestic currency will rise in terms of foreign currencies. If it does appreciate, then, to the extent that residents have net exposure to foreign currencies, this exposure will be devalued, i.e. residents lose money. To the extent that foreigners have liabilities in the domestic currency, then these liabilities will become greater, i.e. foreigners lose money. Conversely, if a country has net foreign liabilities (i.e. net foreign debt) then either residents or foreigners or both are taking a risk that the domestic currency will fall in value, or depreciate.

The current account balance represents the change in the net foreign asset/liability position and hence the change in exposure to currency exchange rate risk. The overall balance of payments 'always balances'. However, the goods and services which make up the current account are purchased for the use which can be derived from them and do not represent currency exposure. If Ms X, who lives in Europe, buys a Japanese VTR, she is unlikely to consider that this has given her an exposure to the Japanese currency. The changes in assets and liabilities which constitute the capital account are a component of national savings and have a direct bearing on currency exposure and risk. Because assets are bought for the return they can give, they imply the risk of gain or loss. If Ms X purchases a Japanese bond or stock instead of a VTR, she is acquiring an exposure to the Japanese currency, and to the risk of loss if the currency depreciates relative to her domestic currency. If there is an imbalance in the current account there must be a matching imbalance in the capital account, and an implicit change in the balance of currency exposure/risk.

If a country has net foreign assets and is running a current account surplus, there is an increasing exposure, held either by residents or foreigners or both, to the risk that the domestic currency will rise in value against foreign currencies. If a country has net foreign liabilities (i.e. it is a net external debtor) and is running a current account deficit, there is an increasing exposure to the risk that the domestic currency will fall in value. This risk is a powerful force, which eventually tends to bring the current account back to balance, and places a limit on the extent to which a country can continue to increase net foreign assets or incur net foreign liabilities, as is explained below.

RELATIONSHIP BETWEEN THE EXCHANGE RATE AND CURRENT ACCOUNT BALANCE

It is clear from the examples given earlier that the exporters and importers whose actions, in a sense, result in a current account imbalance are not necessarily, and in fact not normally, the entities that ultimately adopt the implied exchange rate risk. What is it that makes these entities adopt this risk?

A basic tenet of portfolio theory is that investors will only be prepared to accept a greater degree of risk if there is the expectation of a greater return. As applied to the currency markets, it should also be expected that there will be a positive relationship between risk and return. In the case of the deficit country it means that individuals and entities will be prepared to increase their exposure to the risk of a fall in the value (depreciation) of the deficit country's currency if the return they expect from the assets they are acquiring rises. If the expected domestic currency returns of the deficit country's assets/liabilities remain unchanged, i.e. interest rates are unchanged, this will require the deficit country's currency to be lower in value. The 'cheaper' a currency the greater is the likelihood that it will appreciate in the future, and therefore the greater the return that could reasonably be expected from holding it.

To state this another way, the fact that imports exceed exports for the deficit country requires that foreigners acquire claims on the deficit country. Foreigners will be willing to acquire these assets at a price they feel comfortable with in terms of the return this price would seem to imply. Over time they will only be willing to continue acquiring claims, i.e. continue to finance the deficit, if the return they anticipate rises. This means that the deficit country's currency will fall in value until it offers the prospect of a greater return which is attractive enough to encourage foreigners to continue to acquire claims and finance the deficit. If other factors remain unchanged a fall in the value of the currency in itself will tend to result in a narrowing of the current account deficit. A lower currency makes the deficit country's exports cheaper in terms of foreign currencies and encourages foreigners to buy more of the deficit country's products. It also makes imports more expensive in terms of the domestic currency and leads residents of the deficit country to purchase fewer foreign goods.

If the economy's tendency to lose competitiveness is because its inflation rate is higher than that of its trading partners, then the long-run trend will be for the currency to fall in order to offset the inflation differential and maintain the current account roughly in balance over time. This leads to the currency being drawn to the purchasing power parity level in the long run, as explained in Chapter 3. However, as Chapters 2 and 3 also explained, exchange rates can depart from purchasing power parity levels and current account imbalances arise as a result of business cycles diverging between economies or other factors which affect the demand for funds relative to the supply forthcoming from savings. Nevertheless, as long as a country's current account remains in deficit, foreigners will be continuing to acquire claims on the country and increasing their exposure to the currency. Therefore, a deficit will only be sustainable up to a point. Any particular level of the currency will imply a future level of the current account deficit, in turn representing an increase in foreign exposure to the deficit country's currency. If they act rationally, foreigners will only be willing to acquire claims on the deficit country at an exchange rate which implies future increases in their exposure narrowing along a path they feel comfortable with, in view of the increasing risk associated with increasing exposure.

What if foreigners at some stage become unwilling to increase further their exposure to the deficit country's currency at any price (and domestic residents are unwilling to 'go short', or borrow, foreign currencies)? In this circumstance the deficit country's currency would collapse. It would reach a level which immediately eliminated the current account deficit, balancing imports and exports of goods and services.

The well known J-curve concept implies that, instead of resulting in a narrowing of the current account deficit, a fall in the value of a currency might initially increase the size of the deficit. If the depreciation of a deficit country's currency initially increased the size of its deficit, this could potentially result in an unstable situation. If foreigners were becoming uncomfortable with the risk represented by their increasing exposure, then the currency would fall to a level which offers them a potential return to compensate them for that risk. If this fall in the currency then increased the deficit, it would imply that foreigners' exposure to the currency would have to increase at an increasing rate, raising the threat of a collapse of the currency.

The basis for the J-curve is the notion that the changes in demand for goods and services which result from a move in the exchange rate are initially outweighed by the terms of trade effects. The terms of trade measure the ratio of a country's export prices to its import prices. A rise in the terms of trade can occur as a result of a rise in the country's exchange rate (which tends to lower import prices expressed in domestic currency terms and tends to raise export prices expressed in foreign currency terms) or a general rise in the prices of its exports or fall in the prices of its imports (the latter often being most significant when the goods traded are goods which have an internationally determined price, e.g. commodities). A depreciation of the currency makes the country's exports cheaper in foreign currency terms and imports more expensive in domestic currency terms, i.e. lowers the terms of trade. If residents do not immediately respond to the price change but continue to purchase the same quantity of imports, while foreigners continue to purchase the same quantity of exports, then the total cost of imports will rise in domestic currency terms and the total value of exports will fall in foreign currency terms. This means a deterioration of the current account, whether measured in domestic currency or foreign currency. In fact, even if there were some demand response, the current account could still deteriorate in the short term if the change in demand was not enough to offset the change in the cost of imports and exports.

The important point to note about the adverse terms of trade effect of a currency depreciation is that there must always be an exchange rate at which a current account deficit eventually begins to narrow. This could be an exchange rate which simply makes imported goods too expensive for anyone to afford. At some level of the exchange rate the 'demand' effect will outweigh the terms of trade effect and the current account position will improve. In a foreign exchange market free from interventions by the authorities, where the deficit of a country has become a major source of concern (i.e. investors are very unwilling to continue to increase their exposure to that country's currency), the exchange rate could tend to fall towards this level. If the currency depreciation results in a deterioration of the current account balance over certain ranges of the exchange rate, this could potentially give rise to quite violent moves in the currency of the deficit country. This could lead the authorities to intervene.

OFFICIAL INTERVENTION IN CURRENCY MARKETS

If a currency is under downward pressure intervention to defend a given level for the currency invariably means that the government adopts the exchange rate risk which the private sector is unwilling to adopt at that level of the exchange rate. Taking this further, given that in an economic sense the government is really only the agent of the taxpayer, intervention means that the ultimate exchange rate risk is borne by the taxpayer. Or, in other words, the private sector (as taxpayers) unwillingly, and probably unknowingly, adopt the exchange rate risk they were not prepared to adopt voluntarily at that level of the exchange rate for the currency.

There are two basic ways in which the authorities can attempt to fix, even if only temporarily, a certain level for an exchange rate through taking on the risk implied by the increasing exposure to currency movements. One way is by the government borrowing (or lending) in foreign currencies. The second way is through the central bank using (or adding to) its foreign exchange reserves, or borrowing foreign currencies. In theory, in an open economy, neither approach will enable the exchange rate to be fixed permanently unless it involves implications for monetary policy, as discussed in the next chapter.

Returning to the example of the United States and Japan (from Chapter 3), the United States has a large and increasing current account deficit with Japan and, as a result, an increasing net external debt to Japan. At some point the real exchange rate for the dollar in terms of the yen will be falling, as Japanese residents require lower and lower values of the dollar in order to increase the possibility of the dollar rising in the future, and hence make further increases in exposure to dollar assets an attractive proposition. At this point both the Japanese and US authorities decide they do not want the dollar to fall any further against the yen, but would prefer to defend the current level of the exchange rate. What are their options?

First, the US government could start borrowing in Japanese yen (perhaps by issuing yen-denominated bonds), and finance the current account deficit by selling these borrowed yen and buying US dollars. In this way the currency could, at least for a time, be stabilized. Japanese residents would still be acquiring new claims on the United States (reflecting the continuing current account deficit), but these claims would, to an extent, be yen-denominated (the US government bonds). So Japanese residents would not be exposing themselves to any additional currency risk. Instead, the risk is taken by the US government, which now has an increasing 'short' position in the Japanese currency represented by its yen borrowings. In the event that the dollar fell further, it would cost the US government more dollars to buy back the yen to repay the borrowing. Of course, this loss would ultimately be borne by US taxpayers.

The second, more usual, method is what is commonly known as intervention. The central banks purchase the currency under pressure and sell the currency which is rising in an attempt to prevent the exchange rate from moving in an undesirable direction. 'Sterilized' intervention is intervention that does not involve changing the money supply and therefore does not involve a change of monetary policy. In the example above, sterilized intervention could be conducted by either the US central bank or Japanese central bank, or both. If conducted by the US central bank, it would involve the bank buying a dollar asset (perhaps a US government treasury bill) and selling a yen asset (perhaps a Japanese government treasury bill) which had formed part of its foreign exchange reserves. If the central bank's foreign exchange reserves were drawn down completely, then the central bank could continue intervention by borrowing yen and selling the borrowed yen for dollars. If conducted by the Japanese central bank, the intervention would involve the Japanese authority buying dollar assets and selling yen assets. If it eventually 'ran out' of yen assets, it could borrow yen domestically with which to buy dollar assets.

In the case of intervention by the Japanese central bank, the currency risk is borne by Japanese taxpayers. The current account imbalance between Japan and the United States still results in a build-up of Japanese claims on the United States denominated in dollars, but these dollar claims are, to an extent, held by the central bank. If the dollar later depreciates against the yen, then the central bank loses money on its dollar assets. Because the central bank's profit is periodically turned over to the government and contributes to its financing, a lower profit has to be replaced by higher taxes for any given level of government expenditure.

In the case of intervention by the US central bank, the risk is borne by US taxpayers. Japanese claims on the United States still grow in line with the current account imbalance, but these claims are yen-denominated rather than dollar-denominated to the extent of the central bank's intervention. In fact, this case of sterilized intervention is equivalent to the previously discussed case of the US government borrowing yen funds, most obviously if the central bank itself has to resort to borrowing. Because the central bank's profit is turned over to the government, the potential cost to the taxpayer should be the same for both methods of currency stabilization for any given amount of intervention.

One problem with these forms of interference in the exchange rate determination process by the authorities is that they forestall the process of correction of the current account imbalance. The dollar is under downward pressure in the above example because Japanese residents are no longer willing to increase their exposure to the dollar at the existing level of the exchange rate. To take on the greater risk implied by increasing their dollar exposure they would need to see a lower value of the dollar which would offer the possibility of a greater return from dollar assets, in yen terms. This lower level of the dollar would then help to correct the current account imbalance as described earlier, thereby diminishing the need for Japanese residents to increase further their exposure in the future. If Japanese residents eventually approach a limit to the extent that they are willing to acquire US assets, then the dollar should fall to a level at which the current account imbalance eventually disappears. If the authorities intervene to fix the exchange rate for the dollar and take on the exchange rate exposure themselves, then, other things being equal, there will be no means for the current account imbalance to correct. The imbalance will continue at the fixed exchange rate, and the authorities will need to finance a greater and greater proportion (eventually all) of the imbalance themselves.

The limit to this intervention process occurs when foreign creditors of the deficit country are no longer willing to lend the deficit country any more funds to finance the deficit. The question becomes not one of exchange rate risk but of credit risk. Although, in theory, as credit risk increases rising interest rates should help correct the current account deficit, in practice many countries in this situation have become bankrupt. In the past this has been the case for many Third World debtors – Argentina, the Philippines, Brazil, etc. – whose governments financed current account deficits over a long period by borrowing foreign currencies.

The other, very different form of central bank intervention, which is not ineffective, is unsterilized intervention. Here the central bank allows its intervention to result in a change in the money supply, using its position as the monopolistic supplier of domestic money. For instance, in the above example, the Japanese central bank could pay for the dollar assets it purchases in intervention not by selling yen assets but by creating more yen. This would increase the money supply and result in inflation in Japan which would eventually help to correct the current account imbalance by making Japanese exports less competitive and US products relatively more competitive within Japan. As ultimately this is merely another way of allowing the real exchange rate for the dollar to decline in terms of the yen, in real terms it is similar to nonintervention. This is discussed in greater depth in the following chapter, on monetary policy.

From the above discussion it would appear that intervention in foreign exchange markets by governments or central banks is at best unnecessary and at worst dangerous. Is intervention ever justifiable? Intervention can only really be worthwhile if it is judged that the private sector has estimated the risks and potential returns from increasing exposure to a given currency incorrectly. In the above discussion it has always been assumed that, if all other things remain equal, a lower value of a currency will imply the potential for a greater future return, and hence the private sector will be keener to buy a currency if it is 'cheaper'. However, if the very fact that the currency is falling leads the private sector to anticipate further falls in the currency rather than rises, then there is the possibility of a downward spiral in the currency developing. Such a collapse could take the currency far below the level needed to eliminate the current account deficit. (This is possible because flows of goods and services, i.e. the items in the current account, take longer to adjust to changes in prices than flows of capital, i.e. the items on the capital account.) It could be exacerbated by the adverse terms of trade effects of the currency depreciation. In this event the central bank could usefully intervene to support the currency.

Two things should be noticed about intervention in this case. First, because the central bank is supporting a currency which has already fallen far enough to correct the current account deficit, it – and thus taxpayers – should not lose money from the intervention. This is because the central bank is forming its expectations about the future 'correctly', and the private sector as a whole is not. Secondly, and deriving from this, the fact that the central bank has correct expectations about the future, and the private sector does not, would seem to require that the people working for the central bank are 'smarter', or have better information, than operators in the private sector. On the face of it, this would seem a surprising assumption to make. Nevertheless, the history of the 1980s, which saw extreme swings in exchange rates for the major currencies, would suggest that there might occasionally be a place for central bank intervention in foreign exchange markets. The rule for (sterilized) intervention should be that a central bank should only intervene if it sees the intervention as likely to prove profitable. Then the central bank is only operating as any well informed private entity or individual should, and will be acting to aid the adjustment of the balance of payments and not to hinder it.

MONETARY POLICY UNDER FIXED EXCHANGE RATES 6

LIMITATIONS OF MONETARY POLICY

In Chapter 2 it was described how the business cycle – the medium-term fluctuations in output around the long-term growth trend of an economy – is associated with variations in monetary conditions, but in the long run the only lasting effect of money supply growth in excess of the sustainable rise in money demand is inflation. The implication is that the central bank is not in a position to influence real economic variables except in the short to medium term. Monetary policy can affect only the inflation component of economic variables such as the GNP growth rate in the long term. In an open economy the same also applies to the real interest rate, and the real exchange rate, which eventually tends back to the level which balances the current account. In the long run, the monetary policy of the central bank can affect only the inflation component of the long-term interest rate and the relative inflation element of the movement of the nominal exchange rate.

Further, although the central bank has it in its power to control the supply of money, and therefore the supply of credit, it has no control over the demand for either money or credit, in the short term. In the long run, monetary policy can have important effects on the demand for money and the demand for credit. If, for instance, monetary policy is 'too lax', and the supply of money grows too rapidly, this will ultimately lead to inflation, which will eventually have consequences for the demand for money. In the short run, however, the central bank can have no influence over the demand for money or credit. The central bank is in the position of the monopoly producer in textbook economics: it can either control the supply or the price, but not both independently. If it fixes or manages the supply, the price is determined by demand. If it fixes the price, the supply is determined by the demand at that price.

Given that the (nominal) exchange rate equates to the price of money (Chapter 1), in practice this means that in an open economy the central bank can manage the exchange rate or the supply of money but not both independently. Similarly, because the supply of credit is closely related to the supply of money and the interest rate is the price of credit, it can achieve an independent objective for either the supply of money or the interest rate but not both.

Therefore, the central bank can independently target only one of the three variables: the money supply, exchange rate or interest rate. If it targets the money supply it will have roughly determined the supply of credit. Hence both the exchange rate and the interest rate will be determined by demand. If the central bank targets an objective for the exchange rate, this will determine the money supply and also the supply of credit and hence the interest rate, given the demand for money and for credit. Finally, if it fixes the interest rate, for the given demand for credit the supply of credit will then be determined and therefore also the supply of money.

FIXED RATES IN THE FOREIGN EXCHANGE MARKETS

Here we discuss an approach to monetary policy in which the central bank fixes the exchange rate for its currency in terms of another currency at a constant rate. It achieves this by being always prepared to buy or sell its currency for the foreign currency at that exchange rate. The central bank is in a position to do this because it can create or destroy as much of its own money as it chooses. However, in fixing the exchange rate the central bank will give up its ability to control independently the supply of money. In addition, it was explained in the previous chapters that over the long run, in an open economy, the exchange rate for any currency must return ultimately to its purchasing power parity (PPP) level. If the nominal exchange rate is fixed, it must be the case that PPP adjusts to this fixed exchange rate. This entails an adjustment in the inflation rate such that the PPP level for the currency adjusts to the exchange rate for the currency fixed by the central bank.

Imagine two countries A and B. The balance sheet of A's central bank is illustrated in Balance Sheet 12. Inflation in A is higher than in B and A has an overall current account deficit. If the exchange rate for A's currency is allowed to float, it should float downwards, or depreciate, against B's currency to restore A's competitiveness and bring the current account back to balance. Moreover, if the inflation

Balance Sheet 12

Monetary authority (central bank)	
Assets	Liabilities
Net foreign assets	Currency in circulation (i.e. notes and coin)
Government bonds	Deposits of commercial banks
Loans to financial institutions	Deposits of government
	Net worth

rate in A remains higher than in B, the PPP level for A's currency is falling. Therefore, the exchange rate should also continue to fall in line with PPP to maintain A's competitiveness.

A's central bank now fixes the exchange rate for its currency in terms of B's currency at a constant rate. Because A has a current account deficit, the demand for foreign currencies from importers exceeds the supply of foreign currencies received by exporters. To avoid foreign currencies rising in value against A's currency (i.e. A's currency depreciating against B's in this example) and to maintain the fixed exchange rate, the central bank must meet the excess demand for foreign currency.

When the central bank sells foreign currencies to the private sector, the purchasers of the foreign currency pay the central bank with checks or drafts drawn on the commercial banks. The checks are settled by the central bank debiting the commercial banks' deposits with itself. The balance sheets of the central bank, commercial banks, and the importer, who we assume is buying the foreign currency, alter as shown in Balance Sheet 13 (only balance sheet items which change are shown).

Because the deposit of the importer at the commercial bank is part of the money supply, the money supply has fallen. More importantly, the monetary base has also contracted because of the fall in the commercial banks' deposits at the central bank. This will have a much greater, multiple, contractionary effect on the money supply (Chapter 1). As it continues, the monetary contraction will eventually reduce the inflation rate in A, stabilizing the PPP level for A's currency and ultimately bringing PPP into line with the exchange rate at which A's currency has been fixed.

As long as A's inflation rate remains above that of B, A is losing competitiveness. A's current account will remain in deficit and A will be experiencing a monetary contraction, or a lower than 'normal' rate of monetary growth. The monetary squeeze will be halted only when

Balance Sheet 13

Central bank		Commercial banks		Importer	
Assets	Liabilities	Assets	Liabilities	Assets	Liabilities
Net foreign assets ↓	Deposits of commercial banks ↓	Deposits at central bank ↓	Deposit of importer ↓	Foreign currency ↑ Local currency deposit at bank ↓	

↓ = falling ↑ = rising

A's current account has returned to balance. This will occur when A's competitiveness has been restored, i.e. when the exchange rate is at the PPP level. The difference from a floating exchange rate is that it is PPP that adjusts to the exchange rate, through a reduction in inflation, and not the exchange rate for the currency to PPP.

In the long term, the inflation rate in A will roughly equal that in B. If inflation in A becomes higher than in B then A's current account will tend to slip into deficit. This will cause a monetary squeeze in A which will bring the inflation rate back down. Conversely, if inflation in A falls below that in B, then A's current account will eventually tend to move into surplus and the opposite will occur. The central bank will have to purchase foreign currency to prevent A's currency from rising, expanding the monetary base in the process. Eventually, inflation in A will rise back up to the level in B.

In the long run, therefore, if a central bank fixes its currency to the currency of another country, it means inheriting the inflation rate of that economy. The change in the PPP level for A's currency in terms of B's depends only upon the inflation rate in A relative to that in B. If PPP is to stay roughly constant at the rate fixed for the exchange rate then the inflation rate in A must equal that in B. Importantly, it should be noted that this does not mean that the money growth rate in A must be the same as that in B. The money growth rate in A will be the rate of growth of money supply necessary to generate B's inflation rate. If the long-term rate of real economic growth and the growth in the demand for money in A differ from those in B, then the rate of money growth which generates a given inflation rate in A may be very different from the rate which generates the same inflation rate in B.

Let us return to the original example. After A's central bank sells foreign currency its balance sheet is as shown in Balance Sheet 14.

Balance Sheet 14

Central bank	
Assets	Liabilities
Net foreign assets ↓	Cash currency in circulation ⎫
Government bonds	Deposits of commercial banks ↓ ⎬ Monetary base ↓
Loans to financial institutions	Deposits of government ⎭
	Net worth

The central bank is always able to maintain a fixed exchange rate as long as the value of its net foreign assets exceeds the size of the monetary base. Then, in the event of a balance of payments deficit, the central bank will, if necessary, be able to continue to sell foreign assets until the monetary base is totally destroyed. Because no spending can take place, including spending on imported goods, in the absence of a supply of money, even in the most extreme of circumstances the balance of payments deficit would eventually be corrected. However, a severe monetary squeeze would have very negative implications for the economy in the short run. The central bank might, therefore, be tempted to take measures to offset the monetary effects of its sales of foreign exchange, known as sterilizing the intervention.

The most obvious way that it can do this is through *open market operations* (discussed in Chapter 7). The central bank could increase its holdings of government bonds through purchasing bonds from the private sector. It pays for the bonds by issuing checks drawn on itself. When these checks are paid into banks by the sellers of the bonds, they are presented back to the central bank. These checks are settled through the central bank crediting the banks' deposits with itself, therefore increasing the monetary base. If the value of purchases of bonds exactly equals the value of foreign exchange sold by the central bank, its balance sheet will alter as shown in Balance Sheet 15.

At this stage the monetary base is left unchanged. In terms of the monetary base equation derived in Chapters 1 and 4, in unsterilized intervention (when the central bank is selling foreign exchange) the elements of the identity change in the following way:

$$\Delta M0 \downarrow = PSD - \Delta B - \Delta ED + \Delta D + \Delta R \downarrow$$

Balance Sheet 15

Central bank	
Assets	Liabilities
Net foreign assets ↓	Cash currency in circulation
Government bonds ↑	Deposits of commercial banks ↓↑
Loans to financial institutions	Deposits of government
	Net worth

Monetary base ↓↑ (bracketing cash currency in circulation and deposits of commercial banks)

For sterilized intervention, the following changes occur:

$$\Delta M0 = PSD - \Delta B \downarrow - \Delta ED + \Delta D + \Delta R \downarrow$$

If the central bank is buying foreign exchange, the same variables change in the opposite direction.

In Chapter 5 it was explained that sterilized intervention is generally ineffective because it does nothing to affect the factor(s) originally placing pressure on the exchange rate. In the case of our example, this is a persistent current account deficit caused by higher inflation at home than in trading partners, leading to a lack of competitiveness. Unsterilized intervention, on the other hand, is economically similar to allowing the exchange rate to float. Competitiveness is restored, but through inflation falling (in this example) rather than the exchange rate depreciating. The real exchange rate adjusts in both cases. In the floating exchange rate case, the real exchange rate falls as a result of a depreciation of the nominal exchange rate, and, in the fixed exchange rate case, through an adjustment in inflation or price levels.

In an open economy sterilized intervention may even be a self-defeating process. When the central bank buys or sells bonds it may place pressure on real interest rates which stimulate private sector capital flows which undermine the fixed exchange rate.

In our example, the central bank's purchases of government bonds will reduce the private sector's holdings of government bonds. This is similar to the government running a smaller budget deficit (PSD) or larger budget surplus and will cause real interest rates to be under downward pressure. In an open economy, real interest rates will not actually diverge from the level of real interest rates in the rest of the world. Instead, the downward pressure on the real rate emerges as an increased outflow of capital from the private sector. Consequent pressure on the currency will then require the central bank to conduct more intervention to sell foreign exchange in what becomes a self-defeating process.

In the opposite case of a balance of payments surplus, where the central bank conducts sterilized intervention to prevent its currency from rising in value, an identical process occurs. Then the central bank's sales of bonds could place upward pressure on real interest rates, attracting capital from abroad.

Therefore, sterilized intervention, or offsetting the monetary consequences of fixing the exchange rate, will generally be ineffective. Consequently, in an open economy, rigidly fixing the exchange rate in terms of another country's currency means inheriting the inflation rate of that country and a money supply growth rate which generates that inflation rate.

Moreover, it will also imply inheriting that country's interest rate structure. If two currencies are fixed at one exchange rate, then interest rates for both currencies should be identical. Otherwise, unless they anticipated a devaluation, savers would place all their funds in the higher interest rate currency, bringing interest rates for that currency down.

More formally, it was explained in Chapter 3 that, for two countries A and B:

$$i(A) + E\dot{R}(B/A) = i(B)$$

where i is the interest rate and $E\dot{R}(B/A)$ is the expected appreciation of A's currency against B's currency. If A is fixed to B at a constant rate then $E\dot{R}(B/A) = 0$ and so $i(A) = i(B)$, i.e. interest rates are equal for the two currencies. If real interest rates are equal for all open economies (Chapter 3) and two countries have a fixed exchange rate between their currencies, they will have the same inflation rate over the long term, and hence their nominal interest rates must also be equal.

Nominal interest rates can only differ if investors anticipate a devaluation of one country's currency versus the other. For instance, if the one-year interest rate in A is 5 percent and in B it is 8 percent, then because:

$$i(A) + E\dot{R}(B/A) = i(B)$$
$$E\dot{R}(B/A) = i(B) - i(A) = 8\% - 5\% = 3\%$$

investors must expect A's currency to be revalued against B's by 3 percent within one year. For differences in longer-term interest rates to exist, investors must implicitly believe too that inflation rates will differ (because real interest rates are the same).

FIXED EXCHANGE RATES IN PRACTICE

The preceding discussion of the mechanics and implications of a currency fixed to another currency at a single invariant exchange rate described an extreme version of the fixed exchange rate mechanism. In practice, if a central bank adopts a fixed exchange rate for its currency, it is likely to maintain the exchange rate with one or more other currencies within certain specified ranges, allowing room for a degree of exchange rate variability. In addition, rather than choose one or more specific currencies as an anchor, it may tie its currency to a 'basket' of other currencies.

In the currency basket approach, the central bank sets its currency equal to a specified basket of currencies. For example, one unit of the currency, let us call it the X dollar, could be set equal to US$0.80 + DM 1.0 + ¥50. If, at day 1, the exchange rates for the DM and the yen versus the dollar are US$1 = DM 2, and US$1 = ¥150, then one X dollar will be set equal to US$1.6333 in terms of US dollars (0.80 + 0.50 + 0.3333 = 1.6333). That is, the exchange rate at day 1 will be X$1 = US$1.6333. If, at day 2, the exchange rates have moved such that now US$1 = DM 2.05 and US$1 = ¥155 then the exchange rate for the X dollar in terms of US dollars will be set at X$1 = US$1.6104 (because 0.80 + (1.0/2.05) + 50/155 = 1.6104). The X dollar will be depreciated somewhat *vis-à-vis* the US dollar, reflecting the fact that the other currencies comprising the basket have fallen in value against the US dollar.

If the central bank sticks rigidly to pegging the value of its currency to the fixed basket, then it will inherit an inflation rate which will be some weighted average of the inflation rates obtaining in the countries whose currencies make up the basket. The *weights* are the relative weightings of each of the currencies in the basket. In our example, the central bank of X will inherit an average of the inflation rates existing in the United States, Germany and Japan. In practice, however, many central banks which adopt a currency basket approach leave themselves with the flexibility to appreciate (or depreciate) their currency *vis-à-vis* the basket if they wish to do so. Sometimes, the central bank does not even publish the composition of the basket of currencies, but instead keeps it secret in the hope that market participants will not realize if it is appreciating or depreciating its currency *vis-à-vis* the basket.

Nations that link their currencies to a basket of other currencies include Poland, Hungary, Chile, and the majority of the South East Asian countries, at least prior to their exchange rate difficulties of 1997. However, rather than being pure, fixed exchange rates, most of these are managed exchange rate regimes, which are discussed in the following chapter.

The European Currency Unit (or ECU) is a basket of the currencies which constitute the European Monetary System (EMS). A number of central banks have used the ECU as an anchor unit against which to fix or manage their own currency, including Norway (from October 1990 until December 1992) and Greece (since 1993). The ECU was designed to play a pivotal role in the exchange rate mechanism (ERM) of the EMS, and under the plans for European economic and monetary union (EMU) the new single currency, the Euro, will come into being at a one-to-one rate with the ECU. Nevertheless, throughout its existence, at least under the narrow 2.25 percent bands which operated until August 1993, the ERM functioned as a fixed exchange rate regime in which all member currencies were tied to the Deutschmark as their anchor currency and therefore to the monetary policy of the German Bundesbank.

The ERM has provided some useful examples of the implications of fixed exchange rates for interest rates, the money supply and inflation. It should be borne in mind that, for a substantial part of the period of existence of the EMS (since March 1979), the member countries have not had completely open economies, as most maintained various exchange controls until late in the 1980s. The existence of exchange controls may delay or prolong the fixed exchange rate adjustment process because it can make possible sterilized intervention (see also Chapter 7).

Figure 21 shows how France's inflation rate converged with Germany's after France, together with other continental European members of the European Union committed itself to the ERM. The convergence process took a particularly long time, with French inflation and long-term interest rates not falling to German levels until 1991. The reason for the drawn-out convergence process was that France maintained very strict exchange controls (i.e. controls on outward and inward capital movements) until 1985. Exchange controls were gradually relaxed from 1986 but only entirely removed for both companies and individuals alike at the beginning of 1990.

Controls over capital movements gave scope to the French authorities to pursue an easier monetary policy than the Bundesbank

FIGURE 21 France and Germany: inflation rates

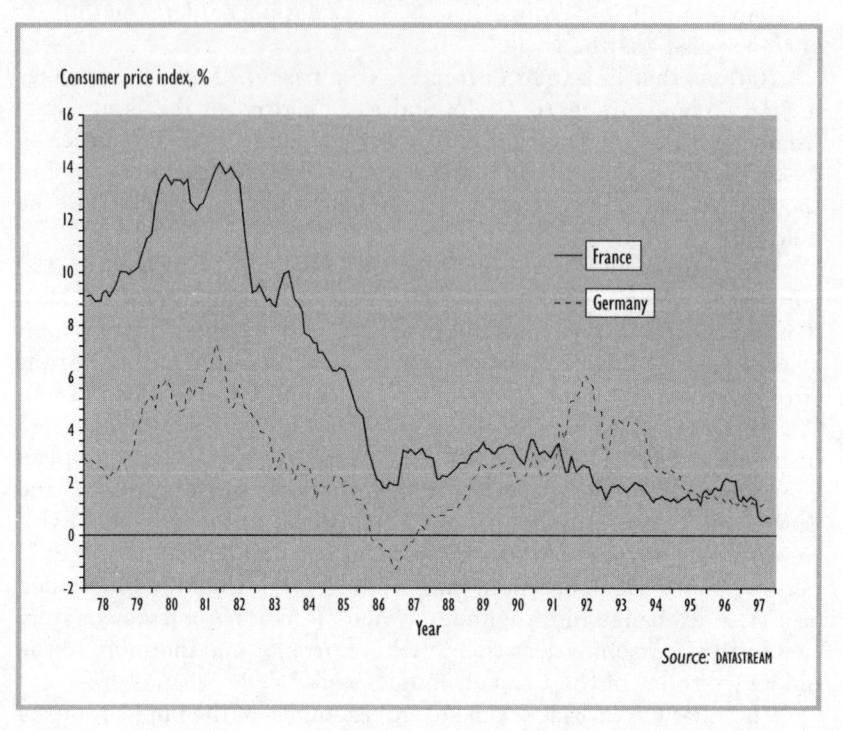

without suffering excessive capital outflows. It did this during 1981/82 – the socialist government's famous 'dash for growth' – and again over 1984/85. Both episodes of easy money were followed by successive devaluations of the franc *vis-à-vis* the Deutschmark, necessary to correct for loss of competitiveness resulting from higher inflation.

The two episodes are clearly shown in Figure 22, which depicts the slope of the French yield curve, as measured by the difference between long-term interest rates and three-month rates, and the slope of the German yield curve measured in the same way. It was explained in Chapter 1 that the slope of the yield curve can serve as a measure of the ease or tightness of monetary policy. In this case it is a much better indicator of monetary conditions than the growth of the money supply itself. During the 1980s, extensive financial deregulation distorted the monetary aggregates rendering them poor yardsticks of monetary policy. The introduction of new financial instruments, abolition of credit and interest rate controls, and various changes in the regime of taxation applying to financial instruments all affected the demand for measured money supply.

FIGURE 22 France and Germany: yield curve slopes

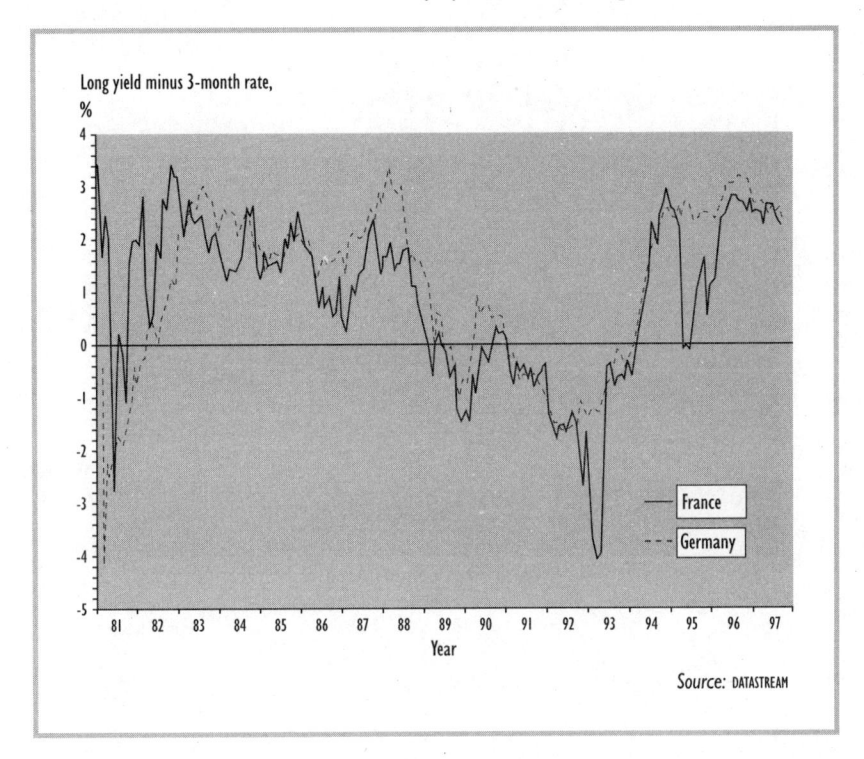

France and Germany: yield curve slopes chart. Long yield minus 3-month rate, %, from 1981 to 1997. Source: DATASTREAM

In Figure 22 the periods of relatively easy money in France show up as a more positively sloped yield curve in France than in Germany. When the slope of the French yield curve exceeded that of the German yield curve, as occurred in 1981/82 and 1984/85, devaluation of the franc ultimately proved necessary.

The chart of purchasing power parity (Figure 23; see Chapter 3 for an extensive discussion of the theory and application of PPP) sheds more light on the franc devaluations of the early and mid-1980s. Easier monetary policy in France led to higher inflation in France than in Germany. As a result, the purchasing power parity rate for the franc *vis-à-vis* the Deutschmark was falling. The implied loss of competitiveness for France and associated pressures on the balance of payments led to the periodic devaluations to alleviate what would otherwise have been painful monetary contractions necessary to restore French competitiveness.

After exchange controls were relaxed from 1986, it became increasingly difficult for the French authorities to implement an independent monetary policy in a way that would ultimately lead to a

FIGURE 23   France: franc/DM rate versus PPP

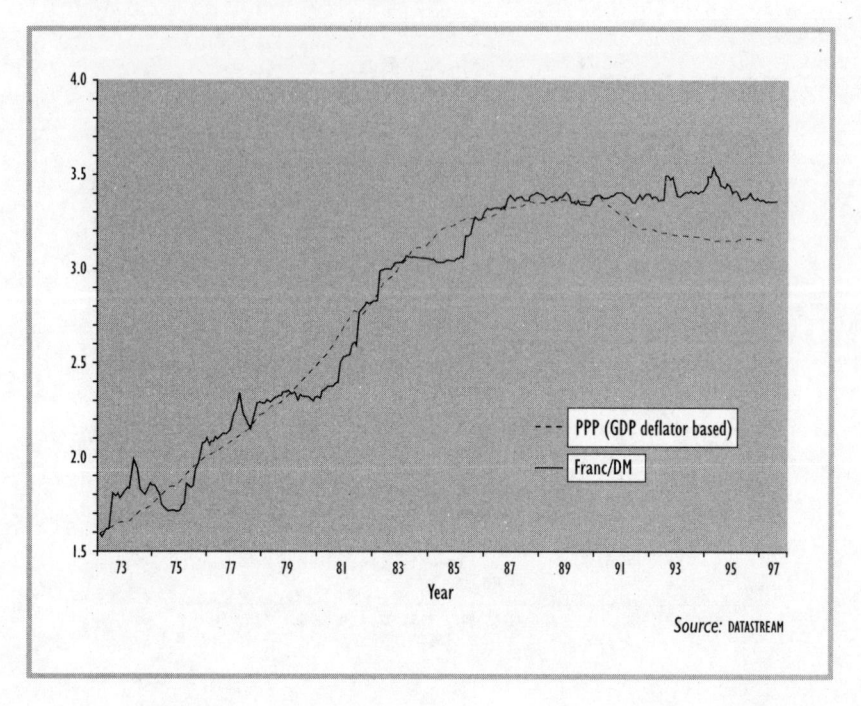

Source: DATASTREAM

realignment of the franc/Deutschmark exchange rate. The 'openness' of the French economy meant that French interest rates became in effect tied to German interest rates.

Even though the convergence process was interrupted by speculative attacks on the franc during and after the ERM turmoil of 1992/93, the ERM central rate for the franc was not devalued, and by 1997, as the markets began to anticipate EMU, French inflation and long-term interest rates had dropped slightly below German rates. A franc devaluation was avoided because in the 1990s French monetary policy had not been easier than German policy, the franc was not overvalued and consequently the current account of the balance of payments was in surplus rather than deficit.

Critics of fixed exchange rates often argue that fixed rates are inevitably untenable in a world of very mobile capital, without capital controls to insulate the currency from speculative attacks. They point to the 1992/93 ERM crisis as evidence. The reality is rather different.

Although there have been examples of central banks forced to submit to a fundamentally unwarranted devaluation (the January 1993 devaluation of the Irish punt is a clear example), most of the devaluations which occurred during the ERM crisis subsequently afflicted markedly overvalued currencies of economies which consequently had substantial current account deficits. This was certainly the case for the UK, Italy and Spain, the exchange rate crises of which began the ERM turmoil in September 1992. In most cases (not the UK example), currency overvaluation under fixed rates arises because of divergent and inconsistent monetary policies temporarily protected by capital controls (the example of France in the 1980s, discussed above), or because of capital inflow which follows the removal of exchange controls (see Chapter 10). Once capital movements have been freed for an extended period, monetary conditions in the fixed rate economy become so locked into the monetary policy of the anchor currency economy that it becomes much more difficult for ultimately unsustainable divergences in the key variables – inflation and the balance of payments – to develop. Austria, the Netherlands and Belgium, none of which faced sustained currency pressure during the ERM crisis, are good examples of this. In contrast, with widespread capital controls there is no automatic aligning of the monetary stance in the fixed exchange rate economies, and adjustment will ultimately occur through the current account of the balance of payments which is economically painful and in many cases ultimately involves a change of exchange rate. Therefore, without capital controls the permanence of a fixed exchange rate can certainly be threatened; with capital controls a fixed exchange rate is simply not permanent.

Austria, the Netherlands and Belgium have maintained much tighter exchange rate bands than the normal ERM bands. There is an argument that the operation of an exchange rate band – when the rate of exchange between two currencies is not fixed rigidly at one rate but is instead allowed to vary within a specified range – makes a currency more prone to speculative attack than a completely fixed exchange rate, and that this was one of the flaws of the ERM. Once a currency exchange rate is allowed to fluctuate within a band, even for two completely open economies there may be some, limited, scope for divergence of interest rates. It will be possible for either one of the two countries to have alternatively an easier, or a tighter, monetary policy than the other, within the limits made possible by the band. The reason is that, depending on the width of the band, there is scope for depreciation or appreciation of the exchange rate within it. Medium- or longer-term interest rates will diverge to the extent of this anticipated depreciation or appreciation according to the following identity:

$$i(A) + E\dot{R}(B/A) = i(B)$$

If the expected depreciation/appreciation is realized, then, assuming the exchange rate is to be maintained within the specified range, the central bank which previously had the easier policy will need to adopt a relatively tight policy. Then, in theory, the interest rate relationship should be reversed to reflect an expected appreciation of the previously weaker of the currencies.

It should be apparent that the wider the band within which the exchange rate is allowed to vary, the greater will be the scope for interest rate divergence. In the extreme, if the specified band were so wide as to encompass the whole range of likely floating exchange rate movement, by definition interest rate behavior would be similar to what it would be under the floating exchange rate.

An example of interest rate divergence under 'fixed' exchange rates is given by the experience of the UK, when sterling entered the ERM in October 1990. At the time of entry, UK short-term interest rates, at approximately 15 percent, were substantially higher than European interest rates, with German rates at roughly 9 percent. Many economists had believed that once sterling had entered the ERM, UK interest rates would be forced down closer to German rates. However, sterling entered the mechanism with a wide band, allowing the exchange rate to fluctuate by 6 percent either side of the central rate with the other EMS currencies. Against the Deutschmark, sterling could fluctuate by up to 6 percent either side of a central rate of £1 = DM 2.95, with the potential for the exchange rate to vary between DM 2.778 and DM 3.132.

Immediately after entry, sterling did rise above DM 3.0 towards the top end of its band. Subsequently, contrary to most expectations, following an initial 1 percent cut in interest rates to coincide with ERM entry, there was no pressure to reduce interest rates further. Sterling was fundamentally overvalued (relative to purchasing power parity) at the central rate chosen. Therefore, given that, over time, sterling was likely to be under pressure to depreciate, at exchange rates over DM 3.0 there was the potential for a significant fall in value (towards DM 2.778). To compensate for this expectation of depreciation within the ERM band, interest rates for sterling had to remain higher than for the Deutschmark. Eventually, the band proved untenable, as even at the lower end sterling was so overvalued as to make the overvaluation impossible to correct through superior inflation performance particularly against a background in which monetary policy in the anchor currency country – Germany – was being held very tight (see also Chapter 10).

COMMODITY AND CURRENCY EXCHANGE STANDARDS OR CURRENCY BOARDS

The tightest form of currency link, and the most robust form of fixed exchange rate, occurs under a commodity exchange standard, or currency board. In this monetary arrangement the central bank is completely passive. The central bank stands prepared always to sell or redeem its domestic currency notes in return for a fixed amount of a given foreign currency or commodity such as gold, silver or copper. For instance, the central bank could set one unit of its currency equal to one US dollar or equal to 0.003 ounces of gold or perhaps 0.15 ounces of silver. If the central bank of country A set one unit of currency equal to 0.003 ounces of gold, then it would always be prepared to create new currency notes and sell them for gold at a rate of A$1 = 0.003 ounces, and to redeem notes presented to it in return for gold, paying out 0.003 ounces of gold for each A dollar redeemed.

Let us consider an example in which the central bank of A sets one unit of its currency (the A dollar) equal to two units of country B's currency (i.e. A$1 = B$2). It always stands ready to issue new A dollar currency notes as long as it is paid B$2 for every A$1 issued, or to accept back A dollar notes, paying out B$2 for every A$1 redeemed. Now assume that at the time that A's central bank makes its currency notes freely convertible into B's currency at the A$1 = B$2 fixed rate, the inflation rate in A is far higher than in B. Because A is rapidly losing competitiveness, its current account will be moving into deficit and its currency will be under pressure to depreciate *vis-à-vis* B's currency.

The exchange rate for A's currency in the foreign exchange market might fall towards A$1 = B$1. There will then be an incentive to people or companies that have 'excess' notes, which they would normally deposit in their own local banks, to sell the notes to the central bank to obtain the A$1 = B$2 rate. For example, a small shopkeeper would receive notes during the course of business and normally deposit them in his bank. Now instead, he could sell any notes received to the central bank for B dollars, at a rate of A$1 = B$2. He could sell the B dollars acquired back to a commercial bank at the market exchange rate of A$1 = B$1. If he received A$10,000 in currency notes during the course of a day's business he would obtain B$20,000 at the central bank's exchange rate. Selling the B$20,000 to a commercial bank would give him an A dollar deposit in the bank of A$20,000 (at the assumed market exchange rate for deposits of A$1 = B$1). These two simple transactions would leave him with a profit of A$10,000, doubling his initial sum of money. The shopkeeper is *arbitraging* the difference between the central bank exchange rate and the market exchange rate.

The actions of the shopkeeper and others taking advantage of the arbitrage between the central bank and market exchange rate would have the effect of supporting the market exchange rate. This is because the arbitrageur obtains foreign currency (B dollars) from the central bank and uses it to buy domestic currency, representing additional demand for the domestic currency. The arbitrageur's actions also have a more important consequence, which is to shrink the monetary base, and hence the domestic money supply.

After the arbitrageur (the shopkeeper in the example) sells notes to the central bank, the central bank's balance sheet initially will be as shown in Balance Sheet 16 (numbers in the example in brackets).

Because the currency notes that the central bank has purchased are no longer in circulation, they are subtracted from both sides of the balance sheet, leaving the central bank balance sheet as shown in Balance Sheet 17.

Therefore, on the central bank balance sheet the counterpart to the sale of foreign assets (B dollars to the shopkeeper) is a fall in currency notes outstanding, part of the monetary base.

Note that in the example net worth is also shown dropping by A$10,000. On a 'flow' basis, the loss arises because the central bank has sold B dollars at a rate of two for every one A dollar when the market rate of B dollars is the same (that is 1:1) as A dollars. This notional 'loss' of the central bank is the counterpart to the profit made by the arbitrageur. In reality the net worth of the central bank

Balance Sheet 16

Central bank of Country A		
Assets	Liabilities	
Net foreign assets ↓ (−B$20,000)	Currency notes	Monetary base
Government bonds	Deposits of commercial banks	
Loans to financial institutions	Deposits of government	
Currency notes ↑ (+A$10,000)	Net worth (−A$10,000)	

Balance Sheet 17

Central bank of Country A	
Assets	Liabilities
Net foreign assets ↓ (−B$20,000)	Currency notes ↓ (−$A10,000) ⎫ Monetary
Government bonds	Deposits of commercial banks ⎬ base ↓ (−A$10,000)
Loans to financial institutions	Deposits of government ⎭
	Net worth (−A$10,000)

will not have fallen, because the rate of its remaining holdings of B dollars has (temporarily) doubled in A dollar terms. In the long run, because the exchange rate for A dollars returns to the exchange rate fixed by the central bank (A$1 = B$2) there is no change in net worth from this source.

The contraction of the monetary base results in a multiple contraction of the money supply. If the public initially still desires to hold the same amount of notes and coin (and there is no reason why the public's demand for notes and coin should have changed) then the commercial banks must acquire back the currency notes which have been 'lost'. They must pay for the notes by running down their reserve deposits at the central bank. They would not pay for the notes with foreign currency i.e. B dollars, because at the central bank's rate (i.e. A$1 = B$2) they would incur a large foreign exchange loss (compared to the market rate of A$1 = B$1). In a fractional reserve system the fall in banks' reserves results in a larger fall in the total money supply. If, for this example, we assume a reserve ratio of 5 percent and the public's cash-to-deposit ratio at 10 percent (i.e. the nonbank private sector tends to wish to hold $10 of notes for every $100 of bank deposits they hold), then the balance sheet of the central bank of A would ultimately be as in Balance Sheet 18.

Deposits held at the commercial banks by the nonbank private sector have fallen by A$66,666.6 (ten times the fall in currency notes because the cash-to-deposits ratio is assumed to be 10 percent, and twenty times the fall in the reserve deposits because the reserve ratio is 5 percent). The fall in the total money supply (currency plus deposits in the banks) is therefore A$73,333.3 (6,666.6 + 66,666.6).

Balance Sheet 18

Central bank of Country A	
Assets	Liabilities
Net foreign assets ↓ (−B$20,000)	Currency notes ↓ (−$A6,666.6) ⎫ Monetary
Government bonds	Reserve deposits ↓ (−A$3,333.3) ⎬ base ↓ (−A$10,000)
Loans to financial institutions	Deposits of government
	Net worth (−A$10,000)

The formula for the final fall (or rise in the case of a monetary expansion) in total money supply as a multiple of the initial reduction (or rise) in the central bank's foreign assets and currency issue outstanding is:

$$M = F \times \frac{(c+1)}{(c+r)}$$

where M is the money supply, F is the fall (or, alternatively, increase) in the monetary base (i.e. the initial fall in currency), c is the cash-to-deposit ratio (0.1 in the example) and r is the reserve ratio (0.05 in the example). The formula derived as follows. If Cp is total cash currency in circulation, BD total bank deposits and BR bank reserves, then

$$Cp = c \times BD$$
$$BR = r \times BD$$
$$F = Cp + BR = cBD + rBD$$
$$\therefore BD = \frac{F}{c+r}$$
$$M = Cp + BD = cBD + BD$$
$$= (c+1)BD$$
$$\therefore M = F \times \frac{(c+1)}{(c+r)}$$

Money supply will continue to contract for as long as the exchange rate for the currency remains under downward pressure. This will only cease to be the case when inflation (in country A) has been brought down and competitiveness has been restored such that A's current account moves back to balance. The argument is exactly equivalent to the case of the exchange rate fixed through intervention.

In the opposite case, of a country with a low inflation rate and a current account surplus which pegs to the currency of a country with a higher inflation rate, the reverse transactions will take place. Then the exchange rate will tend to be under upward pressure, translating into a monetary expansion. Inflation will rise and competitiveness will be lost until the current account moves to balance. In the long run, inflation in A (the country pegging the exchange rate) must equal the inflation rate in B (the country whose currency forms the basis for the peg).

Analytically, the two approaches to fixing the exchange rate – either through intervention or through adopting a currency board – are exactly equivalent. In most cases, in any given situation and for any exchange rate chosen, the monetary consequences will be identical whichever the arrangement for pegging the exchange rate. In an open economy the central bank will not be able to sterilize effectively the monetary effect of the exchange rate peg under either method. There may be a marginal difference between the two systems if the private sector believes an exchange rate devaluation or revaluation to be imminent. Under a currency board, fear of imminent devaluation or revaluation may to some extent discourage arbitrage, leading the market exchange rate to diverge from the central bank's exchange rate for currency notes. (Normally, under a currency board the market exchange rate will remain extremely close to the central bank rate because the possibility of a risk-free arbitrage profit would quickly reduce any divergence between the two.) In this case, capital flight (or inflow) may cause monetary contraction (expansion) to take place at a somewhat quicker pace if the central bank actively intervenes to fix the exchange rate.

A practical difference between the two pegged exchange rate arrangements is that under a currency board there is no need for bank reserves. This is because the central bank is entirely passive. All the currency transactions are initiated by the private sector, and the initial contraction (expansion) in the monetary base occurs via a contraction (expansion) in the note issue. If banks do not hold reserve deposits, money supply will contract (or expand) with the contraction (expansion) in currency in circulation, in accordance with the public's cash-to-deposit ratio. If banks hold no reserves, this is just a special case of the general example discussed, where the reserve ratio is zero. (In the formula $M = F(c + 1)/(c + r)$, setting $r = 0$, reduces the expression to $M = F(c + 1)/c$.) Because, in the long run, the money supply growth rate must be that which generates the inflation rate of the country of the anchor currency, the reserve ratio makes no difference. Therefore, it might as well be zero, i.e. banks hold no reserves. A zero reserve ratio is less advisable under a firm peg which is maintained through active central bank intervention. It is actually the reserve component of the monetary base which is affected by the central bank's foreign exchange interventions.

The best known example in history of an operating commodity or currency exchange standard was the gold exchange standard, which existed in most of the major nations over the period 1925–31. However, subsequent to the successful implementation of a US dollar exchange standard in Hong Kong in 1983, currency boards have found renewed popularity, particularly as a method of achieving financial stabilization during a monetary crisis, and have a number of influential advocates in the financial and academic economic community. Apart from Hong Kong (which operates a modified currency exchange standard), currency board systems are now in place in Argentina, Bulgaria, Estonia and Lithuania.

INTERNATIONAL MONETARY SYSTEMS

Fixed exchange rates in a monetary system

The preceding sections have discussed the mechanics of fixed exchange rates and the economic implications for a country fixing the rate of exchange for its currency in terms of another currency. It was concluded that if country A pegged its currency at a fixed rate in terms of the currency of country B, then in the long run, A would have the same inflation rate as B: the money growth rate in A would be such as to generate that inflation rate. What about country B? Will the fact that country A has pegged its currency to B's have any implications for the economy of country B?

The answer is that it may have, particularly if country A is fairly large in relation to country B. For an open economy operating a fixed exchange rate, mechanistically the growth of the monetary base, and hence the money supply, must be directly related to the growth of the central bank's foreign assets. The monetary base only expands when the central bank is purchasing foreign currency and in return crediting banks' reserve deposits at the central bank or issuing more notes (i.e. increasing the monetary base). If the central bank attempts other methods to expand or contract money growth (e.g. sterilizing interventions), then these actions will tend to be offset by external payments flows. It has been shown that in this way the growth of money takes place via the overall balance of payments.

However, in a growing economy some growth in the money supply is required to 'finance' real economic growth. From the identity MV = PY, assuming velocity is stable, if the economy is capable of a long-term rate of growth of 5 percent (i.e. $\dot{Y} = 5$ percent) then money supply growth must be 5 percent (i.e. $\dot{M} = 5$ percent), even if inflation ($\dot{P}$) is to be kept at zero. Therein lies a theoretical 'problem' of the fixed exchange rate arrangement.

A growing economy which operates a fixed exchange rate will require to run a small balance of payments surplus. This is in order for the central bank continuously to acquire the foreign reserves which represent the counterpart to the growth of the monetary base. Because the economy is growing, there will be some growth in the transactions demand for money, necessitating this growth of the monetary base even under conditions of zero inflation. If this growing economy has a continuous balance of payments surplus, then, by definition, the rest of the world has a persistent balance of payments *deficit*.

Imagine that countries A and B are the only two countries in the world. Furthermore, their respective economies are both of the same size and both have a long-run trend rate of real economic growth of 5 percent. In both economies the income velocity of money remains stable and unchanging, and both monetary authorities have been targeting an inflation rate of zero. Therefore, the annual money growth rate has been kept to 5 percent in both economies.

Now the central bank of country A decides to fix the exchange rate for its currency in terms of B's currency at a constant rate. We will assume that the A dollar had previously been floating against the B dollar, but is at purchasing power parity when the decision to fix the exchange rate is taken. Therefore, there are no 'adjustment' problems (see Chapter 10). Also, we assume that A and B conduct a large amount of trade with each other, but that trade and external payments flows are perfectly in balance at the time that the A dollar is pegged to the B dollar. What will now happen, assuming that the central bank of B keeps to the same monetary policy as previously, i.e. a constant rate of money growth of 5 percent? What will be the new 'equilibrium' after the exchange rate for A's currency has been pegged in terms of B's?

First, if external payments remained perfectly in balance (i.e. an overall balance of zero) then because A's foreign reserves would not be growing, money growth in A would become zero. With A's real economic growth rate at 5 percent inflation would fall to −5 percent, assuming velocity remained stable, i.e. there would be deflation in A. This would not be a stable, or equilibrium, situation. If A's price level were falling, A would be becoming increasingly competitive in trade with B. Consumers in both A and B would be buying cheaper goods produced in A rather than in B, meaning that A's exports to B would be growing, and A's imports from B shrinking. This increasing trade surplus would put upward pressure on A's currency and, under the fixed exchange rate, lead to growth in A's foreign reserves and money supply. Higher money growth would eventually raise A's inflation rate back towards the rate (of zero) prevailing in B.

The stable situation would occur when inflation in A was running at a rate fractionally (in theory imperceptibly) below that in B, so as to generate a current account surplus for A which grows gradually over time. This would provide for a constant rate of monetary base growth equal to that in B. Country B will experience a gradually increasing trade deficit.

The effect on the conduct of monetary policy in B and on B's economy is not obvious, and depends on a number of assumptions. With regard to the behavior of the economy, we could assume that it is domestic demand in B which responds to money growth in B rather than total output or GNP. This would make sense because the net export component of output is more a function of the external environment. Then the rate of growth of output in B will initially tend to drop below the original 5 percent rate, because of the negative contribution to the GNP of the growing current account deficit. By definition, given the assumption that money supply growth is unchanged, the velocity of money would be dropping. A move back to the long-run achievable growth rate of 5 percent would take place via some fall in the prices of the factors of production (i.e. nominal wages would be under downward pressure). This would impart a tendency to deflation in B which would also be reflected in A, where the inflation rate must be roughly the same as in B in the long run. Therefore, if A and B are seen as one economic system, there may now be a slight tendency to deflation in the system where previously there was none.

The problem is that by permanently fixing the exchange rate for its currency in terms of B's, A's central bank has in most senses become passive. Although it is acting to keep the exchange rate for the A dollar fixed in terms of B dollars, this is in essence a passive process, merely entailing the central bank standing in the foreign exchange market to accept or provide for any 'excess' or 'deficiency' of B dollars which emerges at the fixed exchange rate.

Control over the supply of money in the domestic economy rests, indirectly, with the central bank that issues the currency to which the domestic currency has been pegged (i.e. the central bank of B). Therefore, once A has fixed its currency to B's, B's central bank has implicitly become the central bank for both countries. Ideally, it should take A's economy into account when setting its own monetary policy. This is particularly obvious if country A's achievable real economic growth rate is substantially higher than B's. Then the growth rate of the two economies combined will be higher than the growth rate of country B alone, justifying a somewhat higher target rate of money growth for central bank B. Even if the real growth rate of A is not higher than that of B, as in the example discussed previously, it may still be that a somewhat higher target rate of money growth in country B is appropriate. The higher rate of money growth stimulates a higher rate of growth of domestic demand in country B, necessary to generate the appropriate current account deficit with A.

In this example we have supposed that the central bank of A takes a unilateral decision to fix its currency to that of B, and the central bank of B continues to implement monetary policy as before. In an international monetary system (e.g. the European Monetary System, or EMS) the decision to fix exchange rates is taken by all participants in the system. The important difference is that all the member countries in the system can, and indeed will be expected to, intervene in the foreign exchange markets to 'defend' the chosen exchange rates. In our example, in contrast, only country A intervenes or acts to fix the exchange rate, while country B takes no action, either active or passive, with regard to the exchange rate.

Let us now assume that the decision to fix the exchange rate between A's currency and B's is not a unilateral decision by A, but the result of an agreement between the governments of A and B. How should the central banks of A and B share the responsibility for maintaining the fixed exchange rate? If the exchange rate is tending to move away from the chosen rate, which central bank should intervene to maintain the parity? If, for example, there is an excess demand for B dollars at the fixed rate, should these B dollars be provided by the central bank of A, from its foreign reserves, or by the central bank of B creating more B dollars?

It might be thought that the answer to which central bank should intervene to defend the exchange rate at any time would be given by the state of the current account balances for the respective economies. This might be true if, for instance, the A dollar were under downward pressure against the B dollar and A had an obvious chronic current account deficit problem. The appropriate course of action could then be for the central bank of A to sell B dollars and buy (i.e. destroy) A dollars, causing a monetary contraction in A until the current account deficit problem righted itself.

In practice, it is not always obvious that this is the right course of action. Over periods of several years, countries with growing current account deficits can experience upward, rather than downward, pressure on their currencies (see Chapters 2, 3 and 10). In this example it could be that the downward pressure on A's currency stems not only, or perhaps not at all, from A's current account deficit, but more from the fact that monetary policy pursued by B's central bank is, in some sense, too tight. Then the correct solution could be for the central bank of B to intervene to buy A dollars and create more B dollars, easing monetary conditions in B.

The problem is that with two currencies, A and B, with a fixed exchange rate, the rate of money growth and hence the rate of inflation for the system (i.e. A and B together) is indeterminate. If currency A is under downward pressure against currency B, either central bank A can intervene, causing a monetary contraction in A, or central bank B can intervene, causing an expansion in B. Either action would work to ease pressure on the exchange rate between the currencies, but they each have very different implications for the overall rate of money growth and hence inflation for both A and B together. In the first case the overall rate of money growth would fall, and in the second case it would rise. Obviously, this creates the possibility of disinflationary or inflationary biases in the system.

This problem of a fixed exchange rate monetary system is sometimes referred to as the $N - 1$ problem. In our example there are two countries, A and B, but there can be only one exchange rate between them – the A\$/B\$ rate. If this rate is fixed, the price of A dollars is determined in terms of B dollars but the price of B dollars is determined only in terms of A dollars. Money growth in A is constrained by the rate of money growth in B, and vice versa. However, there is no absolute determinant of the rate of money growth and hence inflation. To put it simply, it would not be possible in the long run for A to have a very high rate of inflation and B a very low inflation rate, or vice versa. However, either a very high or a very low inflation rate in both countries could be consistent with the maintenance of the fixed exchange rate between their currencies.

In a monetary system involving a number of countries, e.g. the European Monetary System, the problem of *symmetry*, i.e. which central bank should intervene if exchange rates threaten to become out of line, can be addressed through rules based on exchange rate bands. Once there is a number of countries participating in a monetary, or exchange rate, system any one country's currency will have a number of exchange rates, i.e. the exchange rates for its currency in terms of each of the other participating currencies. In contrast to the two-country system, it should become somewhat clearer which central bank(s) should take action if pressures emerge in the system.

However, the presence of a number of countries and exchange rates does not solve the $N - 1$ problem. If there are N countries there will still be N − 1 independent exchange rates and so there will still be one degree of freedom in the system. (Note that the various cross-exchange rates between currencies depend arithmetically only upon the 'independent' rates and do not provide any additional constraints. In a three-country system comprising countries A, B and C there will be only two (3 − 1) 'independent' exchange rates, the A$/B$ rate and the A$/C$ rate. The cross-rate, the B$/C$ rate, is simply calculated from the other two exchange rates and does not provide any additional constraint on the actions of A, B or C.) The rate of money growth and hence inflation for the whole system is indeterminate.

One 'solution' to this problem is for the price of one anchor currency (and hence all currencies, because they are fixed to each other) to be linked to an external *numeraire*, e.g. the price of gold. Put in the context of our original example the value of the A dollar could be fixed in terms of gold, say at A$1 = 0.003 ounces of gold. This then introduces another price or 'exchange rate' into the system and in a mathematical sense it becomes fully determined.

In practice, this introduces a rough link between the rate of inflation for the system and the increase in the supply of gold (or whichever commodity is chosen) over time. If inflation is tending to rise because the rate of money growth in all the member countries of the system is too high, then the demand for gold will be tending to increase. If the supply of gold is increasing at a similarly rapid pace, then the price of gold may remain roughly constant. No intervention will be required to maintain the fixed rate for gold in terms of the currencies of the system. However, if the supply of gold is not increasing so rapidly, then the price of gold will be under upward pressure. The currencies of the monetary system will tend to be depreciating in terms of gold. The commitment to maintain the fixed rates in terms of gold will then require the central bank of the anchor country, or alternatively of all countries acting simultaneously, to defend the value of its currency by selling gold from its foreign reserves and buying (i.e. destroying) domestic currency. Slower money growth in the anchor country will then translate into slower money growth for the system as a whole, bringing down the inflation rate.

In this case, the fixed exchange rate monetary system is similar to a gold exchange standard, although possibly with a somewhat greater degree of flexibility accorded to the central banks in the system. The Bretton Woods system of fixed exchange rates, which operated between 1947 and 1973, was roughly of this type. In this system the US dollar was the anchor currency for the fixed rate system. The US dollar was freely convertible into gold (by other central banks in the system) at a fixed rate of US$35 per ounce of gold.

The alternative solution to the N − 1 problem in a fixed exchange rate system is for one central bank to take on the commitment to maintain an 'appropriate' rate of money growth in its own economy and, as a consequence, throughout the system as a whole. In the EMS this role has, up until now, been taken by the German Bundesbank. The Bundesbank was able to assume this role because it had the most credibility among the EMS central banks, supported by its record of maintaining a consistently low inflation rate in Germany. Over time, it was perhaps able to maintain this leading role because it usually appeared to desire a tighter monetary policy than the other EMS central banks, all of which operate under different political constraints. Any one of the other EMS central banks which wanted to assume the mantle of 'monetary policymaker' for the whole EMS would have had to have been prepared to tighten monetary policy beyond the degree desired by the Bundesbank, thereby forcing the Bundesbank and the other central banks to follow suit.

The problems of the EMS and its exchange rate mechanism, the ERM, over 1992–93, highlight the shortcomings of a monetary system which relies on the monetary policy of one national central bank, which are particularly acute if the anchor country suffers some form of economic shock. The monetary and economic union of West and East Germany in July 1990 was such a shock. The Bundesbank took the view that the diversion of Germany's large savings flows from capital outflows to domestic capital financing needs, in the wake of economic union, would necessitate a rise in the real exchange rate of the Deutschmark. The Bundesbank was keen to ensure that this real exchange rate appreciation did not take the form of higher inflation in Germany, and so progressively tightened monetary policy. At the same time, the Bundesbank pressured the German government to control the burgeoning fiscal deficit in an effort to contain the domestic requirements for capital.

The tight German monetary policy posed problems for the other EMS member countries, forcing on them, through the fixed exchange rates of the ERM, tighter monetary conditions than appropriate to their domestic economic circumstances. In effect, the Bundesbank was forcing any real exchange rate appreciation to occur via a painful deflation in the other European economies rather than through inflation in Germany.

The French government, in particular, was severely critical of the German authorities, accusing them of taking economic policy decisions on the basis of purely domestic concerns when they should have been considering the need to coordinate policies with their European partners. The Bundesbank, believing that its responsibility was solely to maintain a low level of inflation in Germany, took the view that any tendency to deflation in any other EMS country was the responsibility of that country's central bank. In the Bundesbank's view, the authorities of other EMS members could always devalue their currencies against the Deutschmark within the ERM if that proved appropriate or necessary to avoid recession. In short, the Bundesbank did not see a tendency to real appreciation of the Deutschmark as a problem, because it could always take place via a nominal exchange rate adjustment, i.e. the Deutschmark could simply be revalued in the ERM. For the other governments, however, this was a serious political problem − particularly for the French − because, in their eyes, to accept a devaluation against the Deutschmark would undermine the credibility of their currencies further, and so serve to enhance further the position of the Bundesbank as European monetary policymaker at the expense of the national interests of the other EMS members.

European economic and monetary union

It was precisely political strains such as these that helped to give such rapid momentum to the movement towards European economic and monetary union (EMU). Under the proposals for EMU the role of monetary policymaker for the member countries is to be taken over by a European monetary authority comprising a European central bank (ECB) and a coalition of the existing national central banks, known as the European System of Central Banks (ESCB). The European central bank is to be modeled on the Bundesbank, governed by a full-time executive board and a council comprising the governors of the national central banks.

The original framework for the creation of EMU was set out in the Delors Report, published in April 1989. It envisaged a three-stage process to EMU. Stage 1, beginning 1 July 1990, required the removal of capital controls, the completion of the single market and, in theory, a reduction in exchange rate volatility via all EMS countries joining narrow ERM bands. Stage 2 foresaw the establishment of a central monetary institute, the introduction of guidelines governing member countries' budget deficits and a further reduction in the permissible degree of exchange rate fluctuation. Much of the content of the Delors Report was incorporated in the Maastricht Treaty of December 1991.

The Maastricht Treaty is a treaty on European union, of which monetary union is a part. Maastricht established the European Monetary Institute, as the forerunner of the ECB, from the second stage of the EMU process (1 January 1994). Maastricht also introduced the 'convergence criteria', setting guidelines for convergence of inflation rates, government debt and deficits, long-term interest rates and exchange rate stability which would need to be satisfied by aspiring EMU member countries. The treaty set 1999 as the last possible date for the third stage of EMU, when exchange rates between member countries' currencies would be irrevocably fixed, the ECB would take over the operation of monetary policy, and arrangements would be put in place for a single currency which would be introduced at a 1:1 rate with the existing ECU (confirmed at the Madrid Summit of December 1995).

The ERM crises of 1992/93 and the prolonged period of weak growth in Europe during the 1990s have made the path to EMU less smooth than envisaged at Maastricht. Nevertheless, the Madrid Summit of December 1995 established a more detailed three-phase timetable for the implementation of EMU from 1 January 1999. During phase A (1998), the membership of EMU, based on those countries deemed to have satisfied the convergence criteria, should be announced, the ECB should prepare for the operation of monetary policy and the legal framework for the single currency – the euro – should be in place. EMU is scheduled for phase B, from 1 January 1999 to 1 January 2002. Exchange rates between participating currencies will be locked at a single fixed rate and the new European unit, the Euro, will exist for banking transactions alongside existing national currencies. Monetary policy for the EMU will be implemented by the ECB. Euro banknotes are not planned to be introduced until phase C, from 1 January 2002 to 1 July 2002, at the end of which national currencies will cease to be legal tender and the Euro will be the only legal tender money throughout the EMU bloc.

There has been some concern amongst independent economists and analysts as to whether or not the transitional process set out in the Madrid timetable is workable. One focal point has been whether the existence of two monies in each EMU member state (the national currency and the euro) is viable, particularly during phase C when euro and national currency notes will exist simultaneously.

These particular concerns are likely to prove to be a red herring. Because exchange rates between all the EMU member currencies are irrevocably locked, each national currency will function merely as a different denomination of the same currency, which ultimately will be the euro. The total supply of money within the EMU will be under the control of one central bank – the ECB – which has the responsibility to conduct monetary policy in the interests of the whole EMU (unlike the Bundesbank under the EMS/ERM). If there are shifts of funds between the Euro and the national currency or vice versa in any member country, then these will merely be shifts in relative demand between the different units of account. As long as the ECB explicitly or implicitly maintains control over the total money supply, comprising both national currencies and euro, throughout the whole euro area then these changes in relative demand for the different EMU currency denominations should be irrelevant. The situation is not fundamentally different from that in existing monetary unions such as the Belgium/Luxembourg monetary union, albeit made more complicated by inconvenient exchange rates between national currencies and the single currency. This creates a practical problem akin to decimalization in the UK, which would become very apparent prior to or during phase C.

The serious problem of EMU is not the potential for shifts in relative demand between the different currency units, but the potential for large real exchange rate adjustments between the EMU member countries. Chapters 2 and 3 (and also Chapter 10) explain the major causes of substantial real exchange rate adjustments between economies. These include divergence of business cycles or fiscal policies (both of which affect the demand for funds relative to the supply of funds) and external shocks impacting different economies to varying degrees. With separate monetary systems, the exchange rate plays an important role in the adjustment process, appreciating or depreciating or undergoing discrete adjustments such as during the ERM crisis of September 1992. Under a monetary union, these same real exchange rate adjustments must occur through shifts in relative prices, which are likely to involve painful periods of recession for some economies or inflation for others. In particular, if an economy experiences a real exchange rate appreciation, within a monetary union this will manifest itself in an inflationary boom and deteriorating external balance. The problem occurs when the original force for disequilibrium has disappeared or diminished and the economy adjusts back. Whereas under floating exchange rates there would be a fluctuation of the exchange rate around purchasing power parity, within monetary union this is replaced by a cycle of boom and bust in the economy.

There are a number of factors which can minimize or eliminate the threat of boom/bust for a region of a monetary union. First, if there is substantial flexibility of the real economy across the union then the burden of adjustment can be borne more easily by shifts in relative prices for, and movements of, factors of production across the union, such as labour. Failing this, if the economic structure of the different countries or regions of the union is similar, then the possibility of a shock impacting one or more regional economies more severely than others is reduced. Thirdly, with regard to fiscal policy, if there is a substantial degree of fiscal centralization, the transfers of funds (from higher centralized tax receipts) from regions which are booming to regions which are weak will help to dampen real exchange rate adjustment. Alternatively, national fiscal policy can be prevented from becoming a source of divergence and potential real exchange rate disequilibrium through controls or guidelines governing national budgets.

More straightforwardly, it is important that at its inception, the monetary union is not established in a way that immediately threatens the potential for real exchange rate disequilibria. This is most obvious if exchange rates are fixed at levels which are clearly over- or undervalued. For instance if the UK, in October 1990, had been entering a monetary union rather than merely the ERM, at what was then a very overvalued exchange rate, the UK would have faced prolonged depression rather than merely an exchange rate crisis. Beginning the EMU at an appropriate starting point is the purpose of the convergence criteria of the Maastricht Treaty. Unfortunately, there is room to doubt that the Maastricht criteria are appropriately specified. The important criteria should be exchange rates at purchasing power parity levels, and therefore consistent with long-run balance of payments equilibrium, and roughly uniform inflation expectations across the union.

If inflation expectations are substantially different across economies, then these can be a further source of real exchange rate variability during the transitional phase and in the early stage of the monetary union. As monetary union approaches, inflation expectations implied in the financial markets, i.e. in interest rates, will necessarily be equalized because monetary union means only one interest rate structure. The risk is that these market-implied inflation expectations are not the same as inflation expectations held across the broad economy in certain member states. This is the phenomenon discussed at the end of Chapter 1, with the example given of the Spanish economy. Under floating exchange rates, this type of 'premature' interest rate convergence would result in an appreciation of the nominal exchange rate for the higher-inflation economy as 'convergence' capital inflows would be attracted by the higher interest rates in that economy. Under fixed exchange rates, the result would be higher money growth and inflation, justifying, in a sense, the higher inflation expectations held. A simple way to view this is that, given that the short-term interest rate must be the same across the monetary union, real short-term interest rates will be perceived as being lower – and therefore credit demand will be stronger – in those economies for which inflation expectations are higher. Higher inflation would not be sustainable indefinitely, of course, because competitiveness would be eroded, making inevitable a later period of painful adjustment during which the high inflation economies would be depressed.

For EMU, this concern is addressed through the inflation convergence criteria of the Maastricht Treaty, under which EMU member countries are supposed to have achieved a consumer price inflation rate averaging not more than 1.5 percent higher than the three best performing EU member states over the year (1997) before the time of assessment. The problem with this is that, even if 1.5 percent is a narrow enough margin to represent convergence, it is likely to take more than a year before there has been a genuine convergence of inflation expectations in the aspiring EMU members which have had a previous history of high inflation (Spain, Italy, Portugal). The achievement of fair value exchange rates was supposed to have been guaranteed by the criterion that successful EMU member states were to have been in the narrow ERM fluctuation bands at the same central rate, and without severe tensions, for at least the two years prior to the date of assessment. Unfortunately, this criterion was undermined by the ERM crisis and the consequent abolition of the narrow ERM bands.

For fiscal policy, both the Delors Report and the Maastricht Treaty recognized the necessity of fiscal convergence: in the Maastricht Treaty expressed through the criteria that government deficits should not exceed 3 percent of GDP at the time of assessment (for 1997), and government debt-to-GDP ratios should be sustainable, ideally no more than 60 percent. The Dublin and Amsterdam Summits of 1996 and 1997 extended this principle to cover the EMU once in place, with the agreement on a Stability Pact. The Stability Pact makes an EMU member state liable to sanctions if the government deficit exceeds 3 percent of GDP, unless the deficit has risen as a result of serious recession (defined in the pact as a fall in GDP of greater than −2 percent, with a margin of flexibility if the growth rate is between −0.75 and −2.0 percent)

The Stability Pact has come in for much criticism on the grounds that because the monetary union deprives members of the ability to pursue an independent monetary policy, they must retain the capacity for an independent fiscal policy. This view is mistaken because seriously diverging fiscal policies could necessitate real exchange rate adjustments between member states, which within the EMU would be manifested in monetary instability. It would be inappropriate and potentially dangerous for the shortcomings inherent in EMU to be addressed through fiscal policy. Furthermore, from a longer-term perspective, the single currency would increase the transparency of the European single market and make convergence of tax rates across the Union – already promoted by French and Italian governments – inevitable. With no possibility for debt or deficits to be monetized under the single monetary policy, sustained higher government spending in one economy would threaten government debt sustainability and potentially require a 'bail out' which could further undermine the political legitimacy of the EMU.

Returning to the factors which define the characteristics of a successful monetary union, it is clear that they are for the most part absent from the EU. In particular, the mobility of factors of production and degree of fiscal centralization are minimal. Nevertheless, economic structure is fairly similar amongst the core countries (Germany, France, Benelux, Austria) and the Stability Pact would impose fiscal discipline. Furthermore, the starting conditions for monetary union are met for these countries because they have exchange rates which have been fixed within a narrow range for an extended period (since 1988) and therefore there has been time for a full adjustment to these rates, i.e. there has been genuine convergence. Figure 24 illustrates a high degree of monetary stability for the hard core bloc considered as a whole. Over the period since 1988 the difference between annual aggregate broad money growth and

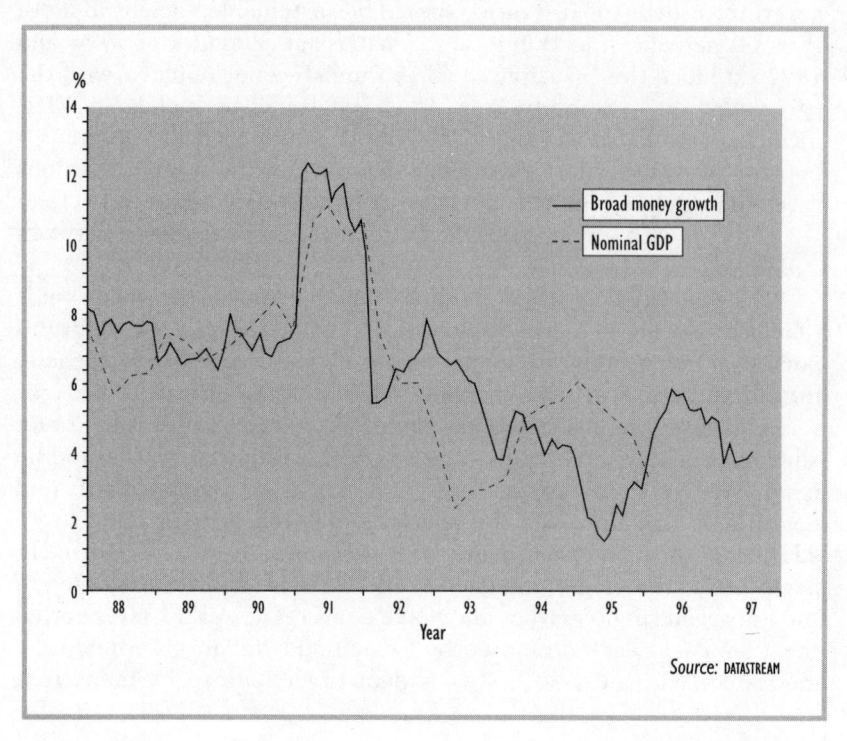

FIGURE 24 Europe: hard core money and GDP

Source: DATASTREAM

aggregate nominal GDP growth for the core bloc has rarely exceeded 3 percent either way, exhibiting greater stability for the whole bloc than for most of the core countries considered individually.

Therefore, if an EMU contained only the core countries it would likely be viable in the sense that the ECB would be able to implement successfully a noninflationary monetary policy. The broader is EMU, on the other hand, the less viable it is likely to prove to be and the more that monetary policy will tend to be inflationary. There is a widespread misconception that the EMU process, as embodied in the Maastricht Treaty, is inherently deflationary, in particular because of the constraints on fiscal policy. In reality, the transition to EMU is an inflationary process because of premature interest rate convergence amongst the peripheral economies. Monetary policy within a broad EMU is also likely to be constrained to accommodate substantial inflation because a high average inflation rate will be necessary to smooth economic adjustments between the member economies. If monetary policy were tight then it would be impossible for member economies requiring a real exchange rate fall to undergo the adjustment because this would entail deflation. This has already been demonstrated by the experience of the ERM over 1992/93, against the background of a tight Bundesbank monetary policy.

If a broad EMU begins before the end of this century and the ECB sticks doggedly to a tight, noninflationary monetary policy then the result is likely to be financial crises in one or more of the peripheral economies. More likely the ECB will be forced to maintain an easy monetary policy in order to prevent or alleviate financial catastrophes, with the result that inflation in the core economies will be high. Therefore, under a broad EMU, high inflation across Europe is likely to be an economic feature of the early years of next century.

IMPLEMENTATION OF AN INDEPENDENT MONETARY POLICY 7

MONETARY POLICY UNDER A FLOATING EXCHANGE RATE

An independent monetary policy

Independence in monetary policy tends to be associated with central bank independence from government control or interference. A movement towards greater central bank independence has been a worldwide trend since the late 1980s, partly influenced by studies showing that independent central banks have been more successful at sustaining low inflation rates in their economies. Over this period more than twenty-five countries have increased the legal independence of their central bank, a recent addition to the trend being the UK where, in 1997, the Bank of England was granted autonomy over interest rate policy.

In practice, the implementation of a monetary policy designed to achieve independent national targets or objectives requires a freely floating exchange rate. As outlined in the previous chapter, a fixed exchange rate involves subjecting the economy to the influence of monetary conditions in the anchor currency country and ultimately inheriting the inflation rate of that economy. To this extent the independence of central banks is rarely complete because in most countries the government retains an influence, or potential influence, over exchange rate policy, even if only over the basic framework of exchange rate arrangements (e.g. for an EU country, whether or not the currency should be in the ERM).

Nevertheless, a central bank which has a free floating currency by definition need not conduct any intervention in the foreign exchange markets and therefore is in a position to control the monetary base, and hence money supply growth. Over the long term, the price of its money in terms of other monies, i.e. the exchange rate, will then be determined as a consequence of the central bank's actions with regard to the supply of money. If the money growth rate is 'too high', inflation will result and the purchasing power parity level of the currency will fall, as will the currency, over time, in order to maintain the economy's competitiveness and balance on the current account. With no intervention, the balance of payments can have no impact on the monetary base and the exchange rate takes on fully the role of adjusting to external influences.

With a floating exchange rate, then, the central bank is free to pursue a domestic objective. In the 1990s there is an almost universal consensus that this objective should be price stability, or in terms of a practical objective, a low rate of measured inflation (usually somewhere between zero and 3 percent). Furthermore, there is a strong consensus that the inflation rate is the only economic variable which the central bank has the ability to control over the long run, and that an independent central bank should be held accountable for it. This is in line with monetarist orthodoxy, which is something of a paradox in that the monetarist analytical framework is by no means universally accepted.

Skepticism about monetarism finds its expression in skepticism of the value of targets for money supply growth as an intermediate objective for monetary policy. Of the major central banks, although the US Federal Reserve (the Fed) and the Bank of Japan retain guidelines for broad money supply growth, only the Bundesbank and, to a lesser extent, the Swiss National Bank, place targets for money supply growth at the heart of decisions regarding the monetary policy stance. In the late 1990s the fashion amongst central banks and economic commentators is for direct inflation targets. The Bank of England, Bank of Canada, Reserve Bank of Australia, Swedish Riksbank and others, all conduct policy with a view to maintaining the inflation rate within an announced target range. Money supply targets have fallen into some disrepute because the demand for broad money in most industrialized countries has been affected by the globalization of financial markets (as outlined in Chapters 1 and 2) and therefore has not always appeared stable. Inflation targeting as a concept has the benefit of simplicity. However, as explained previously, the lags between monetary policy and the inflationary consequences of the policy are long, and therefore, in practice, judgements by the central bank about whether the current monetary stance is appropriate to achieve the inflation target will implicitly, if not explicitly, require consideration of monetary indicators, including the money supply.

The advantage of floating exchange rates is that they make it theoretically possible for the central bank to achieve an objective for the inflation rate. This may be a target of the central bank's own choosing or a target set by the government. The latter is the case, for instance, in the UK, where the government sets the inflation target and the central bank has the freedom to implement monetary policy as it sees fit to achieve the target. This framework has been criticized on the grounds that it represents a curtailment of central bank independence, but it has, at least, the merit of greater democratic accountability.

Given that the central bank of an open economy has no ability, in the long run, to influence the level of the real exchange rate (Chapter 3), there would appear to be little merit in the alternative approach of fixing or manipulating the nominal exchange rate, except perhaps as a way of restoring credibility as part of a monetary stabilization program following a monetary crisis. Fixing, or influencing, the nominal exchange rate can have no real effect in the long run, but will merely substitute inflation or perhaps deflation, for movement in the nominal exchange rate which would otherwise have taken place.

Opponents of floating rates base their arguments on the notion that exchange rate movements do not always have their origins in economic fundamentals, but sometimes can be purely the result of speculative activity on the part of foreign exchange traders and others. They argue that speculative 'bubbles' can take exchange rates far out of line with the economic 'fundamentals', causing unnecessary economic dislocation in the process. Some of the issues involved have been touched on in Chapter 5. In this chapter we concentrate upon the tools at the disposal of the central bank which wishes to achieve a particular rate of money growth.

Reserve targeting in a fractional reserve monetary system

In a fractional reserve type of monetary system the balance sheet of the central bank is as shown in Balance Sheet 19.

Balance Sheet 19 is abbreviated. In practice, the central bank might hold (on the assets side of the balance sheet) domestic paper other than government bonds, e.g. corporate bonds, commercial paper. In addition, there is nothing to stop the central bank borrowing (on the liabilities side) from the commercial banks and nonbank private sector. However, most central banks restrict their activities largely to government debt and government deposits. With a completely free-floating exchange rate, the central bank does not need to intervene and therefore, in theory, there is no need for it to hold foreign assets. Nevertheless, in practice all central banks continue to hold foreign assets, and many also have foreign

Balance Sheet 19

Monetary authority/central bank	
Assets	Liabilities
Net foreign assets	Currency in circulation ⎫
Government bonds	Reserve deposits of commercial banks ⎬ Monetary base
Loans to financial institutions	Deposits of government ⎭
	Net worth

borrowings. For the rest of this section we assume away the existence of the foreign assets and also the net worth because they have no relevance to monetary conditions in a free-floating exchange rate arrangement. (The extent to which foreign assets grow because of interest receipts from foreign deposits, treasury bills, etc., is reflected in an increase in the net worth. The other items on the balance sheet are unaffected, and so the monetary base and domestic monetary conditions remain unchanged, other things being equal.)

If the central bank wishes to restrict money growth and tighten domestic monetary conditions it can sell part of its holding of government bonds, or any other domestic asset it holds, either outright or under a repurchase arrangement. This sale will lead to a contraction of the monetary base in exactly the same way as when a central bank sells foreign currency. The purchaser of the government bond pays the central bank with a check drawn on a commercial bank. This check is settled by the central bank debiting the commercial bank's deposits with the central bank. The balance sheets of the parties involved alter as illustrated in Balance Sheet 20.

In this example the monetary base (of which the commercial banks' deposits at the central bank are a key part), as well as the actual money supply (of which the bond purchaser's deposits at the commercial bank are a part), have both fallen. Some analysts would make a distinction between this and the case in which the purchaser of the bond is itself a commercial bank. As shown in Chapter 1 only sales of bonds to the *nonbank* private sector are a negative counterpart to the money supply, in the first instance. If a bank purchases the bonds, the initial balance sheet changes as illustrated in Balance Sheet 21.

The money supply is unchanged initially. However, the more important consideration, certainly in a fractional reserve monetary

Balance Sheet 20

Central bank		Commercial banks		Government bond purchaser	
Assets	Liabilities	Assets	Liabilities	Assets	Liabilities
Government bonds ↓	Deposits of commercial banks ↓	Deposits at central bank ↓	Deposit of bond purchaser ↓	Government bonds ↑ Deposit at bank ↓	

Balance Sheet 21

Central bank		Commercial banks (government bond purchaser)	
Assets	Liabilities	Assets	Liabilities
Government bonds ↓	Deposits of commercial banks ↓	Deposits at central bank ↓ Government bonds ↑	Deposits of nonbank private sector unchanged

system, is the contraction of the *monetary base*, which takes place in both these examples. In a fractional reserve system, the fall in commercial banks' deposits at the central bank is ultimately likely to require that they reduce their lending activity, and hence deposits, in order to accord with their new lower level of reserve holdings. The growth of the money supply will then fall in line with the growth of the monetary base.

In practice, banks often cannot adjust their lending activity immediately. Some leeway occurs by virtue of the fact that in most fractional reserve monetary systems banks are required to meet reserve requirements on an average basis over each week, fortnightly period or month, known as a *reserve maintenance period*. Also, in monetary arrangements in certain countries reserve requirements are lagged, rather than contemporaneous.

The required holding of reserve deposits at the central bank is calculated for each bank according to the amounts of the bank's various deposit liabilities and the reserve ratio applicable to each type of deposit liability. Generally, the bank's deposit liabilities (eligible liabilities) are calculated as an average over the relevant period. The bank's holdings of reserves against these eligible liabilities are also calculated as an average over the reserve maintenance period. In the case of lagged reserve requirements, the period for which the reserves have to be held begins and ends somewhat later in time than the period for which the actual reserve requirement calculation is made (the period over which the relevant deposit liabilities are averaged). This obviously gives the banks more leeway in meeting reserve requirements in that, towards the end of the reserve maintenance period they know exactly the total of reserves that they need to hold. Arguably, it may make the central bank's monetary actions less effective. In the case of the United States, the reserve maintenance period is a fortnightly period and the lag is only two days. Because the lag is so short, the US system is considered to be a contemporaneous, rather than a lagged, reserve requirement system. In Germany and Japan the reserve maintenance period is a monthly period, in Japan lagging the relevant liabilities period by fifteen days.

If a bank, approaching the end of the reserve maintenance period, finds that it is in danger of not meeting its reserve requirements, then it can borrow reserves (i.e. holdings of deposits at the central bank) from another bank. In the United States, the overnight interest rate it pays for such borrowings is known as the Federal funds rate. If the banking system as a whole does not hold enough reserves, and the central bank is not prepared to provide them through open market operations, because it will generally not be possible for banks to reduce or call in loans immediately, certain banks will inevitably be forced to borrow from the central bank itself, from the central bank's *discount window*. The interest rate paid on such borrowings is the discount rate (and/or Lombard rate, in Europe). The discount rate may or may not be a penalty rate, above the interbank rate. Whether it is or not, banks tend to view discount window borrowings as temporary because they do not want to be indebted to the central bank for too long, for fear of giving the appearance of being in difficulties. Ultimately, if banks are not able to acquire reserves then they reduce discount window borrowings by cutting back on their lending, and hence reducing their deposit liabilities and reserve requirements.

When one bank borrows reserves from another the total of reserves for the whole banking system is unchanged, reserves having merely been redistributed. If a bank borrows from the central bank itself, on the other hand, reserves for the whole system increase. The central bank credits the borrowing bank directly to its reserve account and the central bank's balance sheet changes as illustrated in Balance Sheet 22.

Often, an individual bank will hold *excess reserves* (i.e. more reserves than it needs to meet the statutory requirement) which it

Balance Sheet 22

Central Bank	
Assets	Liabilities
Government bonds	Currency in circulation
	Deposits of commercial banks, i.e. reserves ↑
Loans to financial institutions ↑	Government deposits

does not wish to lend to other banks for precautionary reasons. If certain banks are short of reserves, but other banks are not prepared to lend their excess reserves, then the banks experiencing a reserve shortfall will have to go to the central bank's discount window. As in Balance Sheet 22, central bank lending will increase the total of reserves for the system. Because of the excess reserves held by certain banks the banking system as a whole will then hold reserves in excess of requirements (Balance Sheet 23).

Balance Sheet 23

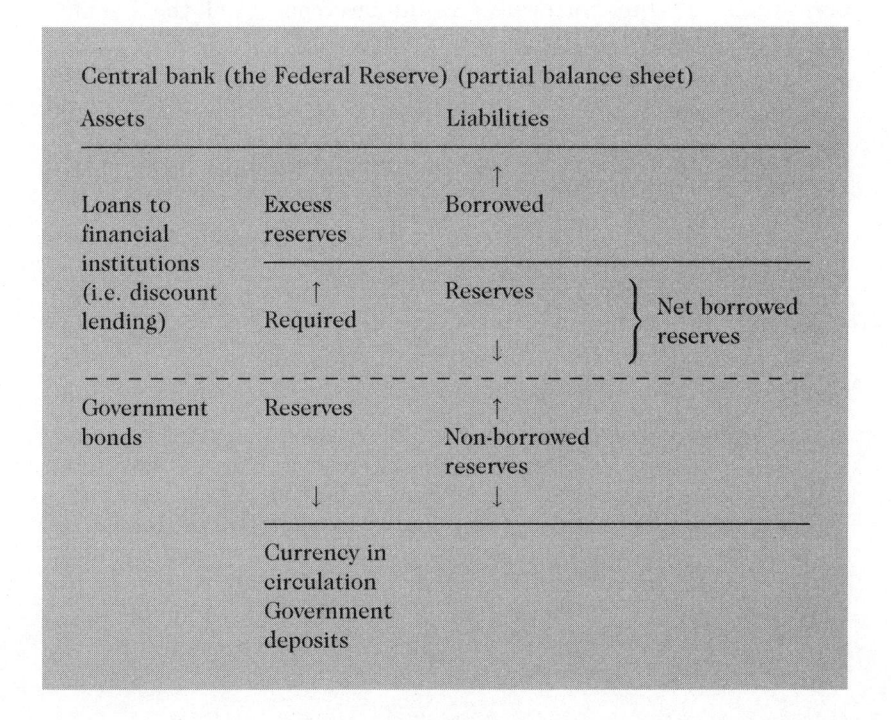

Central bank (the Federal Reserve) (partial balance sheet)		
Assets		Liabilities
Loans to financial institutions (i.e. discount lending)	Excess reserves	↑ Borrowed
	↑ Required	Reserves ↓ } Net borrowed reserves
Government bonds	Reserves ↓	↑ Non-borrowed reserves ↓
	Currency in circulation Government deposits	

Reserve deposits can, in concept, therefore be separated into required reserves and excess reserves. In the US system, in particular, reserves are also often seen as comprising borrowed reserves and nonborrowed reserves. Borrowed reserves are reserves which have their origin in banks' borrowings from the Federal Reserve System (the US central bank). The concept of borrowed reserves is therefore equivalent to the Fed's lending to financial institutions on the assets side of its balance sheet (see Balance Sheet 23). Nonborrowed reserves equal total reserves minus borrowed reserves, i.e. the amount of reserve deposits which originated not from borrowings from the Fed but through changes in the other items on the Fed's balance sheet.

A further reserve concept, to which considerable importance used to be attached by analysts of the US monetary scene, is *net borrowed* or *net free* reserves. Net borrowed reserves are equal to borrowed reserves minus excess reserves. They can be thought of as the amount of reserves that the banking system would still have to borrow from the Fed even if, hypothetically, all the excess reserve positions held by banks were used to pay back discount window borrowings. If this amount is a negative number (i.e. excess reserves exceed borrowed reserves for the system), then it is known as net free reserves or, simply, free reserves. If there is a net free reserve position for the banking system then, hypothetically, if banks with excess reserves were prepared to lend their excess to those with discount window borrowings, all the borrowings could be repaid and the banking system would still have excess reserves left over.

If the Fed wishes to ease monetary conditions, either temporarily or permanently, it can act to increase nonborrowed reserves (and therefore total reserves) through *open market operations*, i.e. sales or, in this case, purchases, of government bills and bonds. If the purchases of bonds are under an agreement by the providers of the bonds to buy them back from the Fed at a later date, i.e. they are repurchase agreements, then the operations are known as *system repos* (i.e. repurchase agreements) or customer repos. If the purchase of bonds is a permanent addition to the Fed's holdings of bonds (i.e. the transaction will not be reversed at a later date) and therefore represents a permanent addition of reserves to the banking system, it is known as a *coupon pass* or *bill pass*.

The Fed's actions to ease monetary conditions through open market operations should show up as a decrease in the net borrowed position, or increase in the net free reserve position. This is because, in the first instance, required reserves have not increased and therefore excess reserves increase. The greater availability of reserves in the banking system puts downward pressure on the Federal funds rate as more banks have extra reserves to lend. Over time, banks will use the extra reserves to increase lending, leading to an increase in the money supply. The excess reserves are eventually 'worked off' as required reserves increase in line with the increase in banks' deposit liabilities.

If the Fed wishes to tighten monetary conditions, i.e. slow the rate of money growth, then it can drain reserves through sales of bonds from its portfolio. Sales of bonds under repurchase agreements (i.e. where it agrees to buy the bonds back after a specified period) are known as matched sales, or matched sale–purchase agreements. An action by the Fed to reduce (the growth of) nonborrowed reserves will initially force some banks to go to the discount window, increasing borrowed reserves and hence net borrowed reserves. The Federal funds rate – and therefore the whole spectrum of short-term interest rates – will also be under upward pressure as banks struggle to meet reserve requirements without borrowing from the Fed, if at all possible. Over time, banks will reduce their own lending and the shortfall of reserves will be met through a reduction in (or slower growth of) required reserves, because of slower bank deposit (i.e. money) growth.

The Fed's open market operations are not the only factor supplying or withdrawing nonborrowed reserves. Intervention in the foreign exchange markets by the Fed obviously affects nonborrowed reserves. However, even in a pure free-floating exchange rate regime, there is a further important factor which can significantly affect the total of nonborrowed reserves. This is the inflows to or outflows from the government's account at the Fed. The monetary base identity presented in Chapters 1 and 4 gives the following:

$\Delta M0$ (i.e. change in total reserves + Currency in circulation)
$= PSD - \Delta ED - \Delta B + \Delta D + \Delta R$

In a pure free-floating exchange rate regime, $\Delta R = 0$ and therefore the identity reduces to:

$$\Delta M0 = PSD - \Delta ED - \Delta B + \Delta D$$

The key factors supplying and withdrawing nonborrowed reserves are the government's fiscal position and foreign borrowing (PSD $- \Delta ED$) and the change in the government bond holdings of the private sector (ΔB). This latter includes the effect of the central bank's open market operations to buy bonds from and sell bonds to the private sector. Much of the open market activity of any central bank, rather than being policy-oriented, is aimed merely at offsetting undesirable effects of shifts in the other influences on the monetary base (particularly the PSD and the government's net bond sales to the private sector). However, because the central bank will always be able to make ΔB whatever it chooses, simply through buying or selling more bonds, it is always able to control $\Delta M0$. The final term in the identity, ΔD, which is the change in the central bank's discount window lending to financial institutions, is the factor supplying borrowed reserves.

If a central bank is following a policy of reserve targeting to achieve a desired rate of money supply growth, the effect of its actions on the money supply is not likely to be instantaneous. A change in the level of net free or net borrowed reserves takes some time to work its way through the system and to translate into a change in bank lending behavior – and therefore in the money growth rate. In the United States, the Fed followed a strict policy of reserve targeting between 1979 and 1983. At that time the leadtime between variations in the rate of growth of nonborrowed reserves and similar swings in the money growth rate was generally in the order of three to four months. This is illustrated in Figure 25, in which the three-month growth rate of narrow money M1 is compared with the three-month growth rate of nonborrowed reserves. This relationship was much used by monetary analysts to forecast M1 growth, which is an important determinant of stock market behavior.

FIGURE 25 United States: nonborrowed reserves and money growth

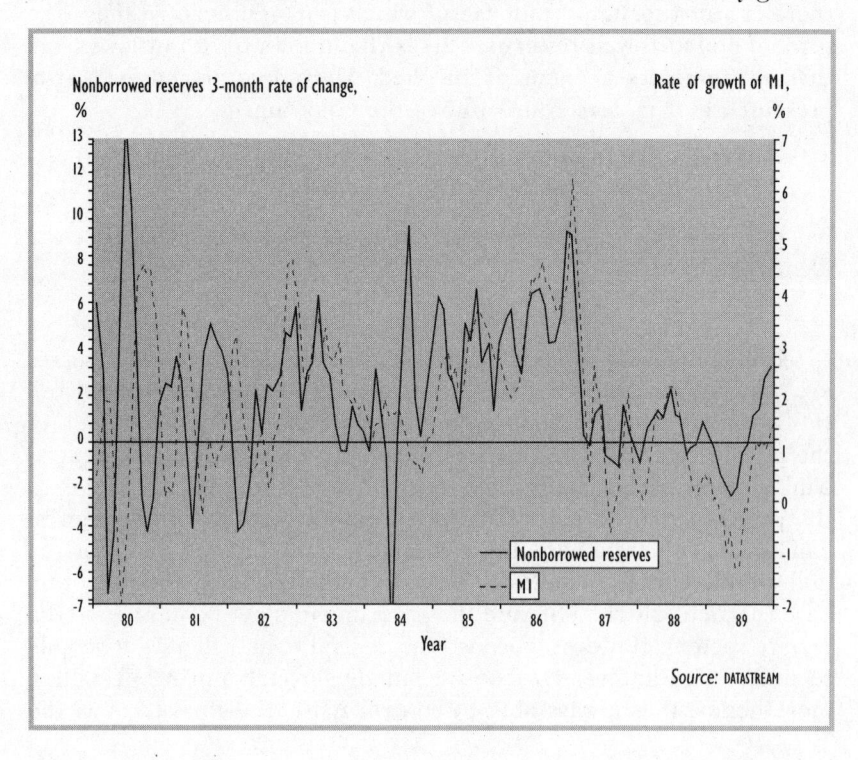

Source: DATASTREAM

Interest rate targeting in a fractional reserve monetary system

At the beginning of Chapter 6 it was explained that, in the long run in an open economy, the central bank can achieve an independent objective for only one of the three variables, the money supply, nominal exchange rate and interest rate. In a free-floating exchange rate regime the central bank has already relinquished control of the exchange rate. If the central bank is following a strict policy of targeting reserve growth to achieve an objective for the money growth rate, then it must also give up any attempt to control interest rates. As explained above, actions by the central bank to increase or decrease provision of nonborrowed reserves to the banking system will have immediate implications for short-term interest rates. If the central bank has specific levels or rates of growth it wishes to achieve for nonborrowed reserves and the other reserve aggregates, it must be prepared to let interest rates move as they will. Even if the central bank is conducting open market operations to keep total reserves on a steady growth path, interest rates could still be volatile because they are subject to variations in the demand for credit in the economy.

The level of the short-term interbank interest rate (the Federal funds rate in the United States) is the result of the interaction of the forces of supply and demand for reserves in the banking system. This was discussed in Chapter 1. To recap, the demand for reserves, in the first instance, depends upon the quantity of deposits in the banks. It is against these deposits that the banks are required to hold reserves, in accordance with the legislated reserve ratios. The potential quantity of deposits is, in turn, related to the demand for bank credit (the other side of the banks' balance sheets). If the demand for bank credit rises, banks require more reserves to back the deposits created by their new credit extensions.

Other things being equal, at lower interest rates the demand for credit and hence the demand for reserves, will be greater. At higher interest rates it will be lower. Therefore, we can imagine a demand for reserves schedule which looks like the curve DR in Figure 26.

At an interest rate (Federal funds rate) of i the demand for reserves by the banks is Q. As the interest rate rises to i_1, the demand for reserves associated with a reduced demand for credit at the higher interest rate, would be a lower Q_1. Over time, economic growth (and inflation if the central bank's policies result in inflation) will mean that the demand for credit, and hence reserves, will be greater at all levels of interest rates. So the DR curve will shift to the right, towards (and beyond) position DR'.

FIGURE 26 The demand for reserves

If the Fed is targeting reserves, then the supply of reserves will be the result of the Fed's open market operations to add and withdraw reserves, and will be independent of interest rates. In this framework, the supply curve for reserves will be vertical (i.e. the supply will be the same whatever the level of interest rates, because the Fed is not influenced by the level of the Federal funds rate).

In Figure 27, with the Fed supplying reserves of Q (i.e. implying a supply curve of SR), the Federal funds rate is at i, given the demand for reserves curve DR. If a constant rate of real economic growth gradually shifts the DR curve out towards position DR' then the Fed will have to increase the supply of reserves (at a constant rate over time). The Fed will move the supply schedule towards SR' in order to avoid deflation.

It should be noted that if the Fed does not do this, but instead maintains the supply of reserves fixed at Q, it does not mean that the Federal funds rate keeps rising to i' and above. In this case, over the long term, the DR curve is constrained to remain at position DR. Deflation reduces the demand for reserves, offsetting economic growth, i.e. in *nominal* terms the economy is not growing. However, if, instead, a sudden increase in the demand for credit causes the DR curve to jump to position DR' (perhaps a tax change engenders a short-term increased demand for credit), then, given the policy to

FIGURE 27 Reserve targeting

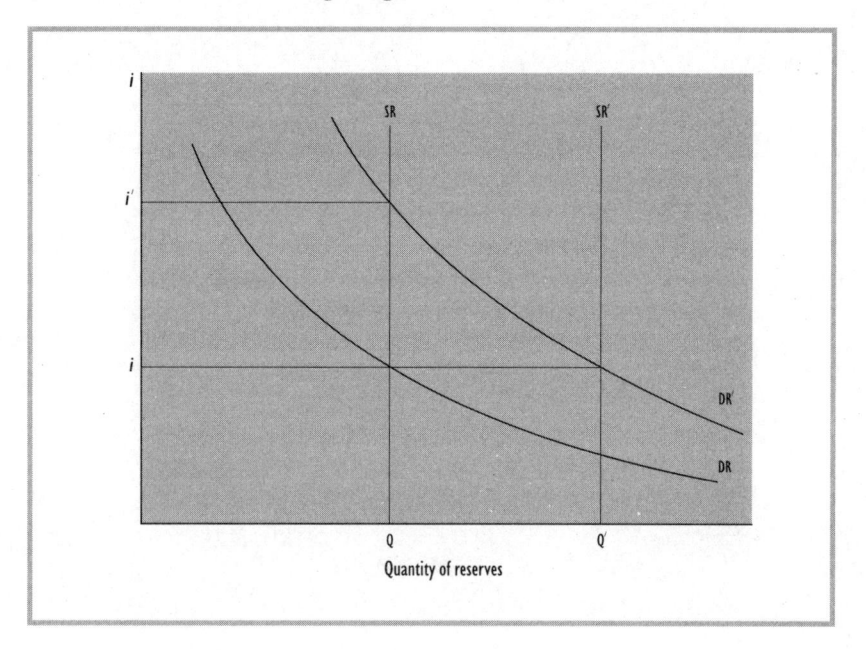

target a fixed level or constant rate of growth for reserves, the Federal funds rate will jump to position i'.

In practice, on a week-to-week or month-to-month basis, the demand for credit can be quite volatile. Therefore, in the real world, the DR curve is moving all the time. A reserve targeting policy will therefore lead to some volatility in interest rates. Because interest rate volatility tends to be unpopular, the central bank is usually steered to an interest rate targeting approach.

If the Fed targets a fixed level for the Federal funds rate, then this will require the Fed to supply whatever quantity of reserves is necessary to keep the Federal funds rate at the desired level. The supply curve for reserves is horizontal, because the Fed is not influenced by the quantity of reserves it is supplying (see Figure 28).

The Fed desires to maintain the interest rate at i and therefore stands prepared to supply whatever quantity of reserves is demanded at that interest rate. If the DR curve suddenly moves to position DR' then, necessarily, the Fed will supply the quantity of reserves Q'. Volatility in interest rates is replaced by volatility in the quantity of reserves, and hence in the money aggregates.

If, over time, the Fed feels that the funds rate it is targeting is associated with too rapid a rate of money growth, it can, of course,

FIGURE 28 Interest rate targeting

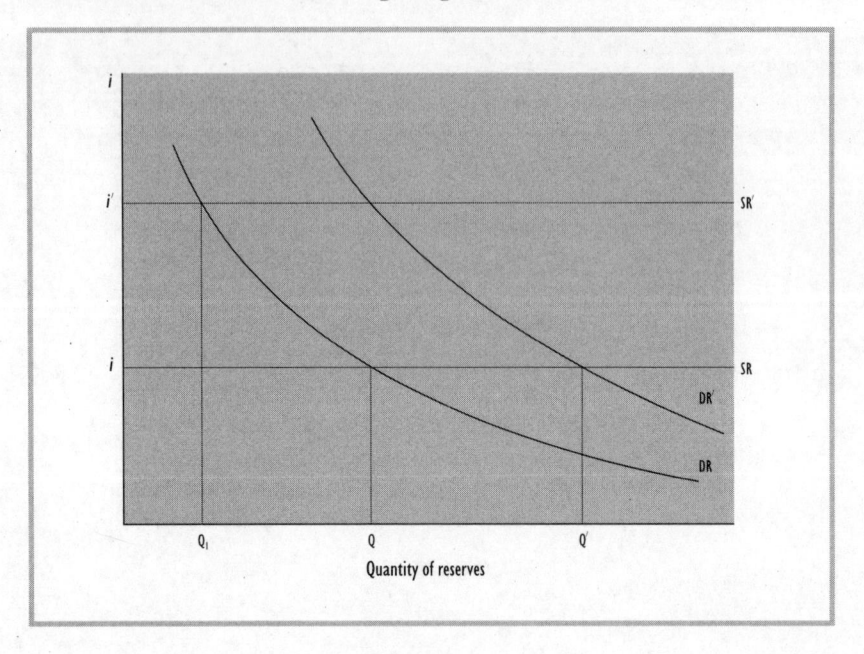

raise the target interest rate. If the demand for reserves curve is at DR and the Fed raises the interest rate from i to i' (i.e. shifts the implicit SR schedule from SR to SR'), then the quantity of reserves supplied will drop from Q to Q_1.

For a central bank, targeting interest rates means relinquishing direct control over the quantity of money, at least in the short term. Nevertheless, this is the operating approach chosen by most central banks which allow their currencies to float. Apart from damping interest rate volatility, an important reason for this is uncertainty about the appropriate rate of money growth, particularly given the possibility of swings in the demand for money. For instance, if the central bank is pursuing a reserve targeting policy aimed at generating a constant rate of money supply growth, an unforeseen large increase in the demand for money to hold could prove deflationary. The fact that individuals and/or companies wished to hold more money would mean that banks would have to hold more reserves against that money. If the central bank is maintaining tight control over the supply of reserves, this will not be possible. Instead, the result would be deflation and probably a recession in the economy.

In the United States, it was uncertainty about shifts in the demand for money (mainly associated with financial deregulation) which was a key factor leading the Fed to abandon its policy of nonborrowed reserve targeting in mid-1983 (a policy which the Fed had initiated in 1979). Since mid-1983 the Fed has been following an interest rate targeting policy, maintaining the Federal funds rate within very narrow bands. Under this operating procedure, 'changes' in policy occur when the Fed alters its target for the Federal funds rate. Figure 29, depicting the Federal funds rate since 1981, shows a clear reduction in interest rate volatility following the change in policy in 1983. Figure 25 on page 146 shows another result of that policy change. Whereas prior to 1983 the growth of nonborrowed reserves tended to lead the growth rate of money by about three months, after the Fed began to target interest rates, nonborrowed reserves grew coincidentally with money. This is because under the interest rate targeting policy the Fed is bound to supply the reserves necessary to accommodate the growth of credit and money at the targeted interest rate. In contrast, as explained previously, under the pre-1983 reserves targeting policy, the growth of money eventually responded to the Fed's policy with regard to reserves.

FIGURE 29 United States: Federal funds rate

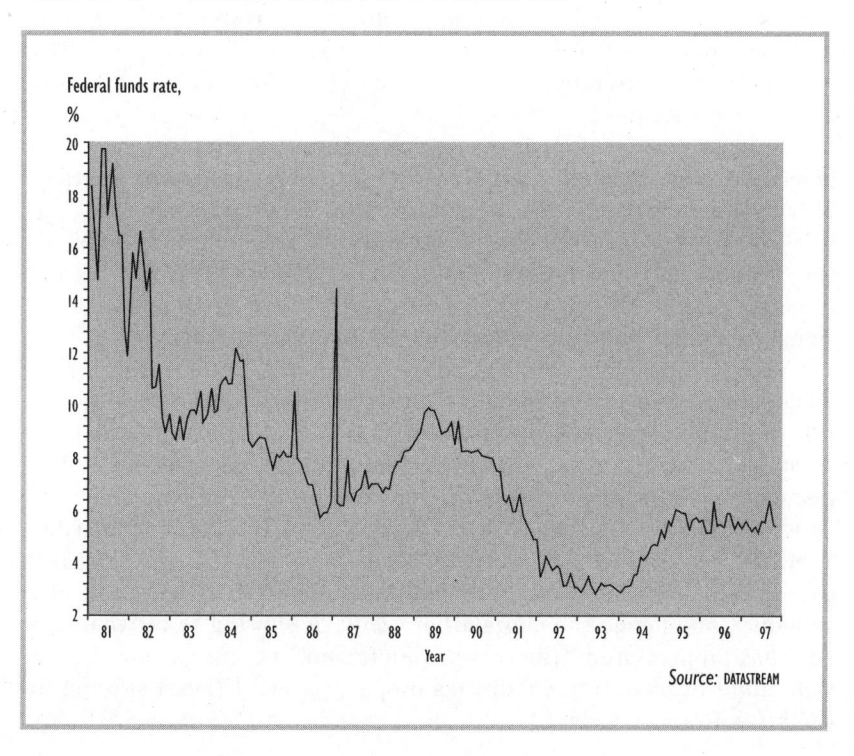

Source: DATASTREAM

In other countries which have fractional reserve monetary systems, monetary policy operates in a similar way with minor differences in the way in which the central bank announces policy initiatives to the banking system and financial markets. The Fed explicitly announces a target for the overnight interest rate at which banks borrow and lend reserves – the Federal funds rate – and then conducts open market operations to keep the funds rate as near as possible to the announced target on a day-to-day basis. In Germany, the Bundesbank signals its intentions through the rate at which it conducts open market operations which take place in weekly repurchase tenders, either on a fixed or variable rate basis. The rate at which it conducts the repurchase operations is the repo rate, and the short-term interbank rate will always tend to be very close to this rate as it is the rate at which the Bundesbank is committed to supplying reserves required by the banking system on a weekly basis. In Germany, and other continental European countries, there is an official corridor within which the repo rate can be adjusted, established by the discount rate at the lower end and the Lombard rate at the upper. These are both discount rates, in effect, but with implicitly freer access than exists in the US system. Interbank rates will not rise above the Lombard rate or fall below the discount rate because then the banking system would either, respectively, borrow from or repay loans to the Bundesbank at these rates. Changes in the official rates are used by the Bundesbank to confirm a clear direction for interest rate policy.

In Japan, the Bank of Japan signals its monetary intentions to the banking system through its policy towards reserve provision, particularly in the early part of the monthly reserve maintenance period. The Bank of Japan releases a reserve deviation figure, which is similar to the US concept of net borrowed reserves. Nevertheless, the official discount rate is the key mechanism through which the Bank of Japan signals its wider policy intentions to the financial markets.

The key problem with a policy of interest rate targeting is analogous to that under a policy of reserve targeting: the appropriate rate of interest is never obvious. The risk is particularly large when the economy is at, or near, a turning point in the business cycle. For instance, if the economy seems to be slowing, the Fed will lower the Federal funds rate, perhaps by 0.25 percent or 0.5 percent initially. Typically, analysts of the monetary scene proclaim that the 'Fed has eased', because the funds rate has been lowered. However, if the economy, and hence the demand for credit, is slowing faster than the Fed has appreciated, the result might not be an easing but a tightening in monetary conditions properly defined (i.e. a slowing in the rate of money growth).

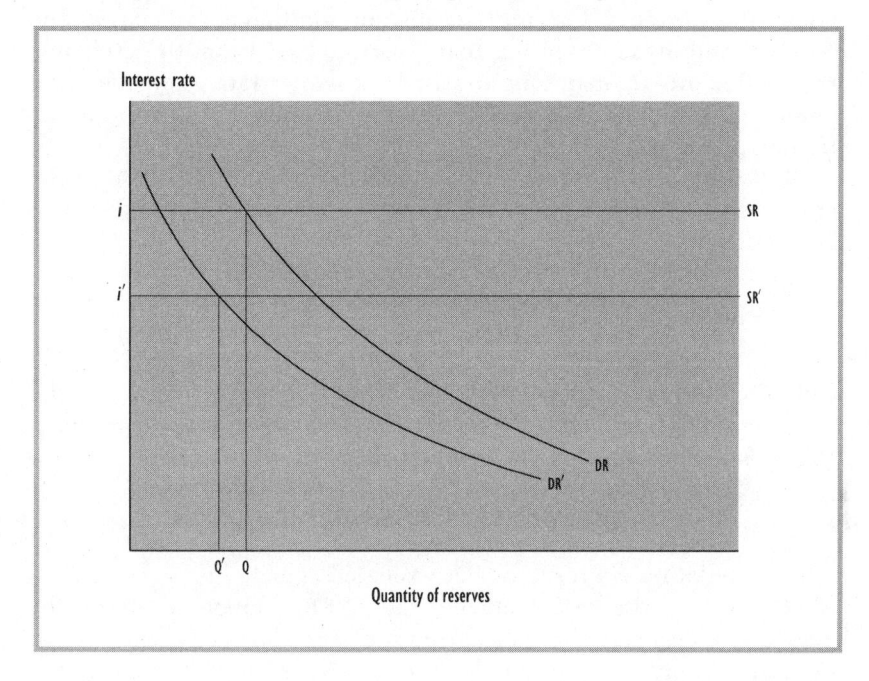

FIGURE 30 Interest rate targeting in a slowing economy

[Figure: Graph showing Interest rate on vertical axis and Quantity of reserves on horizontal axis. Two downward-sloping demand curves DR and DR' (DR' shifted left). Two horizontal supply lines SR at level i and SR' at level i'. Quantities Q' and Q marked on horizontal axis.]

In Figure 30 the Fed, realizing that the economy is slowing, reduces the funds rate from i to i'. However, the economy is slowing more quickly than the Fed realizes, and the demand for reserves schedule has slipped to DR', because of weakening credit demand. The result is that, rather than easing, the quantity of reserves supplied by the Fed falls, to Q', bringing about a monetary contraction.

MONETARY POLICY UNDER A MANAGED EXCHANGE RATE

In an open economy the central bank is operating under the constraints that the real interest rate will equal the world level and it is unable to affect the level of the real exchange rate in the long term. It has the choice between a fixed exchange rate or a floating rate. If it chooses the latter, it can operate monetary policy either by directly targeting the rate of money growth, through targeting nonborrowed or total reserves, or it can peg a level for the short-term interbank interest rate. Pegging the exchange rate means inheriting the inflation rate generated by the central bank which issues the currency forming the anchor for the peg. Floating the currency will mean accepting that, over the long term, the exchange rate will move to maintain the real exchange rate (i.e. offsetting differentials in inflation rates between the home country and its trading partners).

In Chapter 3 the formula for the real exchange rate (RER) for the currency of country A versus the currency of country B was shown to be:

$$RER(A)_T = \frac{100 \times ER(B/A)_T \times P(A)_T}{P(B)_T} \times \frac{P(B)B}{P(A)_B \times ER(B/A)_B}$$

Only the variables which have a subscript T change over time; the others are constants. If we consider this formula in rates of change, the constants disappear. The formula then approximates to:

$$\dot{RER}(A) = \dot{ER}(B/A) + \dot{P}(A) - \dot{P}(B)$$

where the dot over a term means 'expected change in'.

Over time, the real exchange rate, RER, cannot be altered by monetary policy and, therefore, from the central bank's point of view, we can assume that in the long-term $\dot{RER}(A) = 0$. Therefore the equation becomes:

$$\dot{ER}(B/A) = \dot{P}(B) - \dot{P}(A)$$

This equation has already been used in Chapter 3. If the central bank pegs the exchange rate, then $\dot{ER}(B/A)$, the change in the exchange rate, is zero. Therefore,

$$\dot{P}(B) = \dot{P}(A)$$

If the central banks of A and B have a free-floating exchange rate between their currencies, then over the long term, the exchange rate should move roughly according to the differential inflation rates between the two economies.

The pure fixed and pure floating exchange rate arrangements are, in a sense, polar opposite approaches to the monetary and exchange rate policy question. The 'middle way' is the managed exchange rate. A central bank managing the exchange rate can adjust the mix of inflation rate and nominal exchange rate movement to achieve a point somewhere between the two extremes described above.

The hypothetical 'purest' form of the managed exchange rate (which in a monetary sense would be more akin to a fixed rate) would occur if the central bank decided to gradually appreciate the exchange rate for its currency in terms of some other currency, thereby generating an equivalently lower (i.e. lower by the amount of the currency appreciation) inflation rate than in the economy of the other currency.

For instance, the central bank of A could decide to manage its currency against the currency of B (the B dollar), but appreciate the A dollar against the B dollar by 3 percent every year. If the inflation rate in B is constantly running at 5 percent, this will generate an inflation rate of 2 percent (5 percent − 3 percent) in A. That is,

$$\dot{P}(A) = \dot{P}(B) - E\dot{R}(B/A) \quad \text{from before}$$
$$\Rightarrow \quad \dot{P}(A) = 5\% - 3\% = 2\% \quad \text{in this example}$$

The constant managed appreciation of the A dollar against the B dollar will lead country A to have a smaller balance of payments surplus than it would have if the central bank of A maintained a rigid peg for the exchange rate. This in turn will generate a lower rate of money growth, and hence inflation, in A's economy than would otherwise be the case. (Note also that nominal interest rates in A will be equivalently lower (3 percent lower in this example), because $i(A) = i(B) - E\dot{R}(B/A)$ – see Chapter 3.)

In this example it would make sense for the central bank of A to appreciate the A dollar by 5 percent per annum against the B dollar, generating a zero inflation rate in A, i.e.:

$$\dot{P}(A) = \dot{P}(B) - E\dot{R}(B/A) = 5\% - 5\% = 0$$

It will be noted that the central bank of A could obtain the same zero inflation goal if it let the exchange rate float, but targeted money supply to achieve a rate of money growth consistent with zero inflation in the economy. The result would be exactly the same in that the (floating) exchange rate for the A dollar would appreciate by roughly 5 percent each year versus the B dollar, i.e.:

$$E\dot{R}(B/A) = \dot{P}(B) - \dot{P}(A) = 5\% - 0\% = 5\%$$

There are many variants of money and exchange rate policies which could loosely be termed 'managed exchange rate' policies. Central banks in small open economies often closely manage their exchange rates, either against a basket of currencies or against the US dollar.

A much less strict form of managed exchange rate regime is the 'dirty float'. A dirty float is more akin to a flexible exchange rate regime but it is not a pure free float, in that the central bank takes it upon itself to intervene in the foreign exchange markets if the exchange rate for its currency is moving too far in an 'undesirable' direction.

The exchange rate regime which existed among the currencies of the G7 nations (in particular the yen/dollar and Deutschmark/dollar rate) in the late 1980s was a dirty float. Under the February 1987 Louvre Accord between the G7 nations, central banks endeavored to keep the exchange rates between the major currencies within broad, unpublished ranges. These ranges were subject to adjustment when deemed necessary, and the central banks defended the vaguely defined limits of the bands through intervention in the foreign exchange markets. Interventions were occasionally secret, but sometimes coordinated among the central banks and well publicized, depending upon the approach that the central banks felt would be the most effective in defending the agreed ranges.

Although numerous variants of managed exchange rate regimes can be conceived, in an open world economy in the long run, the difference between various regimes boils down to the question of the differing mix of inflation and nominal exchange rate adjustment which comprises any given real exchange rate. The more that nominal exchange rates are prevented from adjusting, the more that economies' inflation rates will converge. Under the post-1987 Louvre Accord international exchange rate regime, exchange rates between the major currencies were flexible at least within broad bands, and perhaps more to the extent that the bands could be altered when pressures became too great. Nevertheless, there was a large amount of intervention by the major central banks to keep the key exchange rates within their desired ranges, and there was a significant degree of inflation convergence among the major currencies.

One analytical way of determining the extent to which intervention, or exchange rate management, is affecting the rate of monetary growth (and therefore inflation) for any given economy is to consider the domestic and foreign sources of the growth of the monetary base. If the central bank is intervening to buy foreign currencies, then its foreign assets should be rising and, other things being equal, the monetary base (on the liabilities side of its balance sheet) will rise equivalently. In principle, over any time period the contribution of the rise in foreign assets to the growth of the monetary base can be calculated as the increase in the central bank's net foreign assets over the period divided by the increase in the monetary base over the period and multiplied by 100 (as a straight percentage). Alternatively, it can be expressed in percentage points of monetary base growth as the increase in the net foreign assets divided by the actual size of the base at the beginning of the period, and multiplied by 100. The 'domestic' contribution to monetary base growth is then the residual (i.e. 100 percent minus the foreign percentage contribution in the first case, and the actual rate of money base growth minus the foreign component in the second method).

In practice, there are complications associated with this type of analysis. The central bank's balance sheet is presented in domestic currency terms. If foreign reserves increase in domestic currency terms simply because the exchange rate for the domestic currency has fallen or because the foreign assets are earning interest (as opposed to rising because the central bank is buying foreign currencies), strictly speaking the increase is not part of the foreign component of monetary base expansion. The increase in the foreign reserves in domestic currency terms is not associated with any increase in the monetary base or any of the other 'true' liabilities of the central bank. If this increase in foreign assets is included, the foreign contribution to the increase in the monetary base will be overstated and the domestic component, which is usually calculated as a residual, equivalently understated.

Often, central banks (including the Bank of England) release figures for the 'underlying' change in foreign reserves (i.e. excluding valuation effects) on a monthly basis. This is of little help when historical central bank balance sheet data are the object of study. Then it is necessary to examine the 'net worth' item on the liabilities side of the balance sheet as this contains the counterpart to any change in the valuation of foreign reserves and also to investment income earnings. If the central bank earns income from its foreign assets or enjoys an increase in their value, this is reflected in an increase in the central bank's net worth. In particular, if the analyst is aware of exchange rate movements which have taken place, changes in the net worth can give a strong clue to how much of any increase or decrease in net foreign assets is due to valuation effects and investment income.

In addition, in many countries (including the United States, UK and Japan) the foreign reserves, or the bulk of the foreign reserves, are held not by the central bank but by the ministry of finance, as assets of an exchange equalization fund. Intervention is usually conducted by the central bank, but strictly speaking as an agent of the fund. In the United States the government body which holds foreign reserves and bears the exchange rate risk associated with the foreign asset holdings is the Treasury's Exchange Stabilization Fund (ESF). In Japan it is the Ministry of Finance's Foreign Exchange Fund.

Intervention in the foreign exchange markets affects the balance sheets of the central bank and government exchange equalization fund/ESF as illustrated by Balance Sheets 24–26.

The ESF acquires a local currency deposit at the central bank by issuing bills to the central bank. In the United States, occasionally, the ESF acquires the deposit (i.e. dollars) by giving foreign currency assets to the Federal Reserve with an agreement to buy them from the Fed some time later at the same exchange rate (i.e. the ESF – the Treasury

Balance Sheet 24

Central bank[a]		ESF[a]	
Assets	Liabilities	Assets	Liabilities
Treasury bills ↑	ESF deposits ↑	Deposits at central bank ↑	Treasury bills ↑

[a]Only balance sheet items that are affected by the intervention process are indicated

Balance Sheet 25

Central bank		ESF	
Assets	Liabilities	Assets	Liabilities
Treasury bills ↑	ESF deposits ↑↓	Deposits at central bank ↑↓	Treasury bills ↑
	Monetary base ↑	Foreign assets ↑	

Balance Sheet 26

Central bank		ESF	
Assets	Liabilities	Assets	Liabilities
Treasury bills ↑↓	Monetary base ↑↓	Foreign assets ↑	Treasury bills ↑

– still assumes the exchange rate risk even though the Fed physically holds the foreign assets). In this case the ESF is said to be *warehousing* foreign currencies with the Federal Reserve.

The ESF sells local currency from its deposit at the central bank and buys foreign currency. Commercial banks end up with the local currency in the form of a credit to their reserve deposits at the central bank, part of the monetary base. Therefore, the monetary base expands.

The central bank can then sterilize the effect of the intervention by selling the treasury bills (or the equivalent amount of other assets), reducing the monetary base back to its original level. Alternatively, if the ESF had originally sold the treasury bills not to the central bank but to the private sector, this would not be necessary, as sterilization would be automatic. Either way, with sterilization the central bank's balance sheet is unchanged. Without sterilization the monetary base increases, but the counterpart on the assets side of the central bank's balance sheet is an increased holding of treasury bills, issued to it by the ESF. Foreign assets rise on the balance sheet of the ESF.

In the case of unsterilized intervention, it will appear that the monetary base has grown because of an increase in the domestic sources of the monetary base (central bank holdings of treasury bills). In reality, the treasury bills are merely the counterpart to the ESF's holdings of foreign assets, a foreign component of monetary base expansion. If intervention is sterilized the central bank's balance sheet will appear to be unchanged when the true picture is that there has been an increase in the foreign counterpart to the monetary base and an equivalent reduction of the domestic counterpart. An accurate picture will require data in which all government bodies with responsibility for central banking functions are consolidated into one balance sheet, for the 'monetary authorities', as is the case, for example, in the IMF's monthly *International Financial Statistics*.

A similar problem can arise in monetary systems in which there is not an exchange equalization fund as such involved in the process of intervention, but there is a separate government entity managing part of the foreign reserves. In the island state of Singapore, for instance, a separate entity of the government – an investment corporation – is responsible for managing the foreign assets representing the foreign reserves. Although reserves accumulate initially at the monetary authority, as the monetary authority intervenes in the foreign exchange markets to manage the domestic currency, part of the reserve is turned over periodically to the investment corporation. The government runs a persistent overall fiscal surplus, resulting in mounting government deposits at the monetary authority. From time to time the government uses these deposits to purchase foreign assets from the monetary authority, transferring the assets to the government investment corporation. When this transfer occurs, foreign assets on the monetary authority's balance sheet fall. Correspondingly, on the liabilities side of the balance sheet, there is a drop in government deposits.

A further variant in which the government – rather than the central bank – also adopts the exchange rate risk inherent in the central bank's foreign asset position, occurs in Turkey. In Turkey, in the past the central bank's foreign currency liabilities exceeded its foreign assets, i.e. foreign reserves were negative. Because over time the Turkish lira depreciates in line with Turkey's high inflation rate, the size of this foreign liability tended to grow in domestic currency terms, eroding the central bank's net worth. The government accepted the obligation for this loss, allowing the central bank to sustain its net worth by assuming an equivalent noninterest bearing claim on the treasury on the assets side of its balance sheet, known as the 'devaluation account'. The devaluation account, being a domestic claim of the central bank, superficially appears to be part of the domestic contribution to the monetary base, but is actually part of the foreign counterpart because it represents the (negative) valuation effect on the central bank's foreign asset/liability position of the exchange rate movement, which, if excluded, would result in the foreign contribution to the monetary base being understated.

An arguably more accurate way of defining the foreign component of money base growth might be to take the increase in total official net foreign assets (i.e. central bank's net foreign assets minus government net foreign borrowing), and not merely the increase in the central bank's foreign reserves, to be the foreign contribution.

For instance, let us imagine that the government runs a deficit (PSD) of $10 billion and finances it entirely by borrowing $10 billion overseas. It sells the proceeds from the foreign borrowing to the central bank for domestic currency, and then spends the domestic money (thereby resulting in the $10 billion PSD). The monetary base and the money supply rise by the domestic currency equivalent of $10 billion. However, on the central bank's balance sheet the $10 billion increase in the monetary base will appear to correspond to a $10 billion increase in foreign reserves, i.e. the foreign currency proceeds from the government's borrowing, which the central bank purchased. From a casual glance at the balance sheet it might therefore appear that the increase in the monetary base has been entirely the result of exchange rate management and that the domestic component of monetary base expansion is zero. In reality the expansion has arguably been more the result of domestic activity by the government.

This problem can be brought into perspective by considering the monetary base identity:

$$\Delta M0 = PSD - \Delta B - \Delta ED + \Delta D + \Delta R$$

At issue is the question of whether the foreign contribution to the increase in the monetary base should be considered to be simply ΔR, or whether it should be $\Delta R - \Delta ED$, i.e. ΔNFR. It is probably usually more accurate to consider ΔNFR to be the foreign contribution, but it should be noted that the foreign contribution will not then correspond to the overall balance of payments. This is, by convention, defined to equal only the increase in the central bank's foreign reserves (i.e. ΔR – see Chapter 5).

Using this type of analysis, for a managed exchange rate regime (and particularly for a closed economy), the increase in the monetary base can conceptually be divided into three main sources:

$$\Delta M0 = \underbrace{PSD - \Delta B}_{\substack{\text{Domestic}\\\text{nonborrowed}\\\text{contribution}}} + \underbrace{\Delta D}_{\substack{\text{Domestic}\\\text{borrowed}\\\text{contribution}}} + \underbrace{\Delta R - \Delta ED}_{\substack{\text{Foreign}\\\text{nonborrowed}\\\text{contribution}}}$$

(The currency in circulation element of the monetary base (M0) is usually construed to be a factor absorbing bank reserves, i.e. a negative component of the increase in nonborrowed reserves.) In a pure free-floating rate regime, the underlying *foreign* contribution, or at least the ΔR term, should be zero. In a pure fixed exchange rate regime, or even the type of 'pure managed' exchange rate regime discussed at the beginning of this section, over the long run the total domestic contribution to the increase in the monetary base should, in theory (but rarely is in practice), be zero. In a dirty float there should be both a domestic and foreign component of monetary base expansion. The relative sizes of each can be used as a guide to determine the extent of the influence of the balance of payments, working through the exchange rate regime, on domestic monetary conditions at any time.

MONETARY POLICY IN A CLOSED ECONOMY

Up to now we have been concerned largely with the monetary policy choices facing a central bank in an open economy. Traditionally, an open economy is one that enjoys free trade in goods and capital. From the perspective of monetary policy, the key feature distinguishing a closed economy from an open economy is the existence of controls on capital movements into and out of the closed economy, i.e. foreign exchange controls. Such controls can either take the form of continuing strict limitations on inward and outward remittances of capital, or they can involve an array of withholding taxes and regulations which can be adjusted at the discretion of the central bank and therefore used as instruments of policy.

Either way, the importance of foreign exchange controls lies in the fact that they permit the real interest rate in the closed economy to diverge from the international level. The freeing of the real interest rate from the international constraint then allows the central bank the possibility of using sterilized intervention to control simultaneously both the nominal exchange rate and the money supply, at least for a period. In other words, the central bank comes into a position to influence the level of the real exchange rate, if it chooses to do so. The addition of the extra policy instrument of foreign exchange controls makes it possible for the central bank to achieve independent objectives for any two of the three variables – money supply, exchange rate and interest rate – rather than just one as in the case of the open economy.

In Chapter 5 it was shown that the current account of the balance of payments for any country should eventually return to balance because domestic residents (in the case of a surplus) and foreigners (in the case of a deficit) will not be prepared to continue to accumulate foreign currency exposure indefinitely. This led to the theory that the nominal exchange rate for any currency must ultimately return to its purchasing power parity (PPP) value. If the central bank is able to exercise control over the level of the real exchange rate this could undermine the market forces which eventually bring the current account back to balance. In the case of a currency which is persistently overvalued (i.e. the real exchange rate is 'too high') persistent current account deficits will lower the credit rating of the country, eventually deterring potential foreign lenders. In the case of a currency which is persistently undervalued (the real exchange rate is 'too low'), current account surpluses can continue to build up much longer if the foreign currency exposure is taken by the central bank. As an official body, the central bank is not subject to market forces determining its behavior. It is this latter case which is discussed here.

Two countries which have in the past made use of foreign exchange controls to maintain an undervalued exchange rate are South Korea and Taiwan. To sterilize the monetary effects of their

Balance Sheet 27

Central Bank	
Assets	Liabilities
Net foreign assets ↑	Monetary base ↑ ↓
Loans to financial institutions	Sterilization instruments ↑
	Deposits of government
	Net worth

purchases of foreign exchange, the central banks of both countries have made extensive use of *sterilization instruments*, i.e. central bank bonds, issued by the central bank for sterilization purposes (when the central bank has run out of other domestic assets to sell). This introduces another item into the central bank's balance sheet, a liability of the central bank but not part of the monetary base (Balance Sheet 27).

The central bank buys foreign currency and sells domestic currency to keep the nominal exchange rate from rising. This initially increases the size of the monetary base because the central bank's purchases of foreign currency are settled through credits to the reserve accounts of the commercial banks. However, the central bank then issues central bank bonds (i.e. sterilization instruments), selling them either to the banks or to the nonbank private sector. When these sales are settled, banks' reserve accounts are correspondingly debited. In essence, the commercial banks sell foreign currency arising from the current account surplus to the central bank but end up ultimately with sterilization instruments, rather than high-powered money, in return. The final position of the central bank balance sheet is as shown in Balance Sheet 28.

Balance Sheet 28

Central Bank	
Assets	Liabilities
Net foreign assets ↑	Monetary base unchanged
Loans to financial institutions	Sterilization instruments ↑
	Deposits of government
	Net worth

Because the monetary base is prevented from growing, the central bank is able to keep inflation under control. Indeed, because it can vary the size of issues of sterilization instruments as it pleases, it can, in theory, make the growth rate of the monetary base whatever it chooses. By using its purchases of foreign currency (i.e. sales of domestic currency) to control the exchange rate, and its issues of sterilization instruments to control independently the money growth rate, it can maintain the real exchange rate at the level of its choice. If it desires a lower real exchange rate, it can issue more sterilization instruments (to bring down the inflation rate). If it desires a higher real exchange rate, it can either reduce purchases of foreign currency (to raise the nominal exchange rate) or reduce issues of sterilization instruments (to increase the inflation rate).

If the central bank manipulates the level of the real exchange rate in this way, it cannot independently control the level of the real interest rate. This can most easily be seen in the case where the exchange rate is maintained at an undervalued level and sterilization instruments are sold through a tender process to the commercial banks. Because bank liabilities (the money supply) are constrained to grow at the rate dictated by the central bank policy, banks' total assets are similarly constrained. As the current account surplus (and hence the issue of sterilization instruments) grows larger and larger, more and more of those assets will necessarily constitute sterilization instruments. As a result, a decreasing amount of new bank funds will be available for lending to the private sector.

A clear example of this process was given by the case of Taiwan in the mid-1980s. As Taiwan's current account surplus surged to a phenomenal US$16 billion (20 percent of GNP) by 1986, a greater and greater proportion of bank asset growth was accounted for by sterilization instruments. As a result, the annual growth of bank lending to the private sector was suppressed to only 5 percent even as the economy was growing at a double-digit rate in real terms.

What would happen in these circumstances if loan demand increased? A rise in loan demand would occur, presumably, if the rate of return to investment in the economy rose. Banks would potentially be able to lend to the private sector at higher interest rates. The central bank, however, would still have to sell to the banks the volume of sterilization instruments necessary to sterilize fully the balance of payments surplus. As banks would only tender for the bonds at rates in accordance with those at which they could lend to the private sector, the interest rates on the instruments would rise to a level at which they would still remain more attractive to the banks than potential new private sector lending. In short, the whole spectrum of interest rates would rise in line with the increase in the rate of return to investment, such that no increase in new bank lending or investment in the economy would take place. The potential new investment would simply be crowded out by the central bank sales of bonds, which represent the counterpart to the accumulation of foreign assets.

In the identity for private sector savings and investment, the addition of sterilization instruments adds another term to the identity, which we abbreviate to ΔZ. The identity then becomes:

$$S - I = \Delta M0 + \Delta Z + \Delta B + K - \Delta D$$

Fully sterilized intervention implies that the monetary base is left unchanged. The private sector's holdings of sterilization instruments, Z, increase, meaning that the term ΔZ is positive. No other term on the right-hand side of the identity changes and therefore either savings, S, must rise or investment, I, must fall. A rise in real interest rates will likely be necessary to bring about this excess of savings over investment (see Chapter 3).

A policy of maintaining an undervalued exchange rate to encourage the growth of the current account surplus will therefore involve the crowding out of consumption and domestic investment. This is not particularly surprising. All that happens is that the maintenance of incorrect 'prices' by the central bank – for money (i.e. the exchange rate) and for credit (i.e. interest rates) – encourages a continuous shift of the economy's resources towards the export and import substitution sectors of the economy, and away from domestic investment and consumption. Although, in the short run, the existence of foreign exchange controls allows the central bank to meet an additional monetary policy objective, in the long run it only distorts the allocation of resources in the economy and leads to problems of imbalanced economic growth.

PUBLIC SECTOR DEFICIT, ITS EFFECTS AND FINANCING   8

PUBLIC SECTOR DEFICIT

The public sector deficit (PSD) is a flows of funds concept. That is, the PSD is equal to the investment of the public sector minus its savings, or the public sector's net incurrence of financial liabilities. Public sector savings equal total public sector receipts (i.e. taxes plus the gross trading surplus of public sector entities plus net factor income from abroad) minus public consumption and net transfers to the private sector, i.e. receipts minus all outlays apart from investment. Therefore public sector savings minus investment is the same as the public sector's receipts minus its outlays. Expressed negatively this is the PSD.

The public sector comprises central government, state or local government and state-owned industries as well as social security funds and other parts of the welfare state apparatus. A consolidation of the public sector balance sheet (including the central bank) would include the major items shown in Balance Sheet 29.

Being a flow of funds concept, the public sector's deficit is equivalent to its net incurrence of financial liabilities. The financing identity for the deficit can be derived from the balance sheet, in the manner presented in Chapter 4, as follows:

PSD = Δ Real assets $-$ Δ Net worth = Δ Government bonds held by domestic private sector $+$ Δ Foreign borrowings $+$ Δ Monetary base $-$ Δ Foreign reserves $-$ Δ Loans to financial institutions $+$ Δ State industries' borrowings from the banking sector $+$ Δ State industries' other debts $+$ Δ State industries' equity held by the private sector

Elsewhere in this book the state, or nationalized industries, sector has been omitted from the flows of funds and monetary identities for

Balance Sheet 29

Consolidated public sector	
Assets	Liabilities
Real assets	Government bonds held by domestic private sector
Foreign reserves	Foreign borrowing
Loans to financial institutions	Currency in circulation } Monetary base Deposits of commercial banks Net worth
	Net borrowing from commercial banks } State-owned industries Corporate debt Equity in private sector hands

the sake of simplicity. Then, the final three terms are removed from the identity and it becomes the PSD financing identity, or the monetary base identity of Chapters 1, 6 and 7:

$$PSD = \Delta M0 - \Delta D + \Delta B + \Delta ED - \Delta R$$

In practice, the existence of a state industries sector opens up another financing possibility for the government. The government can finance itself, at least over a period, by selling off equity in the nationalized industries to the private sector. In Balance Sheet 29 this appears as an increase in state industries' equity held by the private sector. Over the past two decades, privatization has played an important role in government finance in many of the developed and newly industrialized economies, notably in the UK, Japan and France.

As with most aspects of public accounting, the accounting treatment accorded to public sector asset sales differs among nations. A consistent approach would require that government sales of directly owned real assets (e.g. government housing, roads, hospitals or schools) should be treated as negative investment. The asset sale should be deducted from public sector investment, resulting in a lower PSD. Public sector share sales, on the other hand, should be treated in the same way as government debt issues, as a method of financing the PSD.

Privately owned equity in a public enterprise in which the government continues to hold the majority stake pays a dividend to the private sector just as a bond pays a coupon. More important, from a flow of funds perspective, is consistency with the way in which investments are treated in the private sector statistics. For consistency, a real asset sold by the government to the private sector should be treated as a negative investment by the public sector and as an investment by the private sector. The implied reduction in the PSD does not mean that the total 'financing pressure' on the economy has been alleviated. It is merely shifted to the private sector, which must finance the purchase of the government asset. To treat the disposal of a real asset by the government as financing would not be consistent with the treatment of the acquisition of a real asset as an investment, which is standard national accounting practice.

In the same way, logically, government equity sales should not be deducted from government investment unless they are similarly added to private investment. To do this would introduce inconsistency into the flows of funds accounts because an equity purchase, by the personal sector for instance, is viewed as the acquisition of a financial asset and not as a direct investment in real assets.

Correctly measured on a flow of funds basis, the public sector deficit, being the difference between the public sector's investments and its savings, represents the net addition to the demands on private savings imposed by the public sector. This is familiar to financial market participants as the weight of supply of new paper coming onto the financial markets, adding to the pressure on the real interest rate.

It should be noted that if the public sector deficit is measured in this way it does not necessarily imply that a zero PSD is an appropriate target for fiscal policy. If government investment is socially worthwhile, in the sense that it would be undertaken by the private sector if the scope of free markets were wide enough and if the private sector had the resources to undertake it, then the government may be justified in borrowing to finance it. If, on the contrary, the government aimed for a zero PSD and provided for such investment out of current revenues, this could imply the subsidization of future generations of taxpayers by current taxpayers. Current taxpayers would be bearing all the cost of an investment which will continue to provide benefits for future generations (although it is true that they could attempt to offset this by adjusting their savings behavior). This is the basis of the 'golden rule' of public finance, which carries the implication that borrowing to finance public investment is justified.

Some economists have argued for a totally different method of public sector accounting which would account for the public sector as if it were a private corporation. One of the major differences in this approach would be the treatment of investment. Only the depreciation of capital assets would be accounted for as expenditure, rather than the whole of new investment. This would have the advantage of preventing a bias against new public sector investment which might otherwise occur if the government were operating under a zero or near-zero PSD constraint.

Alternative methods of defining a public sector deficit may yield a measure of more use to the government in implementing its fiscal policy. However, the PSD would then cease to be a flow of funds concept and measure of net public demand for private savings. The widely followed budget deficit is generally of limited use in either respect. The exact definition of the budget deficit, comprising the difference between those public sector expenditures and receipts which form part of the government's annual fiscal policy statement, varies from nation to nation. Often it is compiled at the level of the central government and includes as expenditure grants and loans to local government and state industries without accounting for the revenues and self-funded expenditure of those bodies. In these cases the budget deficit is a pure measure neither of the central government's deficit nor of the PSD.

MACROECONOMIC IMPACT OF AN INCREASE IN GOVERNMENT SPENDING

The two basic national income identities are the origins of income identity:

$$Y = C + I + G + X - M$$

and the uses of income identity:

$$Y = C + S + T$$

where T is taxes net of transfers paid by the government to the private sector.

In an economy with limited available underutilized resources, a rise in public sector spending, G, must result in an equivalent decline in private sector expenditure. In the first identity there is a decline in any or all of the expenditures, C, private consumption, I, private investment, or $X - M$, net exports.

MACROECONOMIC IMPACT OF AN INCREASE IN GOVERNMENT SPENDING • 171

If the increase in public sector spending is provided for by an increase in taxation, T, there may be a directly equivalent decline in private consumption (from the second identity). On the other hand, if the private sector meets its greater tax obligations by reducing savings, S, then the change in private sector savings behavior will have consequences for real interest rates which could impact either private investment or the current account balance, X − M, depending upon whether the economy is open or closed.

The same is true for a rise in public sector spending not matched by higher government revenues, i.e. an increase in the public sector deficit. As discussed in Chapter 3, the increase in the public sector deficit is likely to put upward pressure on the real interest rate, crowding out either private consumption, private investment or the current account balance. In either case the fundamental reason is that the public sector has increased its usage of the economy's limited resources, leaving fewer resources available for the private sector. To the extent that the private sector channels fewer resources into investment, investments with a lower return will be cut. Therefore the return on the marginal investment project, equivalent to the real interest rate, will tend to be higher, at least in a closed economy.

In a closed economy an increase in the public sector deficit shifts the I + PSD schedule in the way illustrated in Figure 31.

In Figure 31 the economy is initially at long-run equilibrium, with private savings equal to private investment, prior to the introduction of a public sector deficit (PSD). If the exchange rate remains at purchasing power parity, the shift in the investment plus public sector deficit schedule to new position I + PSD raises the real interest rate to r′. At the higher real interest rate savings are a higher S′. However, private investment is a lower I′ (read off the original I schedule). The difference between the new equilibrium level for investment plus the PSD, i.e. I′ + PSD, and I′ is the extent to which the investment (plus PSD) schedule has shifted to the right. The addition of the PSD causes private investment to fall by I − I′ and private savings to rise by S′ − S. From Figure 31 it can be seen that these adjustments in private sector savings and investment together add to the horizontal difference between the I and I + PSD schedules, i.e. the PSD itself.

Because savings are the inverse of consumption, with unchanged national income a rise in private savings implies a fall in private consumption. Therefore, in a closed economy the increase in the public sector deficit crowds out private investment and private consumption. The extent to which it is consumption which is crowded out rather than investment depends upon the relative sensitivity of savings to the real interest rate compared with investment. The greater is the extent to which savings tend to increase when real

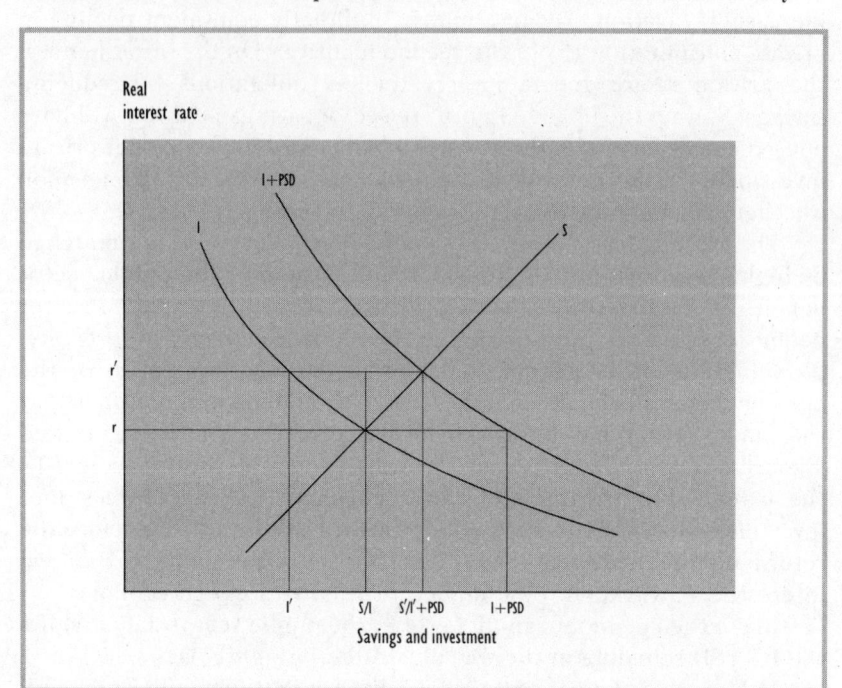

FIGURE 31 Effect of a public sector deficit in a closed economy

interest rates rise (i.e. the shallower, or the less steep, is the gradient of the S curve) the more it will be private consumption which tends to be crowded out. The greater is the extent to which private investment tends to fall when real interest rates rise, the more it will be investment which is crowded out.

In an open economy, the real interest rate should not deviate significantly from the world level. Here we assume that the economy is small and therefore the world real interest rate remains largely unaffected by developments within the economy. In this case, when the I (+PSD) schedule shifts from position I to position I + PSD the real interest rate remains unchanged at position r (assumed to be the world level). Because the real interest rate is unchanged, both private savings and investment are also unchanged, at S and I respectively. The addition of a public sector deficit to financing requirements merely results in a gap between the demand for savings, I + PSD, and the domestic supply of savings, S. This discrepancy represents the current account deficit (because I + PSD − S = M − X). In this case the PSD is financed entirely by a capital inflow, i.e. financed from foreign savings. Therefore, if the economy is both small in relation to the world economy and open, the crowding out effect of the PSD falls entirely upon the current account balance (X − M).

An alternative result is possible if the private sector has 'rational expectations'. Then, in theory, the private sector will recognize that ultimately the government will have to raise taxes to eliminate its deficit and pay back its borrowings. Consequently, individuals and companies will tend to increase their savings to accumulate funds in order to meet their future heavier tax obligations. In the perfect case, particularly if the larger deficit reflects increased government consumption, the rise in private sector savings would match the increase in the deficit. Then, private sector investment and the real interest rate would remain unchanged, the only consequence of the higher public sector deficit being an equivalent fall in private consumption.

To assume this type of behavior on the part of the private sector is logically consistent but unhelpful in practice. During the big expansion of the US public sector deficit in the early 1980s the personal savings rate actually fell. In practice, in an open economy it is more reasonable to believe that most of the impact of an expanded public sector deficit will ultimately fall on the current account of the balance of payments.

The key to the total economic impact of an expanded public sector deficit lies in the way in which the current account deficit is generated. In Chapter 3 it was explained that the process of generating the current account deficit was likely to be associated with a tendency for the exchange rate to appreciate above purchasing power parity as capital is initially drawn from overseas to finance the public sector deficit. The form that this real exchange rate appreciation ultimately takes depends upon the existing exchange rate regime. If the currency is freely floating then the nominal exchange rate appreciates. If the exchange rate is fixed, then the upward pressure on the currency instead translates into a monetary expansion which eventually raises the real exchange rate via inflation of price levels in the economy. In this latter case the rise in the real exchange rate will take considerably longer because there is always a long lag (upwards of two years for many economies) between monetary expansions and resultant inflation. In the meantime it is likely that part of the current account adjustment will occur via a change in the differential rate of growth of demand between the economy and the rest of the world. The monetary expansion stimulates a (temporarily) higher rate of growth of demand in the economy, drawing in imports.

With a fixed exchange rate, therefore, the fiscal expansion tends to be accompanied by a temporarily higher rate of money and demand growth, before inflation takes hold. There could conceivably be a cyclical rise in GNP growth (to the extent that higher demand is not met entirely from increased imports). In the floating currency regime, on the other hand, unless monetary policy is deliberately adjusted there will be no increase in the rate of growth of demand or GNP. If monetary policy is eased in response to the appreciation of the nominal exchange rate, this could stimulate stronger demand in the economy. However, this would imply that the central bank had an objective for the nominal exchange rate and therefore, strictly, the regime would be a managed exchange rate regime, not a free-floating one.

In the floating rate case, real exchange rate appreciation takes place much more quickly via an appreciation of the nominal exchange rate, and the current account balance is quickly crowded out without any, even temporary, beneficial effects for economic growth. It is therefore possible to categorize the relation between economic policy and the exchange rate regime for an open economy as being that under floating exchange rates monetary policy is effective but fiscal policy is not. However, under fixed exchange rates monetary policy is ineffective (strictly the implementation of an independent monetary policy is not possible) but fiscal policy can have a short- to medium-run impact because an expansive fiscal policy leads to an appreciation of the real exchange rate, which is preceded by a monetary expansion.

FINANCING THE PUBLIC SECTOR DEFICIT

The mechanics of the process via which growth of the public sector deficit places upward pressure on the real interest rate involve the financing of the deficit. The PSD financing identity derived above suggests that there is a limited number of ways in which a PSD can be financed. The three distinct methods of financing are by an increase in government borrowing (ΔB or, possibly, ΔED), a rise in the monetary base ($\Delta M0$), or by a fall in foreign reserves ($-\Delta R$).

Borrowing to finance a deficit

In a conventional developed financial system, governments finance deficits by borrowing from the domestic private sector. Borrowing from the central bank, which amounts to printing money, is usually precluded by law. Borrowing in the domestic financial markets has a direct effect on real interest rates through increasing the demand for private savings. This is clear from the identity for the private sector's net acquisition of financial assets, derived in Chapter 4. This identity can be rearranged to give:

$$\Delta B = S - \Delta M0 - I - K + \Delta D$$

Assuming that the growth of the monetary base, $\Delta M0$, is held constant by monetary policy, an increase in government bond issuance exerts pressure for either higher private savings, a reduction in private investment or a greater net capital inflow (or smaller net capital outflow, K). This pressure makes itself felt through a tendency of the real interest rate to rise. In an open economy, a rise in the real interest rate should not be perceived unless the economy is particularly large in relation to the rest of the world (see Chapter 3). Rather, capital is attracted from overseas, keeping the real interest rate down but encouraging an appreciation of the real exchange rate.

If, as would be usual, the government has a specific quantity of borrowing to undertake, the most cost-effective way of issuing debt is through an auction system. In a US-style yield auction, competitive bidders tender for quantities of a preannounced bond issue, bidding in terms of the yield at which they would accept their desired allocation (a lower yield represents a higher bid price). The government allocates the bonds to successful bidders, beginning with the lowest yield (highest price) and working upwards until the issue is exhausted. In a closed financial system the effect on interest rates is clearly direct: the larger the size of the issue, the higher would be the yield accepted by the marginal bidder.

In a closed system, if the government is not prepared to issue debt at real yields above an 'acceptable' level, then it will not be able to determine the size of its borrowings. If it has a real interest rate 'target' for, or constraint upon, borrowings, then, by definition, the amount of debt it issues will be determined by the market. This was broadly the case with tap stock issues in the UK gilt market. A strict interest rate constraint would imply that the quantity of government borrowing would be determined by private sector savings and investment behavior. This state of affairs could exist for only limited periods because of the implied constraint upon fiscal policy.

Assuming that any given increase in the weight of government bond issuance matches an equivalent rise in the PSD, then, according to this identity, the monetary base will be unaffected. In the long run, therefore, the total money supply should also be unaffected. This is despite the fact that government bond purchases by the banking system are a counterpart to the increase in the broad money supply (see Chapter 1). For a given monetary base and, therefore, a given total deposit base, any increase in the bond holdings of the banking system must be offset by a reduction in other bank assets, principally loans. Reduced bank lending for a given level of bank liabilities implies either increased saving or reduced investment by the nonbank private sector, or a larger net capital inflow. Therefore, whether or not new issues of government debt are bought by the nonbank private sector or by the banking system does not alter the consequent pressure upon real interest rates.

Direct borrowing overseas to finance a deficit (i.e. an increase in government external debt, ΔED) is a slightly different matter. The government cannot directly utilize foreign currency funds acquired through foreign borrowing to provide for a deficit unless government spending contains a significant import content. If the government sells foreign currency acquired through overseas borrowings to the central bank, then there will be a rise in the central bank's foreign reserves. There will be an equivalent increase in the monetary base when the government spends the domestic currency funds credited to it by the central bank. The expansion of the monetary base means that the implications for the domestic economy are similar to the consequences of monetization of the deficit, discussed below. The immediate consequences for the exchange rate and the real interest rate are neutral because there is no increased demand for either domestic savings or the domestic currency. However, if the government persists in borrowing foreign currency, over time there will be upward pressure on the real exchange rate via the inflation generated by the monetary expansion. The current account deficit thus created then represents the ultimate counterpart on the balance of payments to the official capital inflow.

'Printing money' to finance a deficit

'Printing money' to finance a deficit is the layman's term for government financing its deficit by expansion of the monetary base, or *monetization*. As explained in Chapter 1, expansion of the monetary base results in a more general monetary expansion which will eventually involve an increase in the note issue. Therefore, literally printing money does play a part in the monetization of deficits, but as the ultimate stage in the process rather than the first. Obviously, this mode of deficit 'financing' is inflationary and, in the extreme, is the primary cause of hyperinflation.

The simplest form of inflationary financing occurs if the government acquires funds by issuing debt directly to the central bank. (In many advanced economies, e.g. the United States, direct issuance to the central bank is forbidden by law.) In return for the bonds, the central bank credits the government with a deposit which the government can then spend. Government checks received by the private sector and deposited in the banking system are settled by credits to the banks in receipt of the checks to their reserve accounts at the central bank. The central bank's balance sheet undergoes the changes shown in Balance Sheets 30–32.

The public sector deficit is incurred as the government spends its funds at the central bank. People and entities in receipt of government checks (contractors, civil servants, etc.) deposit the checks in their own commercial banks. These claims on the government are then settled through debits to the government's account at the central bank and credits to the commercial banks' reserve deposits at the central bank, i.e. an increase in the monetary base.

Balance Sheet 30

Central bank

Assets	Liabilities
Net foreign assets Government bonds ↑	Cash currency in circulation ⎫ Deposits of ⎬ Monetary base commercial banks ⎭
Loans to financial institutions	Deposits of government ↑ Net worth

Balance Sheet 31

Central bank

Assets	Liabilities
Net foreign assets Government bonds ↑	Cash currency in circulation ⎫ Deposits of ⎬ Monetary base ↑ commercial banks ↑ ⎭
Loans to financial institutions	Deposits of government ↑ ↓ Net worth

Balance Sheet 32

Commercial banks (partial balance sheet)	
Assets	Liabilities
Cash currency	Borrowings from central bank
Reserve deposits at central bank ↑	Deposits ↑
Government bonds	
Loans	

Initially, the balance sheets of the commercial banks expand as the banks are in receipt of government checks. The recipients of checks from the government are credited with deposits at the commercial banks while the banks themselves acquire reserve deposits at the central bank. The banks experience an increase in their deposit liabilities, on which they generally have to pay interest, but the corresponding asset they acquire is a noninterest bearing asset, the deposit at the central bank.

The banks will lend out their excess reserves, resulting in a generalized monetary expansion, generating inflation and a consequent greater demand for currency notes. The final result of the process is difficult to portray or analyze within the savings/investment framework because it is distinctly a nominal process, involving the financing of a (nominal) PSD by the creation of inflation. If the government merely maintained its higher level of spending in nominal terms then the PSD would gradually disappear, as inflation eliminated the deficit between real spending and real tax revenues. To maintain stable government spending and a stable PSD in real terms the government would have to create a constant rate of excess money growth and hence inflation. The real deficit would then be financed by the constant devaluing, by inflation, of the outstanding monetary base, including the note issue. This is the *inflation tax* on the holders of the net monetary balance represented by the monetary base, which is a private sector asset but not a liability of the private sector.

If the government persists in deficit monetization and a high rate of inflation is therefore prolonged, the inflation tax will lead the private sector to try to economize on cash currency and other money holdings, shifting savings into other forms and therefore resulting in *disintermediation*, i.e. financial intermediation between savers and borrowers taking place outside the domestic currency banking system. *Dollarization*, i.e. the use of foreign currencies, especially the

US dollar, becomes particularly likely where this is possible. The resultant fall in the demand for the national money and monetary base will reduce the government's ability to finance its deficit through monetization. If the government persists in attempting to extract the same real inflation tax from a monetary base which tends to become smaller in real terms (as inflation tends to outpace monetary base growth as the demand for money falls, i.e. velocity rises), then this will involve creating an accelerating rate of inflation. It is a short step from this point to hyperinflation, a characteristic of which is a rapid decline in the real demand for the monetary base.

Under conditions of hyperinflation or persistent very high inflation there is a natural tendency for the government's deficit, if large in relation to GNP, to be monetized. Very high inflation results in a high risk premium becoming incorporated into the real interest rate, which therefore exceeds the world level, because of the huge uncertainty faced by savers and borrowers with regard to the prospective inflation rate. In this unstable situation the high real interest rate will, from time to time, attract speculative capital which can cause the exchange rate to become temporarily overvalued, i.e. the currency will, for a while, depreciate at a slower rate than the domestic inflation rate. 'Bubbles' can then occur because, with a high real interest rate, if the real exchange rate is rising for a period, speculative capital will be attracted by the possibility of large short-term gains, causing the real exchange rate to rise further. This becomes particularly likely if the government attempts to reduce deficit monetization by increasing domestic debt issues heavily, therefore placing further upward pressure on real interest rates.

The overvaluation of the exchange rate eventually causes the current account deficit to blow out, leading to a bursting of the currency 'bubble' and an exchange rate crisis as the currency undergoes total collapse. A typical situation is that the central bank then has to inject more high-powered money into the financial system to ease stresses there. Alternatively, if the central bank manages the exchange rate in a misguided attempt to prevent it becoming overvalued, then this will amount to monetization 'by the back door', as the monetary base will still grow rapidly but as a result of a rapid increase, for a period, in the central bank's foreign reserves rather than credit to the government.

Turkey, which has a persistent inflation rate in the 60–90 percent range, has undergone both these sequences of events in the 1990s. The central bank's attempt to reduce monetization of the huge public sector deficit in 1993 led to exchange rate overvaluation and created the background for a currency and banking crisis in 1994, while in 1995/96 a further attempt to finance the deficit through debt issuance, with a managed exchange rate succeeded only in creating massive growth in the foreign reserves and hence perpetuating high money growth and inflation. The lesson is that, once hyperinflationary tendencies become established, an elimination of the PSD is likely to be a precondition for bringing inflation under control because it will be difficult for the central bank to prevent the direct or indirect monetization of the deficit.

Even in economies enjoying comparative monetary stability there can be a tendency towards indirect monetization if the government deficit becomes overly burdensome. If the government debt to GNP ratio reaches such a level that it threatens to become unsustainable then a risk premium may become incorporated in the long-term real interest rate. If the resulting upward pressure on long-term interest rates transmits down the yield curve to short-term rates then the central bank may find that it is injecting more high-powered money into the banking system (i.e. expanding the monetary base) in order to keep short-term interest rates at their targeted level. In this way debt will gradually be indirectly monetized. The market, left to its own devices, tends to keep the debt-to-GNP ratio under control by inflating nominal GNP, if the central bank remains passive. According to OECD data, governments' debt-to-GDP ratio (measured by general government net financial liabilities as a percentage of GDP) for the whole OECD has well over doubled since 1980 and is still rising at a level of around 48 percent in the late 1990s. This is a reason for treating claims by many commentators that inflation in the developed world will remain low in future with a great deal of skepticism.

In an attempt to forestall inflation the central bank may raise the reserve requirement on the commercial banks (a fairly common occurrence in developing economies). If the rise in the reserve requirement is equivalent to the increase in banks' reserves, then, by definition, the *adjusted monetary base* remains unchanged (the adjusted monetary base adjusts the monetary base for variations in the relation of total reserves to total deposits which occur as the result of changes in legislated reserve requirements or shifts of funds by the nonbank private sector between types of deposits bearing different reserve ratios. If the monetary base is unadjusted for these factors – as, for instance, in IMF data contained in *International Financial Statistics* – then changes in the observed rate of money base growth need not necessarily signify a change in monetary conditions). There can be no monetary expansion. Instead, the banks have to accommodate their increased holdings of required reserves by cutting back on their other assets, mainly loans. The crowding out of potential borrowers from the banks will involve higher bank lending rates, which will be transmitted to other credit markets as borrowers seek credit elsewhere. The consequences for the real interest rate, savings, investment and/or the net capital inflow follow as though the banks had increased their direct purchases of government debt, a possibility discussed above.

In the short run, financing a PSD by raising reserve requirements will therefore be a low-cost option for the authorities. The cost of the deficit is borne by the banking sector in the form of the hidden tax represented by the reserve requirement. In the longer run, as banks attempt to recoup the cost by a higher spread between deposit and lending rates, marginal borrowers will be driven to other forms of financial intermediation (e.g. commercial paper, the corporate debt market). As with the case of financing the PSD via inflation, there will be disintermediation, resulting in a suboptimal banking system in the long run.

Running down foreign reserves to finance a deficit

A public sector deficit cannot be financed directly by utilizing the nation's foreign reserves. First, these reserves are generally held by the central bank and not the central government. Secondly, they represent foreign currency assets which cannot be used to settle domestic payments. By definition the PSD can be financed by foreign reserves only to the extent that there is a deficit on the overall balance of payments. Then the government can sell bonds to the central bank without monetizing the deficit as long as the central bank is selling foreign reserves to finance the balance of payments deficit. The central bank's purchases of government bonds are offset by its sales of foreign assets, leaving the impact on the monetary base neutral.

The problem is that a PSD cannot be financed indefinitely in this way. The central bank's sales of foreign currency and purchases of domestic currency prevent the domestic currency from depreciating in value, while the government's actions maintain the growth of the domestic money supply. Hence, other things being equal, there is no mechanism by which the balance of payments deficit can be corrected. Eventually, therefore, the central bank's foreign reserves would be exhausted.

NATIONAL INCOME ACCOUNTING   9

REAL AND NOMINAL GDP, GNP AND NATIONAL INCOME

The basic measure of the size of an economy is its gross national product (GNP) or gross domestic product (GDP). Similarly, the most often used measure of economic performance is inflation-adjusted growth of GNP/GDP usually referred to as the *economic growth rate*. GNP or GDP are flow statistics which measure the value of goods and services produced in an economy over a given time period. Usually, but not always, GNP is measured on an annualized basis as the amount of goods and services which would be produced in a year if continued at the same rate as over the particular time period for which it is being measured.

The GNP/GDP can be derived in three different ways: from the measurement of output, expenditure or income. If measured correctly, the three methods yield the same result. Output equals expenditure because all final output must ultimately be bought, and if it is not bought, it is defined as inventory or stock building which is included as expenditure in national income accounting. Similarly, the money proceeds from such spending on output are paid out by firms as income in the form of wages, salaries, dividends, etc., or otherwise held as retained profits, which are included within income. Thus, by definition, output equals expenditure equals income, and all three measurement routes will give the GNP.

The GDP (gross domestic product) of a country represents the value of goods and services produced within the country by residents. The GNP also includes the net income accruing to residents from economic activity carried on by them abroad, including that from rent, interest, profits and dividends ('net' refers to the fact that income paid to overseas residents from their economic activity within the country has to be subtracted). This distinction is discussed in detail later in this chapter, in the discussion of the external contribution to gross national expenditure (GNE).

GDP and GNP can be measured either at market prices or at factor cost. In the market price measurement, goods and services produced are valued at the prices which purchasers pay, and therefore include any indirect taxes and the effect of any subsidies (for instance, for agricultural products). For the factor cost measurement, taxes on expenditure are subtracted and the value of subsidies added back. The measure of output known as national income is, if used correctly, net national product at factor cost. Net national product is equal to GNP minus capital consumption, an estimate of the depreciation of capital resources or the fixed capital 'used up' in the process of production. Capital consumption takes into account the fact that part of the investment spending included in the GNP is for the replacement of existing capital equipment which has become worn out and is therefore not really a new contribution to the overall wealth and living standard of the country. (See below on the output and income components of GNP.)

All the national income concepts can be measured in either real or nominal terms. Nominal GNP is the value of output at today's, or current, prices. When GNP is measured in real, or constant price, terms, goods and services produced are revalued to the prices existing at some given base date.

If the GNPs of a number of different economies at one given time are being compared in order to determine their relative sizes at that time, it would be usual to consider their respective *nominal* GNPs, converted at the appropriate exchange rates into one common currency. When calculating the growth rate of GNP of a specific economy, economists normally use the real GNP. This is because a high rate of nominal GNP growth may only indicate that a country has a high rate of inflation and not a high rate of growth in output.

If nominal GNP is divided by real GNP, then a price index which can be used as a measure of inflation, known as the *GNP deflator*, results. The GNP deflator differs in a number of important respects from the consumer or retail price index (CPI). CPI is a measure of the prices of goods and services which consumers within the country buy, whereas the GNP deflator is a measure of the prices of goods produced by the economy. Thus the CPI includes prices of imports but not exports, whereas the GNP deflator includes prices of exports but not imports. The GNP deflator also includes prices of capital equipment (e.g. machine tools). The CPI may include prices of some secondhand goods, which are not part of the GNP deflator because they are not current output.

It is worth stressing that the GNP deflator does not include prices of imports. However, it is a commonly held fallacy that because imports are subtracted in the calculation of GNP, a rise in import prices actually reduces the GNP deflator. Imports are subtracted in the expenditure calculation of the GNP only because they are already included in consumer spending, investment spending and government spending, and therefore have to be 'removed'. A rise in import prices does not lead to a fall in the GNP deflator, but at best has no impact.

Apart from the GNP, deflators can be calculated for the other concepts of output – GDP and national income – and also for all of the components of GNP.

The most common way in which economists analyze and forecast developments in GNP for an economy is by considering the expenditure components of the GNP. Gross national expenditure (identical to GNP) is divided into four broad categories of spending: private consumption spending, private investment spending, government spending, and exports or foreign spending. The distinction between these four categories is somewhat arbitrary and is arrived at essentially by definition. In theory, an investment is characterized by the fact that it provides a return to the investor either in the form of a flow of income over time or a flow of services. A house could be an investment because it could be rented out to provide income to the owner, or lived in, in which case it provides a return in the form of a flow of services (accommodation). So, also, could a car or a video tape recorder, etc., be classified as an investment on the same principle. However, in national income accounts, only spending on houses and other buildings (construction), and spending on plant and equipment, and inventory-building, by companies is categorized as investment, while all other private domestic spending is included in consumption spending. Similarly, just as private spending is separated into investment and consumption spending, so too is government spending separated.

The sum of private consumer spending, private investment spending and government spending gives total spending on final output (including spending on foreign output) by all persons and entities resident within the economy. This sum is often referred to as domestic demand or total domestic expenditure, because it represents the total spending on final output by residents. Thus,

$$\text{Domestic demand} = C + I + G$$

Sometimes economists omit inventory-building (or the build-up of raw materials, semifinished and unsold goods at the industry, wholesale and retail level) from investment and consider instead a concept known as domestic final sales. The words 'final sales' connote the fact that the goods and services are actually sold to final customers. Thus,

$$\text{Domestic final sales} = C + I - \text{Inventory-building} + G$$

Domestic demand and domestic final sales include consumer spending, investment spending and government spending on foreign goods and services which are not part of domestic output or the GNP. The total of imported goods and services is subtracted from domestic demand to give domestic spending on domestic final output. Thus,

$$\text{Domestic spending on domestic final output} = C + I + G - M$$

The GNP is equivalent to total spending on domestic final output and so also includes a country's exports of goods and services sold to residents of foreign countries. Adding in exports gives:

$$\text{Total spending on domestic final output} = Y = C + I + G + X - M$$

where Y is GNP.

If inventory-building is excluded from investment, then the measure is total final sales:

$$\text{Total final sales} = C + I - \text{Inventory-building} + G + X - M$$

EXPENDITURE COMPONENTS OF GNP

Consumer spending

Standard summary presentations of the broad expenditure components of GNP give statistics for only the total of private final consumption. In more detailed national accounts presentations, consumer spending may be separated into spending on durable goods (defined as goods expected to have a life of at least three years), nondurables (goods expected to last for less than three years) and services.

An aspect of national income accounting principles that often causes confusion is the difference between expenditures that form part of the GNP and transfers of income that, if occurring within the economy, do not. A transfer occurs when a payment is made without goods or services being received directly in return. In the most extreme case, if person A gives away some of his income to entity B, person A may consider that he has 'spent' the money. However, this transfer has not added to output or national income, but merely represents a redistribution of that income.

Treatment of debt and interest payments

A particular area which is often not well understood is the treatment of debt and interest payments. Debt repayments are not consumer spending. In fact, the repayment of a debt is part of saving. If person A borrows money to buy a consumer good, e.g. a car, this allows her consumer spending to exceed (temporarily) her income. Thus, she is dissaving. When she eventually repays the debt, the process of repayment, which can only occur if her income is higher than her spending on consumer goods, represents saving.

Interest payments are usually not part of spending or saving but are transfers. Interest payments which are paid to the banking sector (for instance on mortgage loans, car loans, equipment loans, etc.) are largely paid out by the banks to their depositors. They are transfers of income from the borrowers to the lenders (the depositors), with the banking sector acting as an intermediary. No new goods and services change hands from depositors to borrowers and so national income is not increased, merely redistributed.

However, there is a complication. If interest payments were entirely ignored in national accounting, they would not completely 'cancel out' in this manner. This is because banks do not pay out to depositors all of the interest they receive from borrowers. The difference – arising from the difference between banks' lending rates and deposit rates – is part of the banks' income, and is ultimately paid out to banks' employees or shareholders, or retained as banks' retained profits. This difference might be seen as a payment for the saving and lending service operated by the banks and therefore arguably should be included as part of spending and national income. If it is not included in GNE, then the output and income measures of GNP will exceed the GNE because they will include the output of the banking sector and the incomes paid by the banks to their employees and shareholders.

In practice, rather than the net receipt of interest by the financial sector being included in the GNE, in standard national income accounting it is subtracted as a separate item from the output and income measures of GNP. This item is usually called 'adjustment for financial services' or 'imputed bank service charge'. In practice, therefore, the whole total of interest payments to the financial services sector is treated as a transfer. However, payments for other financial services by consumers – such as investment management fees, financial consulting fees – are considered to be payments for productive services and therefore are included as part of consumer spending and within the GNP.

Treatment of housing

Although mortgage interest payments are not part of consumer spending, the cost of housing is captured through the treatment of rent. Not only is rent for rented accommodation classified as consumer spending, but an imputed rent for owner-occupied dwellings is also included. In the income estimation of GNP, discussed later in this chapter, the rent received by landlords is part of national income. For an owner-occupied house the owner is implicitly deemed to be paying rent to himself, the imputed rent being part of his consumer spending and also his income.

Rent is included in the GNP because it is a payment for housing services, land and property being a factor of production. Given that actual rental payments by tenants to landlords are included in GNE/GNP, it can be seen that an imputed rent for owner-occupied dwellings must also be included. In an extreme hypothetical example we might imagine that every owner-occupier moves to another area of the country, lets out his own house and rents in his new area of residence. Then, if actual rent payments are included in the GNP but no imputed rent for owner-occupied housing, GNP will appear to have increased substantially even though the underlying output of the economy is clearly unchanged. If imputed rents for owner-occupied houses were already included within GNP, then, assuming the estimated rents were correct, there will be no change in GNP in this hypothetical example.

Therefore, mortgage interest payments are not part of GNP, but the cost of housing is captured through the inclusion of an imputed rent for owner-occupied houses. Houses under construction or newly completed appear in GNE under residential investment, while accommodation provided by existing houses is included as part of consumer expenditure in rent and imputed rent.

Private investment spending

Private investment or private capital formation can be separated into gross (domestic) fixed capital formation and inventory-building, or stock accumulation. Gross fixed capital formation comprises residential construction (investment in new houses) and nonresidential fixed investment, or investment in plant and buildings, machinery and equipment by companies. It also includes fixed capital formation within the economy by foreign entities. (Note that private consumption spending, in contrast, includes only consumption spending by residents. Consumption spending by foreigners (i.e. tourists and visitors) is part of exports of goods and services.) Because new houses are ultimately purchased by individuals, in economic analyses economists sometimes lump together private consumer spending and residential construction to consider the concept of total 'household spending'.

Inventory – or stock – building represents materials, semifinished or finished goods which are unsold and left in the hands of companies whether manufacturers, wholesalers or retailers. Because the goods have been produced and hence are part of the output and income measures of GNP, they are also included in the expenditure measure of GNP, where they are categorized as part of gross capital formation. When considered in nominal terms, inventory-building comprises the physical increase in the quantity of stocks held by companies and also an element of stock appreciation (the change in the value of stocks owing to a rise in prices). Physical inventory-building can be either voluntary, when firms increase inventories in anticipation of a rise in demand for their products, or involuntary, when goods have been produced which cannot be sold because of weaker than expected demand.

Gross domestic fixed capital formation includes investment either for replacement or for adding to the stock of fixed assets. If capital consumption, or depreciation, is deducted, then the measure of investment is net (domestic) fixed capital formation.

Government spending

Government, or public, expenditure is separated into government final consumption and public fixed capital formation. General government (including central government and local authorities, etc.) final consumption comprises only government current spending (i.e. not capital or investment spending) which constitutes a direct demand for goods and services. The most obvious items in this category are spending on such things as defense, utilities, maintenance of roads, parks, etc. Although government consumption spending is a separate category in the GNE, the government really only acts as an intermediary between the consumer/taxpayer and the goods and services being provided. For instance, the government could levy a tax to finance the maintenance of a park or, theoretically, it could turn the park over to a private business, which would charge for entry to the park. In the former case the money spent on the park would appear in the national accounts as government final consumption, whereas in the latter case the entry fees paid would be part of private final consumption.

The important point to note is that only government spending on goods and services contributes to the GNP, whereas government *transfers* do not. Transfers are items such as grants (university grants, for instance), unemployment benefits and social security. Government current 'spending' of this nature represents only a transfer of income from the wage-earner/taxpayer to the recipient of the grant and does not constitute spending on goods and services, and therefore is not part of GNE. The exclusion of transfers from the measure of government consumption contained in the GNP means that this measure will be lower than the overall measure of government current spending contained in the government's budget, and probably significantly lower if the country in question has a large welfare state.

The salaries and wages of civil servants and government employees are included in government final consumption and GNE. The taxpayer can be thought of as purchasing the services of government employees, which are deemed part of national output. As civil servants' wages are included as part of GNE and output, they are also included in the wages and salaries component of the income measurement of GNP. In contrast, benefits received by the unemployed, for instance, are not included.

Public fixed capital formation is investment undertaken by the general government and includes such items as the building of roads, airports, hospitals, libraries, schools, etc. Often in presentations of GNE statistics, public fixed capital formation is included together with private fixed capital formation and only government final consumption is shown separately. (This is true, for instance, in the statistics on GNE included in the IMF's *International Financial Statistics*.)

External component of GNE

When the measure of surplus of the nation included is exports of goods and *nonfactor* services minus imports of goods and *nonfactor* services then the measure of output is the gross *domestic* product, or GDP. Exports of goods and nonfactor services is all spending by nonresidents on the economy's output of goods and services. It includes exports of goods, all spending by tourists (i.e. nonresidents) within the country, and overseas earnings from services such as shipping and transportation, communications, the banking and financial services industry, etc. It is output which, if purchased by residents instead of nonresidents, would still have formed part of GNE, i.e. it represents a direct demand for domestic goods and services by nonresidents. If *factor incomes* from abroad are also included within exports and *factor incomes* paid abroad within imports, then the surplus of the nation is part of the gross *national* product, or GNP. Factor incomes from abroad include interest, dividends and profits and also rent received by residents from abroad, which do not constitute final demand for goods and services. If they were received by one entity from another within the economy, they would be merely transfers of income and not part of GNP. (Although, importantly, it should be noted that this does not apply to rent, which, as discussed above, is not treated as a transfer but is included within GDP.) Specifically, factor incomes include repatriated profits, interest receipts, dividends, rental income, and receipts of other investment income from abroad, as well as income remitted to the country by residents who are temporarily working abroad, and also by immigrants. Factor incomes from abroad do not represent a direct demand for goods and services and so do not, in the first instance, increase domestic output. However, because they are transfers of income from outside the country they do add to domestic incomes and are included in national income and hence the GNP.

Thus GDP is a measure of domestic output, or the output of goods and services produced by residents within the country. GNP includes also the results of the economic activity of residents carried on abroad, in the form of income repatriated to the home country. In GNP accounting, this difference between GNP and GDP can either be included within the exports minus imports, or surplus of the nation, component of GNP or be included as a separate item, 'net factor income from abroad', sometimes known as 'net property income from abroad'.

Net property (factor) income from abroad is part of the current account of the balance of payments. Therefore, if in a presentation of GNP statistics it is included within exports minus imports, the surplus of the nation is exactly equivalent to the balance on the current account of the balance of payments. The surplus of the nation in a set of *GDP* accounts, on the other hand, is equal neither to the current balance nor to the trade balance (because it includes foreign net spending on the output of services), but is 'between' the two.

Because net property income from abroad includes interest payments and dividends and repatriated profits, it follows that, in general, countries which are large external debtors, or have in the past been recipients of a large amount of foreign investment, will tend to have a GNP lower than their GDP (i.e. net property income will be a negative item). The opposite will be the case for countries which are large external creditors or large foreign investors. On the other hand, countries which have a large number of nationals temporarily working overseas on contract (e.g. certain Asian countries) may have a larger

GNP than GDP (unless, of course, repatriated income from overseas workers is offset by debt interest payments or other items).

Domestic and external contributions to GNE

Often, the performance of GNE is analyzed by breaking down GNE growth into its domestic and external contributions. The external contribution to GNE is the surplus of the nation, explained above. The domestic contribution includes the remainder of GNE, i.e. consumption spending and investment spending, including government spending. If inventories are excluded from the domestic contribution, then more properly it is the domestic contribution to total final sales.

Arithmetically, a component's contribution to the percentage growth in GNE from any base period (often the same quarter of the previous year, or the previous quarter) is equal to the absolute increment in the component (i.e. current value of the component minus value at the base period) expressed as a percentage of the GNE at the base period. When calculated in this way, the sum of the contributions to GNE growth of all the components of GNE equals the growth rate of the GNE over the period.

Many economic factors can influence the growth of GNE and the domestic and external contributions to that growth over any given period. However, one specific factor merits attention as it affects the relative behavior of the domestic and external contributions to the GNE measured in real terms in an exactly opposite way to that in which it affects the contributions to the GNE measured in nominal terms. This factor is a change in the country's terms of trade (i.e. its ratio of export prices to import prices). A large rise in the terms of trade tends to increase the external component of *nominal* GNE but reduce the external component of *real* GNE, while increasing the domestic component of *real* GNE. The opposite is true for a fall in the terms of trade.

This can best be seen by considering the specific example of the large fall in the terms of trade endured by Japan and other oil-importing countries during the oil crisis of 1979–80. The doubling of oil prices over this period meant a huge decline in the terms of trade for countries such as Japan. The effect was to lead to a sharp deterioration in the current account of Japan's balance of payments as import values rose sharply, and therefore a decline in the external component of the nominal GNE. In volume terms, however, Japan's current account position did not deteriorate but actually improved. Much higher oil prices led Japanese companies to attempt to reduce their imports of oil (in real terms, i.e. in terms of barrels). At the same time, the deteriorating nominal current account position led to a sharp decline in the foreign exchange value of the Japanese currency which boosted Japan's competitiveness and encouraged a rise in Japan's export volumes, or exports in real terms. Thus, in the *real* GNE, the external contribution to GNE growth actually increased sharply over this period. The adverse impact of the terms of trade decline instead showed up in a decline in the real domestic contribution. This was because consumers and companies were having to spend more of their income on oil (and other imports, with the decline in the currency) and so had less income to spend on domestic output, having to reduce the quantities of domestic goods purchased (i.e. reduce demand in real terms).

OUTPUT COMPONENTS OF GNP

The output derivation of the GDP gives the output of goods and services broken down into the main sectors of the economy by which the goods and services are produced. Typically, these sectors are agriculture, mining, manufacturing, construction, utilities, transport and communications, wholesale, retail trade, restaurants and hotels, financial and other services, etc. Because rent and imputed rent is included as part of GNE (see 'Treatment of housing' above) an equivalent item – ownership of dwellings – is included in GDP. Similarly, because the pay of government employees is included within government expenditure in the GNE (see 'Government spending' above), an equivalent item is also included in the output measure of GDP, representing the output of the public sector.

In the output presentation of GDP statistics the output of each sector is measured by the *value-added* of that sector. For an individual company, the value-added of the company is equal to the value of all output produced by the company minus the value of raw materials, parts and components, semifinished goods or services, etc. purchased from other companies which represent the output of those other companies. In this way, 'double counting', whereby a component, for instance, is counted once as the output of the company that produced it and again as part of the value of the manufactured product of which it ultimately forms a part, is avoided. More importantly, the value-added represents the incomes to the factors of production employed by the company, because the revenues from the sale of the company's output which do not go towards purchasing the products and services of other companies must become wages and salaries, rents or profits. Therefore, the value-added of the company is actually the company's contribution to national income, or GNP.

At the sector level, the value-added of each major sector is the sum of the value-added of all the companies operating in the sector. This is equal to the value of goods and services produced by the sector which are either sold to final purchasers (i.e. form part of final output) or to other sectors, minus the value of goods and services purchased from other sectors. When the value-added of all the sectors is aggregated, intersectoral purchases implicitly 'cancel out', making the sum of the value-added of all sectors equal to the final output of goods and services, or the GDP. As in the case of the individual company, the value-added of each sector is the income generated by that sector, and the value-added by the whole economy is the national income (when appropriate adjustments are made for net property income from abroad and depreciation).

Although intercompany purchases of intermediate-stage products are subtracted in the calculation of value-added and are not part of the GNP (because they are not spending on final products by consumers, the government or foreigners), it should be noted that this does not apply to investment goods. A purchase of a capital good by one company from another is included in private fixed capital formation in the GNE and *does* form part of the GNP. If, for instance, a car company purchases a machine tool from an engineering company, this will add to the GNP. The purchase is part of the value-added of the engineering company, but is not subtracted in the calculation of the value-added of the car company, therefore increasing the output measurement of the GNP. It is included as investment spending in the GNE, and it increases incomes to the factors of production employed by the engineering company but does not reduce them at the car company in the income measurement of GNP.

The essential difference between the purchase of the investment good and the purchase of an intermediate-stage product is that the latter forms part of the value of the final product of the company making the purchase, whereas the former does not in a direct way. In the case of the investment good, only the *depreciation* forms part of the value of the final output produced in a given time period. However, depreciation is not deducted in the calculation of *gross* national product, but is part of the GNP (see below on the income components of GNP). Depreciation is, however, deducted from GNP to calculate the *net* national product, NNP, or national income. In the calculation of national income, it is at this final stage that the value of investment goods 'used up' in production – thereby in effect forming part of final output – is taken into account.

As value-added represents the incomes to the factors of production – wages and salaries, rent and profits, including depreciation – it follows that a high value-added good is one for which a high proportion of the value of the good represents the cost of labour and management, depreciation on capital equipment or the profit margin. In general, a high value-added good will be either capital-intensive in production or require skilled labour and/or highly paid management to produce.

The output of service industries, by their nature, often tends to be high value-added, with a large proportion of the value of output comprising the pay of managers and employees and possibly, in the case of business services, depreciation on business equipment. The value-added for a service company, like the goods-producing company, is equivalent to the total value of output produced – in this case the revenues derived from the sale of the services offered – minus the value of goods and services, other than capital goods, purchased from other companies. However, as explained in 'Treatment of debt and interest payments' above, a particular problem arises with respect to the value-added of the banking sector. This is because a significant part of a bank's revenues derive from the excess of interest it receives from its loans over interest it pays to its depositors – a function of the interest rate spread. The problem is that interest payments are treated as transfers of income in national income accounting and not as payments for goods and services produced, and so they are ignored in the calculation of GNE.

To bring the output and income measures of the GNP into line with the GNE, an adjustment is made by subtracting an estimate for the net receipts of interest by the financial services sector, often referred to as the 'adjustment for financial services' or the 'imputed bank service charge'. Thus, although net receipt of interest by the banks is part of the value-added of the insurance, banking, finance and business services component of the GDP, the subtraction of the adjustment factor in the calculation of total GDP means that the banking sector's actual contribution to the measured total GDP is limited to banks' fee-based activities.

Often, a further adjustment is made for the 'residual error'. This is an adjustment factor reflecting the measurement error necessary to bring the estimate of GDP from the output components into line with the estimate from the expenditure components, the GNE. The sum of the value-added of all the sectors of the economy, minus the adjustment for financial services and adjusted for the residual error, equals the gross domestic product (GDP) at factor cost, or the total output of goods and services produced by residents within the country. Net factor, or property, income from abroad would have to be added to obtain the GNE, and depreciation deducted for the NNP, or national income.

INCOME COMPONENTS OF GNP

The income presentation of GNP shows the components of the income stream which results from spending on output, accruing to the different factors of production – land, capital and labour. As explained above, the output derivation of GNP (or GDP) shows the source of value-added (i.e. final output) in the economy by sector of the economy. The income derivation shows the use of that value-added in terms of the form of income resulting from productive activity.

The value-added in production represents income in the form of income from employment and self-employment, 'profits' and rent. It should be clear from the previous discussions of the expenditure and output components of GNP that only incomes which result from productive activity form part of the income estimate of GNP. Personal income which arises from transfers, such as interest receipts, unemployment benefits or other social security payments, etc., is not part of the national income. Also, all income components of the GNP must necessarily be measured gross of tax if they are to sum to the GNP. Tax payment, with consumer spending and saving, is one of the uses of income, whereas GNP/national income statistics show the sources of income and how that income is generated.

The trading or operating surpluses of companies were referred to in the previous paragraph as 'profits' in inverted commas, because profit in the national income accounting sense differs significantly from pretax profits in the corporate accounting sense. Profits here include depreciation on capital equipment which, as discussed in the previous section on the output components of GNP, is not deducted in the calculation of *gross* national product. Depreciation is only deducted as a final step in the calculation of *net* national product, or national income. Profit, or trading surplus, in the national income accounting sense is not even equivalent to cash flow (i.e. profit plus depreciation) in corporate accounting. First, corporate cash flow and profits calculations include items, most notably interest receipts and payments, which in national income measurements are treated as transfers. Secondly, corporate accounts may include receipts from asset sales, for instance, as part of profits. The operating surplus in national income accounting includes only the surplus derived from production of output, which ultimately forms part of final (current) output. This is illustrated in the following section of this chapter.

The total of wages, salaries and supplements and the gross operating surplus of all companies and the public sector (together with rents and imputed rents) deriving from domestic economic activity equals the income measurement of gross domestic product at factor cost. The addition of net incomes accruing to residents as a result of economic activity carried on abroad (i.e. net factor or property income from abroad) gives the income estimate of GNP. 'National income' itself is equal to GNP at factor cost minus depreciation on capital equipment.

GROSS NATIONAL SAVINGS

The direct uses of private income are consumption and the paying of taxes, with the residual use of income being savings. If government savings are included, savings for the economy as a whole are by definition equal to the sum of investment (or gross capital formation) and the current account surplus on the balance of payments. Gross national savings accounts merely illustrate this equality, showing the amount of income saved by each of the major sectors of the economy – the personal or household sector, corporate sector, financial institutions sector (if separated from the rest of the corporate sector) and government sector.

For a correct measure of savings on a sectoral basis, savings must be measured out of total posttax income (i.e. total posttax income minus consumption for each sector), not out of income components taken directly from the national income figures, because incomes there are merely incomes from productive activity, measured before tax and exclusive of transfers. The savings for each of the sectors can be derived from the following simple identities. (The respective items taken directly from the income components of GDP are in block capitals, and the total incomes for each of the sectors in square brackets.)

Personal sector:

[WAGES AND SALARIES + RENTAL INCOME + Net transfers from corporate sector − Net transfers to (or + Net transfer from) financial institutions sector + Net transfers from government sector + Net factor income from abroad] − Taxes − Private consumption spending = Personal savings

Corporate sector:

[GROSS TRADING SURPLUS − Net transfers to personal sector − Net transfers to financial institutions sector + Net transfers from government sector + Net factor income from abroad] − Taxes = Corporate savings

Financial institutions sector:

[GROSS TRADING SURPLUS + Net transfers from (or − Net transfers to) personal sector + Net transfers from corporate sector + Net transfers from government sector + Net factor income from abroad] − Taxes = Financial institutions' savings

Public (or government) sector (could be separated into central government and public corporations):

[GROSS TRADING SURPLUS OF CENTRAL GOVERNMENT + GROSS TRADING SURPLUS OF PUBLIC CORPORATIONS − Net transfers to personal sector − Net transfers to corporate sector − Net transfers to financial institutions sector + Net factor income from abroad + Taxes] − Government consumption = Government saving

Careful examination of the terms within the brackets will show that, if the savings for all the sectors were added together to obtain total savings for the economy, the various transfers between the sectors would cancel out. This must be the case because a transfer, by definition, does not increase total national income but merely reduces it for one sector (or entity) and increases it by the same amount for the sector or entity receiving the transfer. Similarly, taxes also cancel, because they are a payment for each of the private sectors but an equivalent receipt for the government/public sector. The items listed in capitals are the incomes from productive activity, and, for all sectors taken together, sum to the gross domestic product. Thus, as expected, the sum of the savings for all sectors of the economy as listed above reduces to:

GDP + Total net factor income from abroad − Private consumption
− Government consumption = GNP − Total consumption
= Total savings (gross national savings)

From the expenditure components of GNP (i.e. GNE) we know that GNP minus total consumption equals total investment spending (i.e. gross capital formation) plus the net external surplus (i.e. the current account surplus). Therefore,

Gross National Savings (i.e. S(Total)) = Gross Capital Formation (i.e. I(Total)) + Current account surplus $(X - M)$

The important transfers accruing to the personal sector are dividend income (from the corporate sector), net interest receipts from the financial institutions sector (which could be a negative item), and unemployment and social security benefits, as well as interest payments on government debt, from the government sector. These items are all added to wages, salaries and supplements to obtain total household income.

In the UK national accounts, corporate sector total income is defined as follows:

Company sector total income = Gross trading profits (i.e. Gross trading surplus) + Rent and nontrading income + Income from abroad

Income derived from activities which fall outside the generation of final output captured within GDP, and income repatriated from overseas are necessarily included within the measure of corporate sector total income. Corporate savings, or undistributed income, are then equal to this measure of income minus tax and the transfer of

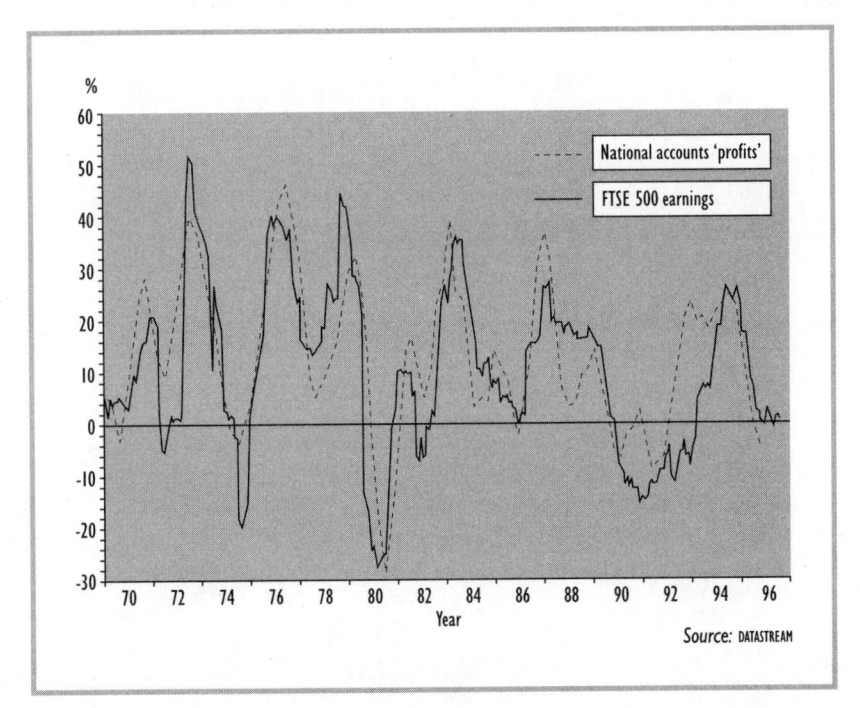

FIGURE 32 UK: profits from stock market and national accounts data

income to the personal and financial institutions sector through dividend and interest payments, i.e.

> Corporate savings = Company sector undistributed income
> = Gross trading profits + Rent and nontrading income
> + Income from abroad − Interest − Dividends − Tax

In the UK statistics, the estimates for rent and nontrading income of companies and interest payments by companies have historically been very close so that, for practical purposes, these two items in the above accounting identity can be 'cancelled out' against each other. The value of this identity is that it then provides a basis for analyzing the development of corporate profits in the UK. The measure of corporate cash flow, or undistributed income plus dividends, derived from the above (cancelling out nontrading income and interest) is:

> Cash flow = Undistributed income + Dividends
> = Gross trading profits + Income from abroad
> − Tax (approximately)

This national accounts measure of cash flow behaves similarly to the measure of implied stock market earnings for the FTSE 500 nonfinancial share index. The relationship is shown in Figure 32.

ECONOMIC INFLUENCES ON FINANCIAL MARKETS

LONG-RUN STOCK MARKET VALUATION AND RETURNS

Real stock market returns

In equilibrium, markets will value assets such that the expected real return from assets of a similar maturity differs only in accordance with the *riskiness* of those assets. That is, the expected total real return (i.e. return adjusted for inflation) from an asset or class of assets can conceptually be separated into the risk-free return, r, plus a risk premium:

$$\text{Expected total real return} = r + \text{ERP}$$

where ERP (equity risk premium) is used to denote the expected return required to compensate for the perceived riskiness of the asset(s).

Within a portfolio of assets, risk can to some degree be diversified away; so that the larger the portfolio, the smaller the return expected to compensate for risk. If we could imagine the investor as being able to have a stake in the productive assets of the whole world economy, then he would have no (relative) risk in his portfolio. The return would therefore be r, the riskless rate, which, in full equilibrium, can therefore be thought of as the yield (in terms of economic earnings) on the productive assets of the world economy which equates to the growth of these assets, and therefore the growth of the world economy. In practice, because the debt of the governments of the major nations is virtually risk-free, the real yield to maturity on long-term government debt will be very close to r. Thus r is the real interest rate, which should be equalized across the open economies of the world (see Chapter 3).

A national stock market does not represent claims on the total productive assets of the whole open world economy nor even on all the productive assets of the national economy. Therefore there is likely to be an element of relative risk built into the expected return, and therefore into the valuation of any national equity market. Hence the stock market will be priced to return, in real terms, the real interest rate plus a positive equity risk premium. This expected real return is the appropriate rate for discounting expected future dividends per share for the market to arrive at the net present value (NPV) of the dividend stream, which equates to the current value of the market. In the appendix it is shown how the NPV formula can be summed to break down the components of the expected return into the dividend yield and the expected growth of dividends.

The investor receives his return from equity investment in two components: the current yield and a capital gain which will equate to the growth of income from the investment:

$$\text{Expected total return} = r + \text{ERP} = \frac{\text{DV}}{\text{P}} + g$$

where DV/P is the dividend yield and g is the expected real growth rate of dividends. From this identity the level of the stock market, P, can be represented as:

$$P = \frac{\text{DV}}{r - g + \text{ERP}} \qquad (1)$$

This will grow at rate g in real terms because the current dividend (DV) is assumed to grow at rate g, and the other terms in equation (1) are assumed to be constants (for these purposes).

In market valuation work, the growth rate, g, is usually assumed to be the real growth rate of the economy. This is a good working assumption for most purposes, although theoretically is not strictly valid. If we imagine again the asset base of the whole open world economy backed by equity, the total real return on this equity will be r, the riskless rate. If the total economic earnings which represent this return were paid out as a dividend, then the dividend yield would also be r and there could be no dividend per share growth. However, savings have to be invested to achieve the growth which r represents. The dividends which represent the yield on the asset base (in this example) would have to be reinvested in new equity to allow the growth of the asset base to be sustained. Therefore dividend per share growth would be zero but, as new shares were constantly issued, total dividends and total earnings (and total market capitalization) would all grow at r.

Therefore, for the world as a whole and to a greater or lesser degree at the level of the national economy, the dividend yield, DV/P, and the real growth rate of dividends per share, g, are not independent. A higher current dividend yield for the market would tend to be associated with a lower expected growth rate of dividends per share.

Either way there is not, contrary to a popular belief, any necessary relationship between the *total return* to be derived from a stock market and the growth rate of the economy. If high future economic growth is anticipated then the market will tend to be valued at a higher level so that the investor will receive a lower portion of the total return in the form of the current yield. From the identity,

$$r + \text{ERP} = \frac{\text{DV}}{\text{P}} + g \qquad (2)$$

if high future growth is expected to be associated with high dividend growth, then g will be higher, but DV/P will be equivalently lower. The price-to-earnings and price-to-dividend ratio (the inverse of DV/P) for the market will simply be higher such that the current yield element of the total return will be lower. Therefore high-growth economies will tend to have high price/earnings ratios and low dividend yields but will not, at least in theory, necessarily provide a higher total return to the investor over the long run. In practice, many investors believe that the market will never be valued highly enough to discount fully the benefits of sustained high economic growth.

It is, of course, a different matter if the long-term rate of economic growth rises in a way that was previously unanticipated, perhaps as a result of deregulation or opening of the economy making possible more efficient use of the economy's resources and the drawing on of external resources. Then the investor who invested in the capital market could make an enormous capital gain through rapid market appreciation.

For example, let us assume that the global real interest rate is 3.5 percent, the equity risk premium is 2.5 percent (both reasonable approximations to reality) and an economy's expected growth rate had been 2 percent. Then from equation (2) the current yield, DV/P, will be:

$$0.035 + 0.025 - 0.02 = 0.04 = 4\%$$

If, as a result of a major economic policy development, the economy's long-run expected growth rate now rises to 3 percent, the yield on the market should drop to 3 percent (because $\text{DV}/\text{P} = 0.035 + 0.025 - 0.03 = 0.03$). The fall in the yield from 4 percent to 3 percent will come about as a result of an appreciation of the market, P, of one-third (33 percent, from 0.04/0.03) to a new level which would represent the present value of the now higher expected future income stream.

Inflation and stock markets

So far the discussion of stock market valuation and returns has been couched entirely in real (i.e. inflation adjusted) terms. However, investment returns are normally stated in nominal (money) terms and it is nominal returns with which investors are familiar. The identity $r + \text{ERP} = \text{DV}/\text{P} + g$ has two terms which can only be real variables (and therefore independent of price levels in the economy and inflation) – ERP and DV/P – and two terms – r and g – which we have considered as inflation-adjusted but could equally well be expressed in nominal terms. If expected inflation is added to the real interest rate, r, then it becomes the nominal interest rate, i, and if inflation is added to real growth, g, then it becomes nominal growth, G, that is:

$$i + \text{ERP} = \frac{\text{DV}}{\text{P}} + \text{G}$$

The equity risk premium, ERP, is a measure of risk and should be independent of inflation, while the dividend yield, DV/P, is also independent of inflation because both dividends, DV, and the level of the market, P, will rise over time with price levels in the economy, and therefore the ratio of the two should not vary, at least in theory, with inflation rates (DV/P is a nominal variable divided by a nominal variable which is therefore a pure number, or a real variable).

Each side of the identity, then, represents the expected total nominal return to the investor, which is simply the expected real return plus inflation. For two stock markets in economies which have very different inflation rates over time, obviously the economy with the higher inflation would be expected to be associated with a higher *nominal* return – and therefore a more rapid rise in the local currency stock market index. However, in equivalent currency terms this difference will vanish because the higher-inflation economy will experience a depreciation of its currency in line with purchasing power parity, and therefore the inflation differential. Over the long term, much of the superficial difference in the performance of different national stock market indices is explained by differing inflation rates. In common currency terms, the returns from national stock market indices exhibit a tendency to a high degree of convergence.

In theory, the valuation level of the stock market should be independent of inflation because, as explained, the dividend yield or earnings yield, or its inverse, the price/earnings ratio, are all real numbers because they are ratios of two nominal variables. In the identity $DV/P = i + ERP - G$, inflation is present in the term i but is subtracted in the term $-G$ and, therefore, however high or low the inflation rate, the yield, DV/P, and by extension the price/earnings ratio (P/E) should be unchanged.

In practice, we observe that the impact of inflation is not as 'neutral' as described here, at least over the course of the cycle. In reality, many national stock markets display a tendency to trade on a lower P/E ratio when the inflation rate is higher and on a higher P/E ratio when the inflation rate is lower. For the US stock market, this phenomenon is encapsulated in a rough rule of thumb often used by investors and known as the 'rule of twenty'. The rule states that the sum of the P/E ratio for the stock market and the US inflation rate should tend towards, and not exceed, a level of twenty (see Figure 33).

FIGURE 33 US: stock market price/earnings ratio and inflation

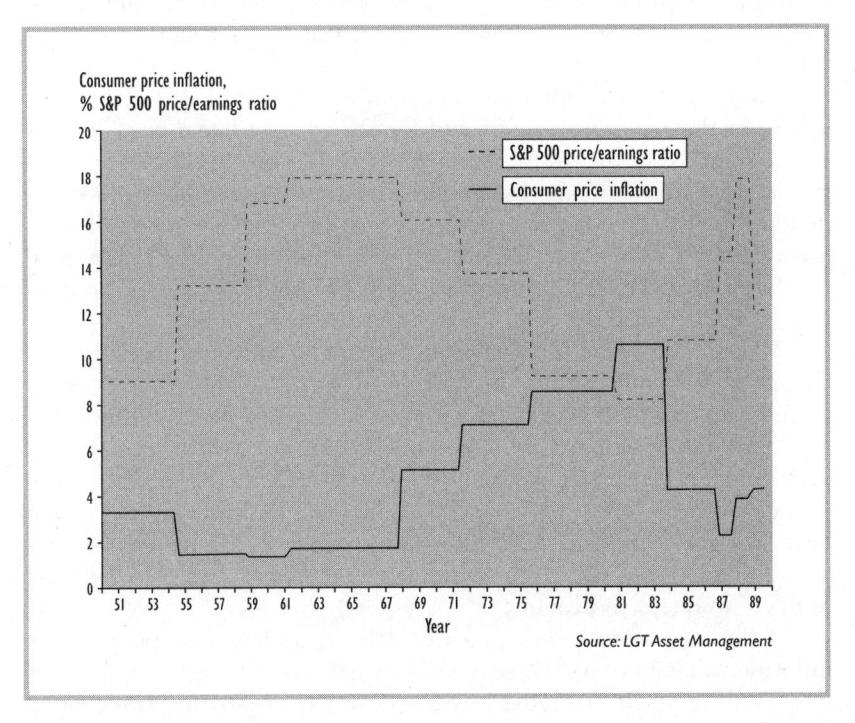

Source: LGT Asset Management

In the real world, accounting conventions and tax systems result in two broad ways in which inflation can affect measured P/E ratios. First, under inflation, measured profits tend to increase at a rate faster than the inflation rate itself if depreciation of capital equipment is accounted for at historical cost rather than at the replacement cost of capital equipment. Because the depreciation cost is fixed in nominal terms, it is understated as the prices of output and other costs rise. The result is an artificial inflation of profits. A similar effect can also occur with other costs, e.g. costs of raw materials, if accounted for at historical, rather than replacement, cost.

In this case, the apparent rise in inflation-adjusted profitability is artificial and not real. True costs are understated because the measure of depreciation does not adequately reflect the replacement cost of equipment. If market participants realize this (which is likely), share prices will not increase in line with measured profits but will instead reflect true profitability. Therefore, measured P/E ratios will decline.

The second way in which inflation can affect profitability and, potentially, P/E ratios is through the effect of inflation on the real cost of debt and debt interest payments and the effect of inflation on the real cost of tax payments. In the most obvious case of unanticipated inflation, inflation will reduce the real value of debts and loans, therefore benefiting the corporate sector if it is a net debtor to other sectors.

However, even if inflation is basically anticipated, it can have an effect on the real earnings stream for the market because of the tax treatment of interest. In most tax systems, interest receipts are taxed in the hands of the lender but interest payments are at least partly tax deductible for the borrower, certainly for corporations for which they are deducted as a cost. With continuous inflation, higher nominal interest rates will raise nominal interest payments for any given debt and therefore raise the real value of the tax deduction.

Additionally, even if inflation is stable and fully anticipated (and, therefore, fully reflected in the yield to maturity on any loan), because of the way in which borrowings are structured in practice, inflation would be likely to have an effect on the future path of real pretax earnings for leveraged companies, and therefore the market as a whole. For inflation to have a neutral impact, the value of debt would have to grow in line with inflation, requiring that interest be accumulated into the debt rather than paid out, which would be unlikely to occur in practice.

If the corporate sector is a net debtor, under most tax systems inflation will lead to higher real earnings growth via the interest effect justifying, in itself, a higher 'true' P/E ratio for stocks. However, a hypothesis of *inflation illusion* advanced by some finance experts (in particular, Modigliani) suggests that the market fails to recognize the potential benefit of inflation to future real earnings growth while it does tend to recognize the overstatement of current earnings (and possible tax consequences of this) resulting from historical cost accounting. The consequence is that measured P/E ratios tend to fall as inflation rises.

The implication of this is that the measured equity risk premium has a tendency to be higher if inflation is higher and lower if inflation is lower. An alternative possible rationale for this might be that the future inflation rate is more uncertain at higher rates of inflation, and therefore the potential effects of inflation on real corporate earnings are more uncertain. The argument here is that uncertainty tends to increase with the inflation rate because uncertainty about inflation and its effects increases. If inflation is running at 1–2 percent, for example, other things being equal, a continuing low rate of inflation is likely to be anticipated and the impact of future inflation on the real economy will be expected to be minimal. If, on the other hand, inflation is running at 1,000 percent (hyperinflation), companies and individuals will probably be unsure whether future inflation is more likely to be nearer 50 percent or 10,000 percent (depending on which policy the government adopts). As a result the degree of uncertainty about the impact of future inflation on the economy and corporate earnings will be very large.

As discussed in Chapter 8, very high inflation rates will also result in a risk premium becoming incorporated into the real interest rate, r, if r is measured as being the real yield to maturity on domestic currency government debt. Therefore, the P/E ratio for the stock market is likely to drop to increase the expected future total return in accordance with a rise in both the r and ERP constituents of the expected return $r + \text{ERP}$. In practice, it may not always be easy to separate out the two elements. The difference between the r and ERP elements of the expected total return is more than anything a matter of definition, as both variables represent the reward for accepting risk to a degree. In practical valuation work, however, a distinction usually has to be made.

A further way in which there may be an apparent inverse relationship between inflation and P/E ratios over the cycle is through the interaction of inflation and monetary policy.

The process by which increases in the rate of money growth above the demand for money tend first to result in higher asset prices, then later in a cyclical rise in economic growth, and then finally in inflation of goods and services prices was described in detail in Chapter 2. If asset prices rise as a result of higher money growth, in the case of stock prices it should mean that the market is 're-rated' (i.e. valued on a higher P/E ratio). Over the course of the business cycle this appears justified by higher rates of earnings growth which follow as a result of the later cyclical rise in economic growth. Over the longer run, the economic growth rate reverts to the long-run achievable rate, and the market P/E falls back to the long-run appropriate P/E. It may fall below it for a time if inflation rises and particularly if a monetary squeeze becomes necessary to bring down inflation. If the central bank's monetary policy is implemented largely in response to inflation then this could result in an apparent inverse correlation between inflation and P/Es. This is discussed further in the next section of this chapter.

Figure 34, for the UK stock market, indicates a reasonable relationship between the measured equity risk premium and the inflation rate. In this chart the earnings yield on the UK stock market (i.e. the inverse of the P/E ratio) has been used rather than the dividend yield to estimate the equity risk premium. This means that the ERP is not a precise measure of perceived risk in equity investment, but it will move closely with the 'true ERP'. This is usual

FIGURE 34 UK: equity risk premium and inflation

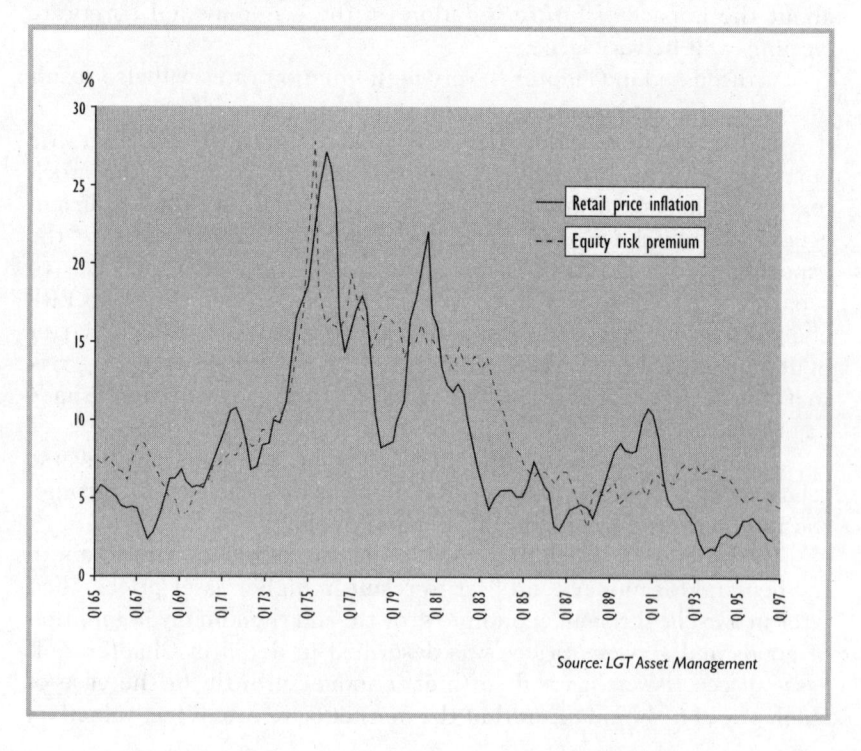

Source: LGT Asset Management

in comparative valuation studies because of the paucity of dividend data for many stock markets. The ERP is therefore estimated as:

$$ERP = E/P + g - r$$

where the E/P (inverse of P/E) is estimated on trend earnings, g is taken as a constant 3 percent average real growth rate of stock market earnings over the period, and r is measured as the long-term gilt yield minus a five-year centered moving average of the inflation rate, but assuming r to be zero at times (in the 1970s) when measured r was negative. The chart shows a clear relationship between the inflation rate and the ERP, which is confirmed in studies of many other markets.

Investors take for granted the relationship between the ERP and inflation in many of the simple valuation tools which are applied to markets. An example is the yield ratio, or the ratio of the nominal long bond yield to the dividend yield (or earnings yield) on the stock market. In the UK, investors traditionally pay much attention to the ratio of the long gilt yield to the dividend yield on stocks and draw conclusions about the 'cheapness' or 'expensiveness' of equities based on this ratio. In theory this is nonsense because, as explained, the dividend yield is a real variable while the gilt yield is a nominal variable. Investors in stocks achieve recompense for inflation because dividends will tend to rise with inflation, while investors in gilts do not because the coupon is fixed. If inflation, for instance, were 50 percent and expected to stay there, the gilt yield would be at least 50 percent. The dividend yield, however, while undoubtedly higher than the normal range, would be nothing like 50 percent.

In the valuation identity expressed in nominal terms, $DV/P = i + ERP - G$, if we assume a constant relationship between DV/P and i, then this identity implicitly carries the assumption of a one-to-one relationship between the equity risk premium and inflation. For instance, if we assume that the gilt yield should 'normally' be double the dividend yield then we can replace the gilt yield with two times the dividend yield, leaving the equation:

$$DV/P = G - ERP$$

This means that an assumption that a constant value of 2 is a fair level for the 'yield ratio' requires the assumption that the dividend yield is equal to the nominal growth rate minus the ERP. The nominal growth rate, by definition, varies with inflation so this can only be true if the ERP also varies with inflation. This is theoretically wrong, but the longevity of valuation notions such as the yield ratio implies that they have some practical validity, and this is borne out by Figure 34.

Models of fair valuation for a stock market can be constructed on the basis of assumptions about the ERP. One approach is to calculate the implied equity risk premium using the current actual yield. Alternatively, historical values for the equity risk premium can be calculated and then some form of historical average ERP used to arrive at a 'correct' earnings yield. In the first case, the implied ERP can be compared to the historic ERP. In the second case the calculated earnings yield can be compared to the current actual earnings yield to attempt to determine whether the market is over- or undervalued. Modifications of these types of valuation model can build in an assumption, or an estimated relationship, for the variability of the ERP with inflation.

MACROECONOMIC CAUSES OF EXCESS RETURNS

Liquidity conditions and cyclical divergence

In Chapter 2 the behavior of financial asset prices, including equity prices, over the business cycle was explained with reference to the cycles in monetary conditions. In an open economy with a floating exchange rate, the key to variations in liquidity conditions is the policy of the central bank with regard to money growth and/or interest rates. Liquidity conditions can be expected to ease (i.e. the money growth rate rise) if the central bank eases policy. Conversely, liquidity conditions can be expected to become more restrictive (the money growth rate fall) if the central bank tightens policy. If the central bank is following a strict policy of reserve targeting to achieve an objective for money growth, a change in policy will involve an adjustment to the targeted path for reserves. If the central bank is following an interest rate targeting policy, then a change in liquidity conditions in the economy could arise either as a result of an increase or reduction in short-term interest rates by the central bank, or because of a shift in credit demand. Liquidity conditions could become easier because either the central bank lowers its objective for short-term interest rates, or credit demand in the economy rises, or both of these.

The problem with a re-rating of P/E ratios that accompanies this sort of liquidity expansion, is that the process is fundamentally inflationary. The rise in the price of stocks is the first element in a generalized rise in prices, as described in Chapter 2. This rise in inflation will require and be associated with currency depreciation that enables the economy's competitiveness to be maintained. The problem for the (unhedged) international investor is that currency depreciation may occur fairly early in the cyclical process. The same excess of liquidity which leads to a cyclical re-rating in stocks is also likely to translate into an increased capital outflow and therefore depreciation of the currency. At first the real exchange rate falls, a real depreciation which is later corrected when inflationary pressures feed through into traded goods prices. If the fall in the real exchange rate is as great as the real appreciation of equity prices in the early phase of the monetary expansion (as, in theory, it might be expected to be) then the international investor will have gained no returns in excess of investing in his home equity market.

Chapter 2 also explained and illustrated that the global real interest rate, r, tends to move cyclically with the world business cycle. If world economic activity is picking up in the recovery phase of the cycle but one economy, for whatever reason, remains weak, then equities for that economy will suffer from a higher r being applied to the valuation of future earnings streams without the benefit of greater prospective growth, g, to boost those earnings.

As explained in Chapter 2, an economy in this situation will be experiencing a fall in its real exchange rate because capital outflows to the rest of the world will be part of the process through which the real interest rate for the economy is equalized with the rising real rate in the rest of the world. The fall in the real exchange rate may help to offset downward pressure on equity prices. From the point of view of investors in the rest of the world, it makes little difference as both are manifestations of the same phenomenon, which is a devaluation of asset values for the economy resulting from the application of a higher rate of discount to future economic earnings.

All of the above points to the conclusion that a characteristic of substantial cyclical outperformance of one equity market relative to another is likely to be cyclical real exchange rate appreciation. If, in an economy experiencing stimulative monetary conditions, the exchange rate does not depreciate, then this is tantamount to a real exchange rate appreciation. Stimulative monetary conditions will have inflationary repercussions. If the exchange rate does not immediately drop then the real exchange rate has implicitly appreciated. The foreign investor can benefit from the liquidity-driven re-rating of equity prices without giving back the capital appreciation on the currency. Under fixed exchange rates, any upward pressure on the real exchange rate will translate into monetary expansion, as outlined in Chapter 6. The investor will benefit from the monetary stimulation of equity prices while the exchange rate remains fixed.

The following sections outline the major categories of circumstance in which a substantial real exchange rate appreciation or depreciation may occur and therefore be associated with divergent performance by the domestic equity market.

Pegging of the exchange rate in an open economy

A major potential cause of real exchange rate volatility can occur when central banks or the authorities fix exchange rates at a time or at a level when long-run equilibrium conditions do not hold. This has already been discussed, with particular reference to EMU, in Chapter 6.

The key elements of the long-run equilibrium for two economies, A and B, which have a fixed exchange rate between them, are as follows:

- the expected inflation rate should be the same in A as in B;
- the fixed exchange rate should be at the purchasing power parity level for the two currencies;
- the current accounts for both economies should be close to balance.

We can consider what happens if the exchange rate between the currencies of A and B is initially fixed when one or more of these long-run equilibrium conditions does not hold.

The first, and easiest, case is when the exchange rate is fixed at a level which is not the purchasing power parity level for the two currencies, say at a level which overvalues A dollars in terms of B dollars. In this case the real exchange rate for A will initially be too high, and for B too low. The result will be a one-off deflation in A or inflation in B (or both), which eventually brings the real exchange rate for the A dollar in terms of the B dollar back down (i.e. brings PPP into line with the fixed nominal exchange rate). Initially, A's balance of payments will deteriorate, reflecting A's lack of competitiveness at the fixed nominal exchange rate. To defend the fixed exchange rate, either the central bank of A has to intervene to buy A dollars, thereby contracting the money supply in A, or the central bank of B has to intervene to sell B dollars (for A dollars), thereby expanding money supply in B. The result will be tighter liquidity in A than in B until the adjustment has been completed.

This was the case of sterling in the exchange rate mechanism (ERM) of the European Monetary System in 1990–92. The central rate overvalued sterling by at least 10 percent against the Deutschmark and other European currencies. The rate was ultimately unsustainable because, over a period, the UK would have had to endure consistently tighter monetary conditions than its European partners, which proved impossible against a background of tight Bundesbank monetary policy and low inflation in core Europe.

The second case is when inflation has been, and is, running at a higher rate in A than in B when the decision to fix the exchange rate is taken. This has already been discussed in relation to European monetary union (Chapter 6).

The potential problem is that if the inflation rate is higher in A than in B, then nominal interest rates will also be higher in A than in B, reflecting the expected depreciation of the A dollar *vis-à-vis* the B dollar. In theory, once the nominal exchange rate is fixed, longer-term interest rates for the two economies should instantaneously be equalized. This assumes that market participants fully expect the exchange rate to remain fixed in the future. Because inflation in A is higher than in B, A's balance of payments on current account should, for a time, deteriorate. This will reduce money growth in A and eventually bring inflation in A down to the rate existing in B.

In practice, nominal interest rates in A may not drop instantaneously. Instead, interest rates in A may only fall as capital is drawn into A, attracted by the higher interest rates and zero exchange rate risk in A relative to B. This capital inflow would initially boost A's overall balance of payments position and therefore lead to upward, rather than downward, pressure on A's currency. This would raise rather than reduce the rate of money growth in A. The adjustment process therefore initially 'goes the wrong way', leading to a still higher rate of inflation in A. If this process is seen through to its end, the later adjustment of the current account is much more severe. Because inflation in A has risen further, the current account eventually deteriorates all the more rapidly, bringing money growth and inflation in A back down. The overall effect is a more vicious cycle and eventual liquidity squeeze.

Many countries have been through this type of cycle in the 1980s and 1990s, arguably the UK (1987–89), Mexico (1994–95), Thailand (1995–97 – see Figure 35) and, potentially, Greece (1995–?). Because the final liquidity squeeze usually proves severe, devaluation is usually inevitable.

The final nonequilibrium case is when the exchange rate is pegged when the current account is not in balance. As illustrated in Chapter 3, for any economy the current account can be out of balance at any one time for reasons other than purely the variations in inflation rates that arise from changes in domestic monetary policies. If a shift in the rate of return to investment or a change in fiscal policy or some other nonmonetary factor alters the savings/investment balance for an economy, then this may engender a (temporary) adjustment of the real exchange rate. If the nominal exchange rate is fixed at any time

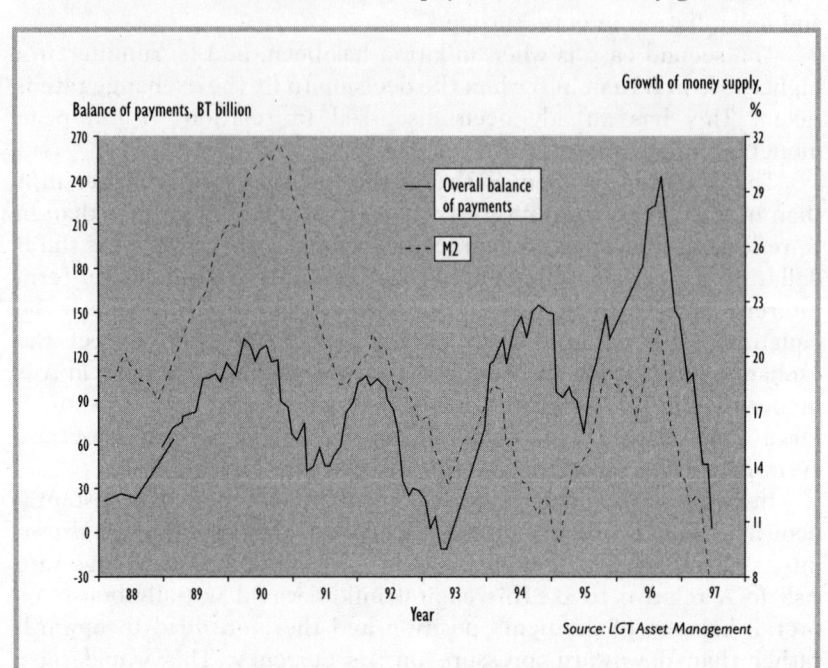

FIGURE 35 Thailand: balance of payments and money growth

during this adjustment process, then the adjustment will be transferred to the economy and price levels, leading to inflation or deflation. In the case when the correction of a chronic current account deficit requires a fall in the real exchange rate, fixing the nominal exchange rate transfers the necessary adjustment to price levels, leading to deflation in the economy. The stock market crash of October 1987 may have been an example of this.

Under the Louvre Accord of February 1987 the G7 governments and central banks agreed to maintain the exchange rates between the dollar and the other major currencies (particularly the yen and the Deutschmark) within broad, roughly defined ranges. The target exchange rate ranges themselves were not announced and were subject to adjustment if deemed appropriate.

The Louvre Accord implied that the world monetary system had moved away from an open economy floating exchange rate regime to an open economy managed, or quasifixed, exchange rate regime. This meant that the central banks had sacrificed a substantial degree of independent control over monetary conditions within their own economies and that, ultimately, inflation rates for the major economies would tend to converge. The issue for financial markets in 1987 was this: had the real exchange rate for the dollar fallen far enough to correct the large US current account deficit, which by then had become a chronic problem of the US economy?

Institutional investors in Japan – where 'excess' savings were to a large extent the counterpart to the 'deficiency' of savings (relative to domestic investment and the government deficit) in the United States – had appeared to show themselves unwilling to continue to finance the deficit at its then existing level (i.e. they were unwilling to take on the growing risk represented by continuous increases in their exposure to dollar assets). Therefore, if the current account deficit did not embark on a clear, narrowing path, the real exchange rate for the dollar would be forced to fall further. Fixing nominal exchange rates would imply that this further real exchange rate adjustment, if it were to occur, would have to take place through deflation in the US economy. This, then, potentially represented an example of fixing exchange rates at a time when the current account is in chronic deficit.

A severe monetary squeeze, leading eventually to deflation, would have been a disaster for the stock market. Seen in this light, it was rational for investors to pay extremely close attention to the monthly trade deficit numbers to seek confirmation that the required narrowing trend in the trade and current account deficits was indeed occurring. Prior to the crash on 19 October, the 14 October 1987 release of the monthly trade report had revealed that the trade deficit had been a larger than expected US$15.7 billion in August, little improved from July's then record monthly deficit of US$16.5 billion. Money supply growth had already been slowing sharply since February. In response to the news that there was still no improvement in the trade deficit, the Dow Jones Industrial Average immediately dropped 95 points, a record fall at that time, which began the freefall which led to the crash on 19 October.

Following the crash, the Federal Reserve immediately eased monetary policy, thereby implicitly downgrading the importance of any objective for the exchange rate. The Louvre Accord ranges were abandoned or adjusted. Consequently, the dollar dropped again, falling to its lowest at the end of December 1987, replacing the need for any deflation in the US economy.

Closed economies becoming open

A number of the examples of interest rate convergence affecting the real exchange rate, given above, are also examples of the greater opening up to capital flows of economies which had previously been closed, or behaved as if they were closed. Fixed or closely managed exchange rates are almost a necessary characteristic of closed economies. If exchange rate controls for a previously closed economy are relaxed or removed there will tend to be interest rate convergence and consequent effects for the real exchange rate.

The likely short-term response of any specific economy to opening cannot easily be determined in advance. It depends upon the return to investment in the economy, the government's fiscal stance, and the relationship between these and the propensity to save, not all of which can easily be ascertained. Two examples will serve to illustrate this.

For the closed economy indicated by Figure 36, with savings schedule S and investment plus public sector deficit schedule I + PSD, the real interest rate has been at r. It should be remembered that in a perfectly closed economy the real interest rate is independent of the world real interest rate and is determined as the outcome of the authorities' policies with regard to the money supply (i.e. inflation) and the nominal exchange rate. In this example the authorities have maintained the nominal exchange rate at an undervalued level (i.e. the real exchange rate has been held down through sterilized intervention) to generate a current account surplus of $S_1 - (I + PSD)_1$. Therefore, the real interest rate is at r. In fact, this is the example of Taiwan, discussed in Chapter 7 (page 164). It should be noted that

FIGURE 36 Closed economy becoming open (1)

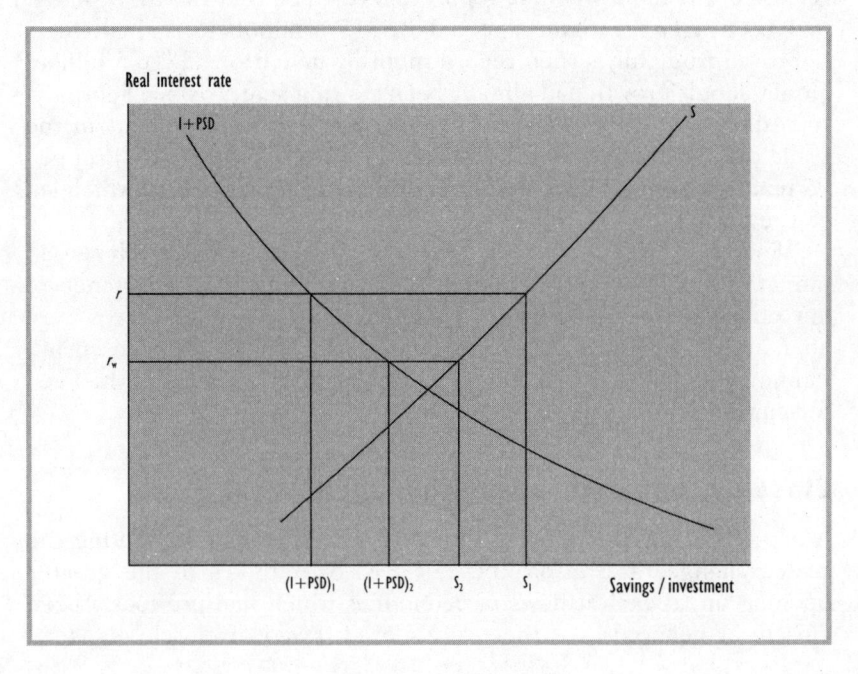

the authorities cannot control the level of the real exchange rate and the real interest rate independently. Each level of the real exchange rate, achieved through sterilized intervention, implies a specific current account surplus (i.e. positive savings/investment gap). In turn, this implies a level for the real interest rate.

If the economy is now opened (i.e. foreign exchange controls are removed so that, in theory, effective sterilized intervention is no longer possible), the real interest rate will fall to the world level, here assumed to be r_w. Initially, capital will be drawn in by the higher real interest rate. Together with the current account surplus, which can no longer be sterilized, this will result in a sharp increase in money growth. Later inflation will rise, bringing the real exchange rate up to a level consistent with a smaller current account surplus $S_2 - (I + PSD)_2$. (If the exchange rate is floated when the economy is opened, the real exchange rate will rise as a result of a rise in the nominal exchange rate rather than as a result of an increase in the money growth rate.)

The result (i.e. higher money growth) may not seem very surprising. Given that the economy in this example had a large current account surplus, the monetary effects of which were previously being sterilized, it might be expected that the exchange rate would be under upward pressure, or that there would be an inflation problem, once the economy was opened.

However, consider the example in Figure 37. Here the average return to investment in the economy is higher (perhaps because taxes are lower or fiscal policy is easier), so that the I + PSD schedule is further out to the right.

The real exchange rate has been held at a level consistent with a current account deficit of $(I + PSD)_1 - S_1$. The exchange rate is therefore overvalued relative to the level which would bring about current account balance, i.e. private savings equal to investment plus the government deficit. At the existing level of the current account deficit the real interest rate is at r. However, this real interest rate is higher than the world level, r_w. Therefore, when the economy is opened the real interest rate will be forced down to r_w and the current account deficit will tend to *widen* further, to $(I + PSD)_2 - S_2$. Assuming the exchange rate remains fixed, this will happen as capital inflows are attracted by the initially higher level of the real interest rate, resulting in an improvement in the *overall* balance of payments position. With the nominal exchange rate fixed, the rising *overall* balance of payments surplus translates into higher money growth and higher inflation. The real exchange rate therefore rises further (i.e. the nominal exchange rate becomes even more 'overvalued'), generating a larger current account deficit.

FIGURE 37 Closed economy becoming open (2)

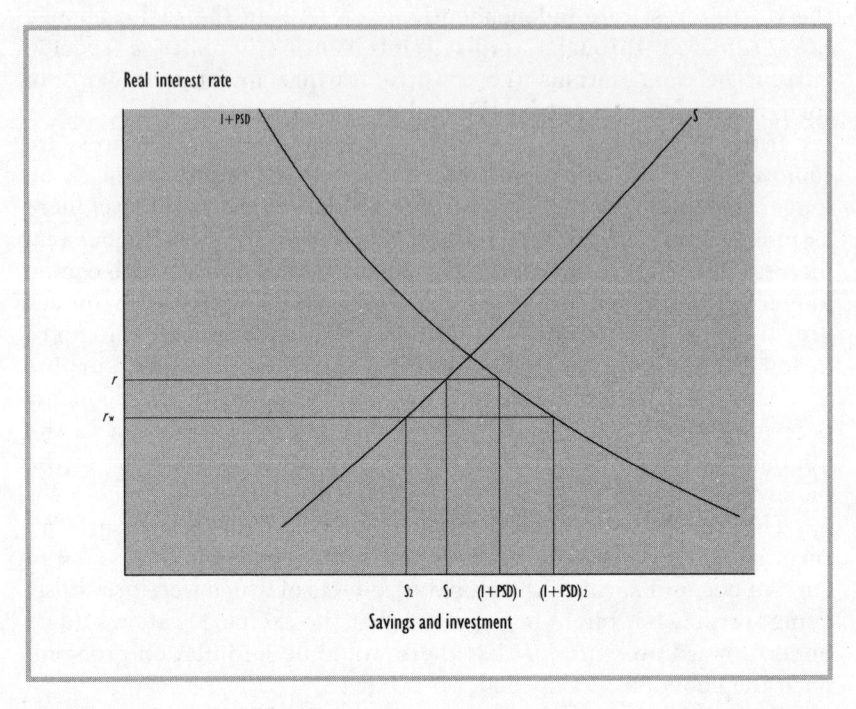

Figure: Real interest rate (y-axis) vs Savings and investment (x-axis). Curves labelled I+PSD and S, with a second curve (I+PSD). Horizontal lines at r and r. X-axis points: S₂, S₁, (I+PSD)₁, (I+PSD)₂.*

In this second example, liquidity expands when foreign exchange controls are removed even though the current account is in deficit. One way this might happen is if the government is running a large budget deficit. Because the economy is closed, this deficit has had to be financed primarily internally. Therefore real interest rates are 'high' to encourage a high level of private savings to finance the government deficit in addition to the private investment which needs to be financed. In our example, some of the financing has also come from the central bank, which has kept the real exchange rate at a level consistent with a small current account deficit. The central bank finances the current account deficit by selling foreign reserves, and can therefore buy an equivalent amount of government bonds or private debt without changing its liabilities (i.e. the monetary base). Once the economy is opened the real interest rate must be at the world level. At this lower real interest rate, private savings are not large enough to finance the government and private sector and so part of the financing occurs through private capital inflows. The current account deficit therefore becomes larger.

This latter process was seen in Italy in the run-up to 1992, particularly when foreign exchange controls were removed between

October 1988 and May 1990. The important point to note is that the initial way in which liquidity conditions adjust cannot be determined solely by reference to the state of the current account of the balance of payments. The key is where the real interest rate is relative to the world real rate. Unfortunately, this is not always easy to determine because of the difficulty in ascertaining inflationary expectations, and the possibility that there might also be a credit risk factor in the government long bond yield.

Commodity prices and the real exchange rate

If a large proportion of a country's traded output is made up of commodities which have an internationally determined price and therefore the unit value of exports is largely unrelated to inflationary conditions in the domestic economy, then the economy may well experience real exchange rate variability dependent upon the movements of those commodity prices in the international markets. An extreme example is given in Figure 38, which shows that the real exchange rate for the Zimbabwe dollar was in secular decline from the

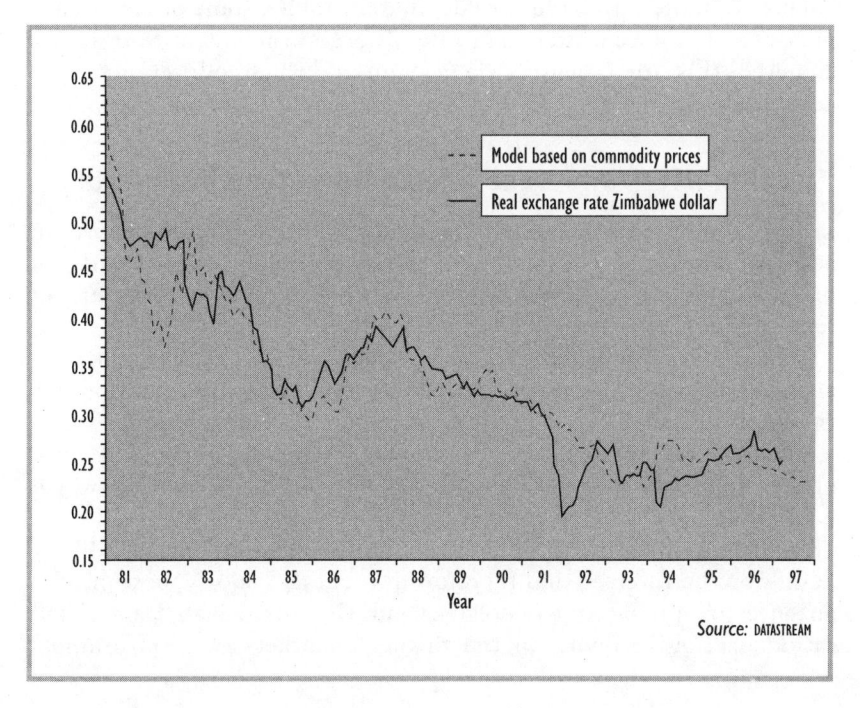

FIGURE 38 Zimbabwe: real exchange rate and commodity prices

Source: DATASTREAM

beginning of the 1980s until the beginning of the 1990s, as the prices of three of its major commodity exports – tobacco, cotton and gold – declined in real terms. The prolonged depreciation of the real exchange rate in line with the commodity prices in this case implied a lack of flexibility in the economy and a failure of the nonagricultural sector of the economy to capitalize on improving real competitiveness.

An opposite case is the case of the sharp real appreciation of sterling when oil prices soared over 1979/80, and the manufacturing sector of the UK economy was seriously undermined. This represented, in effect, the crowding out of the manufacturing sector by much greater oil revenues. However, the rise in oil prices, in itself, does not necessarily draw the economy's real resources out of manufacturing and into the oil sector. Instead this can easily occur via the influence of the government.

Generally, a substantial part of commodity revenues accrue to the government in tax – petroleum revenue tax in the UK. If the government spends any part of the increased revenues arising from higher commodity prices (in this case PRT), then this will constitute an increased real claim on the resources of the economy and play a large part in crowding out other sectors of the economy. The responsible action for the government to take is not to spend any of the extra revenues but instead to allow the public sector financial balance to move into large surplus, thereby taking some of the upward pressure off the real exchange rate. The government of Norway has achieved this to a degree via a fund in which oil revenues are accumulated.

'Irrationality' and real exchange rate movements

In the real world, economic variables do not always behave in accordance with the rationality of economic theory. 'Irrationality' in financial markets and in the economy more generally can be a cause of real exchange rate variability and volatility.

The most obvious case is capital shocks, when capital flight from an economy occurs for no good fundamental reason. By definition this is almost impossible to predict, although the most usual case is 'contagion' effects, when one or more economies are affected because of their perceived association – often geographical – to another which is in difficulties.

Although difficult to predict, an irrational capital shock will, by definition, be reversed and therefore presents a major opportunity to an investor prepared to look beyond the immediate panic, and rationalization of panic, in the financial markets. A good example was Sweden in 1994/95 or France at various times through the ERM crisis.

In the case of Sweden, a panic by foreign investors caused the real interest rate to rise sharply relative to the world real rate, and the exchange rate to drop to heavily undervalued levels in 1994. Monetary policy had been very tight and by 1995 money supply growth was negative year-on-year and the exchange rate for the krona was substantially below purchasing power parity levels (see Figure 17 on page 59), even though the current account was in surplus and the real long-term interest rate was exceptionally high. The combination of current account surplus, high real interest rate and low real exchange rate was caused by the heavy withdrawal of capital and could not be sustained indefinitely. The investor prepared to look beyond the scaremongering at the time could have made very handsome returns in Swedish government bonds through to 1997.

More complicated effects for the real exchange rate can occur as a result of 'inflation illusion' in the broad economy. A good example is the UK, where the existence of inflation illusion in the personal sector has contributed to the volatility of the UK's business cycle in the past. The evidence for this is given by the definite relationship between the personal savings rate and the *nominal* interest rate, illustrated in Figure 39. To the extent that the savings rate should be related to an interest rate, it should be the *real* interest rate, not the nominal rate.

The influence of nominal interest rates on the personal sector in the UK is probably explained by the importance of owner-occupied housing in personal wealth. When mortgage interest rates fall (i.e. nominal rates fall), mortgage borrowers have income freed up and may well tend to increase their consumption. The recipients of the interest receipts – those with bank and building society deposits – experience a fall in their income but, in aggregate, probably do not reduce consumption by as much as borrowers increase consumption because they are likely to be wealthier and have a lower marginal propensity to consume. Therefore, for the economy as a whole, consumption will be higher and the savings rate lower when mortgage interest rates fall. If the fall in interest rates is a nominal fall, i.e. it reflects a decline in inflation and future inflation, then the behavior of mortgage borrowers is irrational. Although they experience an improved immediate income position they are no better off because lower inflation will reduce the rise in house prices and therefore the accumulation of personal equity in the housing stock (or, another way of looking at it, raises the real burden of the outstanding mortgage debt). The improvement in mortgage borrowers' income position is exactly offset by the decline in the present value of their future housing equity. They would need to

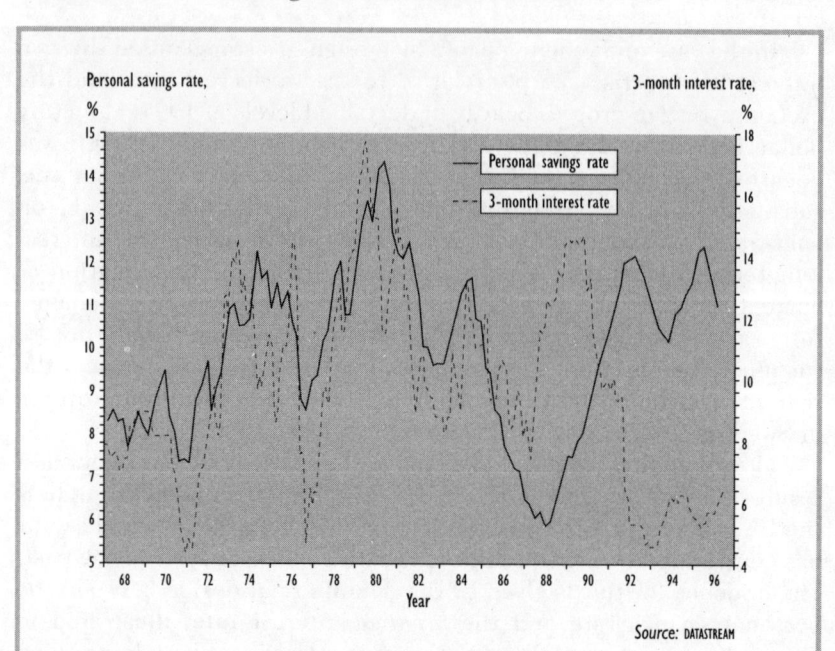

FIGURE 39 UK: savings rate and interest rate

save the extra income gained from the mortgage rate cut to maintain future wealth at its previous level.

In practice, the evidence of Figure 39 suggests that the UK personal sector does not behave according to the dictates of economic theory when mortgage rates change. This, then, could be a source of cyclical outperformance by UK financial assets in the late stages of the monetary cycle downturn and early stages of the upturn. As inflation is falling and interest rates are being eased – with both a nominal component and real component to the fall in rates – the savings rate is likely to decline. This would imply a tightening of the demand/supply of funds position for the economy. As the savings rate falls, there would be a tendency for the economy to draw in capital, supporting the real exchange rate. This could mean that the nominal exchange rate does not fall as much as might otherwise be expected in the early stages of the monetary upturn.

This phenomenon probably played a part in the developing overvaluation of sterling and the sequence of events which eventually led to the overheating of the UK economy in the late 1980s. At that time the authorities were attempting to peg sterling within a narrow band against the Deutschmark (between March 1987 and March 1988) as a possible prelude to Britain joining the ERM. Interest rates, which had been much higher in the UK than in Germany, came down sharply in the spring of 1988, falling to a low of 7.5 percent for base lending rates. As Figure 39 indicates, the savings rate plunged. As the exchange rate was under upward pressure, money supply growth soared and the economy overheated, causing house prices to explode, the current account to deteriorate sharply and the inflation rate to rise further into 1989. During 1989, as the current account deteriorated further, sterling eventually began to come under pressure in the foreign exchange markets and the real exchange rate began the process of adjusting back down.

APPENDIX

The formula relating the value of the stock market to real dividends, the real growth rate, and the real interest rate can be derived as follows. The net present value of the dividend stream is given by:

$$P = \frac{DV1}{(1+r)} + \frac{DV1(1+g)}{(1+r)^2} + \ldots + \frac{DV1(1+g)^{n-1}}{(1+r)^n} \qquad (1)$$

Multiplying through by $(1+g)/(1+r)$, we have:

$$\frac{P(1+g)}{(1+r)} = \frac{DV1(1+g)}{(1+r)^2} + \frac{DV1(1+g)^2}{(1+r)^3} + \ldots + \frac{DV1(1+g)^n}{(1+r)^{n+1}} \qquad (2)$$

Subtracting (2) from (1) gives:

$$P - \frac{P(1+g)}{(1+r)} = \frac{DV1}{(1+r)} - \frac{DV1(1+g)^n}{(1+r)^{n+1}}$$

or

$$P(1+r) - P(1+g) = DV1 - \frac{DV1(1+g)^n}{(1+r)^n}$$

As n becomes extremely large, the final term on the right-hand side tends to zero, because in the long run it must be the case that $g < r$, and therefore $(1+g)/(1+r) < 1$. Therefore we have:

$$P(1+r-1-g) = DV1$$

or

$$P = \frac{DV}{r-g}$$

where we use DV as a short form for DV1.

If the discount rate is $r + \text{ERP}$, rather than simply r (i.e. incorporating a risk premium into the discount rate) then the formula would reduce to:

$$P = \frac{DV}{r + \text{ERP} - g}$$

or

$$\frac{DV}{P} = r + \text{ERP} - g$$

which is the formula which shows the constituents of the return that investors expect from investing in equities.

BIBLIOGRAPHY

LGT Asset Management

Greenwood, J., 'How to rescue the Hong Kong dollar: three practical proposals', *Asian Monetary Monitor*, September–October 1983

Greenwood, J., 'The stabilisation of the Hong Kong dollar', *Asian Monetary Monitor*, November–December 1983

Greenwood, J., 'The monetary theory of asset price movements through the business cycle', *Global Trends*, November–December 1996

Lee, T., 'The impact of monetary policies on world markets', *The LGT Guide to World Equity Markets*, Euromoney Books, 1997

SBC Warburg, *EMU opportunity or threat?: The SBC Warburg Guide*, December 1996

SBC Warburg, 'Conversion rates and the Euro', July 1997

Shearson Lehman

Spencer, P., *'Portfolio Disequilibrium - Implications for the Divisia Approach to Monetary Aggregation'*, April 1992

UBS

Benzie, R. (ed.), *Central Banks*, February 1996

INDEX

A

adjusted monetary base 180
adjustment for financial services (in national income accounting) *see* imputed bank service charge
Amsterdam Summit 133
appreciation (of a currency) 50, 95, 132, 155, 175
arbitrage 94, 188, 121
assets 39, **70–73**, 84, 201
    of banks 13, 41, 164
    of nonbank private sector 2, 4, 13
asset sales by government 168–169
auction *see* bond auction

B

balance of payments **83–84**, 87–88
    basic 83
balance of services *see* invisible trade balance
bank clearing system 8–9
bank credit *see* bank lending
bank deposits 4, 11, 20, 23
banking sector 12, 14, 20
    central bank 7–9, 13
    banks' deposits at **8–11**, 141, 144
    see also reserves
    crisis 179
    in balance of payments 88
    in determination of money supply 14
    in national income accounting 187, 195
bank lending 8–11, 14–16, 81, 141–147, 164–165, 176, 180

Bank of Canada 138
Bank of England 137–138
Bank of Japan 138, 152
bank reserves *see* reserves (of banks)
bank share prices 42
basket of currencies *see* currency basket
bear market 39
Belgium/Luxembourg monetary union 131
bill pass 144
bonds **22**, 39, 42, 45, 50
    auction or tender 175
    prices of 22, 39, 42
    return from 46
borrowed reserves 144–146
borrowing 71–72, 86
    government 174–175
Bretton Woods 127
budget deficit 170, 218
    see also public sector deficit
bull market 40
Bundesbank 36, 111, 128–129, 135, 138, 152, 213
business cycle **29**, 31, **34**, 208, 211

C

capital account (of balance of payments) **83–84**, 86, 95, 102
capital consumption 184, 189
capital controls *see* exchange controls
capital formation/spending *see* private investment, investment
capital gain 202, 203

capital inflow 43, 65, 85, 94, 115, 172, 175–176, 213
capital outflow 35, 65, 85–86, 94, 109, 111, 211
capital shocks 220
cash currency 2–3, **6–7**, 9–10, 117–118, 120–121, 161, 176–177
    demand for **7**, 9–11, 119, 177
cash flow 196, 200
cash-to-deposit ratio 119–120
central bank independence 137, 139
central (exchange) rate 114, 116
civil servants (wages in national income accounting) 190, 193
closed economy 68, **162**, 171, 215–216
collapse (of a currency) 102, 179
commodity standard 117, 122
competition 37
competitiveness 52–56, 62, 97, 101, 105–108, 113, 121, 138, 211–212, 220
consumer price index 57, **184**
consumer spending *see* consumption
consumption 36, 65–66, **70**, 173, **185–186**, 188–190
    government final 68, 189–190
contagion 220
contemporaneous reserve requirements 141–142
contribution analysis 156, 192
convergence 111, 114, 133–134, 156, 204, 214
    criteria 129–130, **132–133**
convertible currency standard 117, 127
corporate income 199
corporate saving 78, 197, 199
coupon pass 144
crash (of stock market) *see* stock market
credit 13, 21
    demand for **13–14**, 23–24, **40–41**
credit risk (of a nation's debt) 101, 162

crowding out 68, 70, 165, 172–173, 180
currency basket 110
currency board 117, 121–122
currency exchange standard **117**, 122
currency in circulation *see* cash currency
current account (of balance of payments) 52, 54, 58, 61–62, 67, **83–84**, 91, 95–101, 115, 121, 164, 173, 191, 213, 217
customer repos 144
cyclical stocks 42

D

debt repayment (in national income accounting) 187
deficit (on the current account of the balance of payments) 97–102, 115, 125, 176, 179, 213–218
deflation 129, 135, 148, 150, 214–215
deflator 184
Delors Report/program 129, 133
demand deposits 4
depreciation
    in corporate accounting 170, 194, 196, 206
    see also capital consumption
    of a currency 36, 56, 95–98, 102, 116, 210–211
Deutschmark 36, 111, 128, 214
devaluation 113, 115, 121, 129, 213
devaluation account 160
direct investment 87
dirty float 155, 161
discount rate **142**, 152
discount window 142–143, 145–146
disintermediation 20, 178, 181
dissaving 65
divergence 43, 108, 115–116, 131–132, 162, 210
dividends 200
    growth of 202–204
    per share 202–203

dividend yield 202–204, 209
Divisia money 5
dollar (US) 62, 122, 179
dollarization 178
domestic contribution to
    GNE 192–193
domestic demand 34, 36, 124, **185**
domestic expenditure *see* domestic
    demand
domestic final sales 186
Dublin Summit 133
durable goods 66, 186

E

earnings 202, 206–7, 211
    (per share) 206
    growth 202, 207–209
    multiple *see* price/earnings
        ratio
    yield 205, 209–210
economic activity 5, 34, 37, 41
economic growth rate 29, 32, **183**,
    201, 203, 208
economy balance sheet 76
eligible liabilities 141–142
emerging economies 29
EMU *see* European economic and
    monetary union
equity risk premium 201–202, 204,
    207–210
ERM *see* exchange rate mechanism
Euro 111, **130–131**
European Central Bank
    (ECB) **129–130**, 135
European Currency Unit (ECU) 111,
    130
European economic and monetary
    union (EMU) 26, 36, 111,
    129–135
European Monetary Institute
    (EMI) 129
European Monetary System
    (EMS) 111, 125–126,
    128–129, 212
European single market 129, 133
European System of Central Banks
    (ESCB) 129

European Union 129, 134
excess reserves 142–145
exchange controls 111, 113–115,
    129, **162**, 165, 217–218
exchange equalization fund 157–159
exchange rate 21, 52–57, 62, 93, 98,
    102, 121, 131, 137, 222
    crisis 102, 132, 179
    fixed *see* fixed exchange rate
    floating 62, 108, 131, **137–139**,
        145, 174
    managed *see* managed exchange
        rate
exchange rate band 115–116, 126,
    156
exchange rate mechanism
    (ERM) 111, 115–116,
    128–129, 132–133, 212
    crisis 114–115, 130–131, 133
    narrow band of 111, 129, 133
    wide band of 116
exchange rate risk *see* foreign
    currency risk
Exchange Stabilization Fund
    (ESF) *see* exchange
    equalization fund
expected inflation rate *see* inflation
    expectations
expenditure *see* consumption 17, 32,
    65, 183
    household 189
    total final 186
exports 38, 67, 92, 189–190
external contribution to GNE 190,
    192–193

F

factor incomes 84, 191
Federal funds rate 23, **142**, 144–145,
    147–149, 151–152
Federal Reserve 23, 138, 144–146,
    148–149, 151–153, 215
financial assets 70–72, 76–77, 85
    prices of 39, 42–43
financial deregulation 112
financial institutions' savings 198
financial liabilities 71–72, 77

financial service fees (in national income accounting) 187–188
fiscal policy 35, 131–133, 170, 174
fixed exchange rate 99, 101, **104–106, 109–111**, 114–115, 119–126, 130, 139, 161, 174, 212–215
flows 71
flows of funds **77**, 84
foreign assets 71, 83, 93
    see also net foreign assets, foreign reserves
foreign currency risk 92–100, 162, 215
foreign debt see net foreign liabilities
Foreign Exchange Fund see exchange equalization fund
foreign reserves 88, 91, 99–100, 107, 118, 120, 125, 140, 156–160, 176, 179–181, 218
forward contracts 92–94
forward exchange rate 94–95
fractional reserve system **10–12**, 23, 119, 139, 141, 147, 152
franc (French) 112–114
free reserves see net free reserves

G

G5/G7 156, 214
German monetary union 36, 128
gilts 175, 209
    index linked 46–47
globalization 37, 138
GNP deflator 184–185
gold exchange standard 122, 127
government bonds 21, 175
government borrowing 174–175
government current spending 189–190
government debt 133–134, **179–180**
government expenditure 185, 189–190
government final consumption 67, 189–190

government foreign borrowing 87, 99, 101, 145, 160, 176
government foreign debt 87, 101, 176
government investment see public fixed capital formation
government net foreign assets 79–80, 88, 160
government outlays 167
government saving 67–68, 79, 198
government savings/investment gap 68
government sector 68, 73, 76, 79
gross capital formation 188–189
gross domestic product (GDP) 84, 183–184, **190–191**, 193, 195
gross fixed capital formation 188–189
gross national expenditure (GNE) **184–185**, 192, 194–195
gross national product (GNP) 31, 67, **183–186**, 189, **191**, 193–196
gross national savings 48, 197–198
gross operating surplus see gross trading surplus
gross trading surplus 197–198
growth rate see economic growth

H

hedging (currency risk) 92–93, 95
high-powered money see monetary base
historic cost accounting 206–207
housing (in national income accounting) 188
hyperinflation 14, 19, 176, 179, 180, 207

I

imports 38, 67, 92, 186
imputed bank service charge 187, 195
imputed rent 188, 193

income 65–67, 70–71, 183
    household 197, 221
    in national income accounting 170, 196–197, 199
income velocity of circulation of money *see* velocity
index-linked bonds 46
industrialization 57
inflation 13, 19, 30–34, 37, 39, 46, 50, 104, 110, 121, 126–127, 131, **135**, 138, 178, 180, **204–210**, 213–214, 221
    expectations 25, 40, 42, 45–47, 132–133, 221
    illusion 206, 221
    targeting 138–139
    tax 178–179
interest payments and receipts (in national income accounting) 187–188, 195–196
interest rate **20–21**, 24–25, 49, 104, 109, 116, 147–150, 213, 221
    ceilings on 20
    convergence 129, 132, 135, 213, 215–216
    differential 94, 109, 116
    effect on velocity of circulation of money 19–20
    expectations 25, 40, 42, 45–47, 132–133, 221
    Federal funds *see* Federal funds rate
    long-term **21–22**, 24–25, 39–40
    overnight *see* overnight rate
    short-term **23–25**, 39–40, 145, 147, 152
    targeting 147, 149–152, 180, 210
International Financial Statistics (IMF) 159, 180, 190
intervention (in the foreign exchange market) **98–102**, 108–109, 121, 125–126, 145, 156–158

inventory building 183, 185–186, **189**
inverted yield curve *see* yield curve
investment 29, 48, 59–61, **65–66**, 69, 72, 77, 85, 165, **184–185**, 189, 194
    see also private investment
    relation to real interest rate **48**, 50, 59
invisible trade balance 83–84
irrationality 220

J

'J'-curve 97

K

krona, Swedish 59, 221

L

'L' (liquidity) 4
lagged reserve requirements 141–142
leading indicator 25
legal tender 130
liabilities 71–73, 84
    of banks 4
liquidity
    conditions 40, 210, 219
    indicator 36–37, 43
lira (Turkish) 160
loan demand 16
    see also bank lending
Lombard rate 142, 152
Louvre Accord 156, 214–215

M

Ml **3**, 11, 146
    velocity of 18–19
M2 **4–5**, 11
M3 **4–5**, 11, **15**, 20, 81
    velocity of 18, 20
Maastricht Treaty 129–130, 132–133, 135
Madrid Summit 130
managed exchange rate 111, **154–155**, 161, 180
matched sales 145
means of payment 1, 4

234 • INDEX

merchandise trade balance 83
Modigliani, Franco 207
monetary aggregates **3**, 6, 112
monetary assets 5–6
monetary base **7**, **9–13**, 76, 91, 105, 107, 118–119, 122, 137–141, 145, 157, 164, 176, 179–180
    domestic component of 156, 159–160
    foreign component of 156–157, **159–161**
monetary capital flows 88, 91, 94
monetary cycle 36, **39–43**
monetary formation 15
monetary policy 24, 37, 40, 103–104, 113, 115, 124, 135–138, **152**, 162, **174**, 207, 210
monetary services index see Divisia money
monetary squeeze 105–107, 208
monetary stability 12
monetary systems 9–10, 12, 1222, 125, 127–128, 131
monetary union 129, 131–132, **134**
monetization (of deficits) 133, **176–178**, 179–180
money 1, 13–17, 21, 81
    demand for **13–14**, 16, **18–20**, 26, 31, 33, **43**, 103, 106, 112, 130, 138, 150, 179
    growth 12, 25, 31–323, 40, 43, 106, 123, 126–128, 135, 141, 145–146, 150, 180, 210, 217
    price of 21
    quantity theory of 17–18
    see also money supply
money multiplier 10–11
money supply 3–4, **7–11**, **14–19**, 23, 25, 31, 81, 91, 101, 104–105, 119, 120, 130, 140, 145, 150
    targets 138
mortgage interest payments 188, 221

mortgage interest rates 221–222
MZM 5

N

'N – 1' problem 126–128
national income 184, 194–197
nationalized industries 168
net assets 71–73
net borrowed reserves 144–146
net factor income from abroad see net property income
net financial assets 77–78
net fixed capital formation 189
net foreign assets 63, 73, 76, 83, 85–86, 91–92, 95–96
    of banking sector 15, 88
    see also monetary capital flows
    of central bank see foreign reserves
net foreign liabilities 85, 91–92, 94–96, 99
net free reserves 144, 146
net national product see national income
net present value 202
net property income from abroad 191
net worth 73, 118, 140, 157, 160
nominal exchange rate see exchange rate
nominal GNP 184, 192
nonborrowed reserves 144–147, 151
nonfactor services 190

O

official discount rate see discount rate
official net foreign assets see government net foreign assets
oil crisis, effect on Japan 192
open market operations 107, 142, **144–145**, 147–148, 152
operating surplus (of companies) 196
output gap 30
overall balance of payments 83, **88**, 122, 181, 217

overnight rate 142, 152
overvaluation (of exchange
 rate) 57–58, 115–116, 132,
 162, 179, 217, 222

P

personal income (in national income
 accounting) 196
personal savings (rate) 197
petroleum revenue tax 220
portfolio investment (in balance of
 payments) 86, 88, 91
pound (sterling) 116, 212, 220, 222
present value 202, 221
price/earnings ratio 203–208, 210
prime lending rate 20
private capital formation *see* private
 investment
private final consumption *see*
 consumption
private investment 48, 68–70, 169,
 171, 188
private sector 73, 76, 78
private sector financial
 surplus 78–79, 85, 175
private sector savings 68–70, 79,
 171, 173, 175
 see also saving
privatization *see* asset sales by
 government
productivity growth 29, 31, 41, 57
 effect on price levels 57
profits 200, 206
 in national income
  accounting 196, 200
 see also earnings per share
public expenditure *see* government
 spending
public fixed capital formation 68,
 189–190
public sector 167
public sector borrowing requirement
 (PSBR) *see* public sector
 deficit
public sector deficit 67, 133, 160,
 167–174, 177, 180–181,
 218
public sector savings 167

purchasing power parity 23, 50,
 54–59, 62, 97, 104–106,
 113, 131–132, 138, 204,
 212, 221

Q

quantity theory of money 17–18

R

rational expectations 173
real assets 70–72, 76–77
real effective exchange rate **54**, 58
real exchange rate 35, 43, **52–53**,
 57, 62, 99, 101, 103, 108,
 128, 131–132, 135, 162,
 164, 173–174, 176,
 211–213, 215–221
real GNP 31, 184, 192
real interest rate 23, 35, **42–51**,
 58–61, 69, 108–109,
 162–165, 171–172, 175,
 179–180, **201**, **207**, 209,
 211, 216–218, 221
real money growth 4, 34
real return 201–202
real wages 38, 57
recession 29–30, 131, 150
rent (in national income
 accounting) 188, 191, 193,
 200
repo rate 152
repurchase agreements 144–145
repurchase tenders 152
required reserves 144–145
Reserve Bank of Australia 138
reserve deviation 152
reserve maintenance
 period 141–142, 152
reserve ratio **10–12**, 119–122, 141,
 147, 180
reserve requirements 10, **12**,
 141–142, 145, 180–181
reserves (of banks) **10–12**, 23–34,
 119–122, **141–142**,
 144–145, 148–150, 177, 180
 demand for 23, 147, 149–150,
  153
 supply of 23, 147, 148–150

reserve targeting **139, 146–150**, 210
residential construction 188
residual error (in national income accounting) 195
rest of the world financial deficit/surplus 180
retail price index *see* consumer price index
Riksbank 138
risk 96, 201–202
risk-free return 49, 201
risk premium 22–23, 45, 179–180, 201, 207
rule of twenty 205

S

sales (total final) 186
saving(s) 48, 59, 61, **65–72**, 77, 80, 165, 171–172, **197–198**, 202, 221–222
    government 67–68
    of nonbank private sector 81
    of private sector *see* private sector savings
    relation to real interest rate **47**, 59–61, 171, 218
savings curve 47–48, 59, 172
savings deposits 4, 11
savings investment gap 69, 77–78, 80, 85
service prices 57
service sector 195
speculative bubbles 139, 179
spot exchange rate 94
Stability Pact 133–134
sterilization (of foreign exchange transactions) 100, 108–111, 121, 159, 162, 164, 216–217
sterilization instruments 163–164
stocks 71, 189
stock appreciation
stock building *see* inventory building
stock market
    capital appreciation of 39, 204, 211
    crash 86, 214–215
    cycle 39
    dividends 202
    earnings 200
    returns 201–204, 207
    value of 202, 204–205, 209–211
stock (prices) 39
    and money growth 39
surplus of the nation 84, 191
swap rate 94
Swiss National Bank 138
symmetry 126
system repos 144

T

tap stock issues 175
tax 67, 170–171, 173, 189, 196, 198
    burden 29
    convergence 133
terms of trade 98, 102, 192
Third World debtors 101
time deposits 4–5, 11
trade balance 83, 191
traded goods 55
    prices 55, 57
transactions demand for money 18, 31, 123
transfers 84, 170, 186, 191, **198**
    in balance of payments 84
    in national income accounting 84, 186, 190
treasury bills 4
trend growth rate 29–31

U

undervaluation (of exchange rate) 193–196
unemployment benefits 190
unsterilized intervention 108, 159

V

value added 193–196
vault cash 10
velocity (of circulation of money) **146–150**, 31, 33, 39, 179

W

warehousing 159
wealth 73
    of an economy 76

Y

yield **21–22**, 201–202, 206, 209
    on stock market *see* earnings yield and dividend yield

yield curve 6, 20, **24–27**, **40–43**, 112–113
    effect on velocity 20
    inverted 24–25, 27, 40, 42–43

Z

Zimbabwe dollar 219–220